The Last Roundup
On
The Llano Estacado

A Novel Based On Family History

Chuck Olson

This Book Is Dedicated

To

My Sons

Leland J. "Lanny" Olson
1961-2012

Charles Matthew Olson
1967-

Michael Christian Olson
1969-

And
In Memory Of My Mother
Agnes Ada Pruit Olson
1911-1996

Acknowledgements

I want to thank Alton R. Pruit who authored "The Search for David", a history of the Pruit family published in 1984. Without his research, this book would not have been possible. Alton was the grandson of John David Pruit who was my Great Grandfathers brother.

My first cousin, Morris Warren Pruit of Jacksboro, Texas regaled me with stories of our family that contributed to this book and provided insight into life on the range.

Diane Indorf provided technical assistance in formatting of the manuscript that was invaluable. She made a painful process painless. Thank you, Diane.

I must give a big thank you to my wife Kathy. She has been my proofreader and editor-in-chief serving without pay while offering encouragement and motivation to finish the book.

Introduction

This book was born of conversations with a generation of my family all now deceased. I remember sitting spellbound talking with my uncles Charles Curry Pruit, Samuel Morris "Geter" Pruit and my aunts Tommie Pruit Goodwin, Clarabell Pruit Gore, my mother's double cousin Buck Hill Pruit and her first cousin Roy Lee Mayes about their life in the early southwest. My mother, Agnes Ada Pruit Olson, one of eight siblings was born January 11, 1911, in a dugout house on a cattle ranch at Pearl, NM. Seven of those children survived to adulthood. There was no inside plumbing, no running water, no electricity, no telephones, no doctors or hospitals. Automobiles and airplanes had not yet affected their life. In my mother's eighty-five years, she lived to see all of the aforementioned conveniences and see a man walk on the moon.

The first marriage license issued in Gaines County, Seminole, Texas was to my maternal grandfather, Charles Thomas Pruit and my grandmother Ada Stamps in 1906. My grandfather served as the Marshall in Lovington, NM for many years. His reputation was such that lawbreakers when told Marshall Pruit was looking for them, would usually turn themselves in voluntarily. What a heritage he left us.

They were tough people. They had grit.

Table of Contents

Chapter 1

The Battlefield

Franklin, Tennessee November 30, 1864

He could not identify the sound. Faint at first, a buzzing humming noise became more and more intense. Was he asleep? His head spun and pounded with pain. He remembered drinking too much moonshine when he was fourteen but this was different. He could not see. Only his right arm functioned. He wiped his eyes. They felt crusty. He picked at whatever kept his eyes shut. After a few minutes, he saw a faint glimmer of daylight through his left eye. Everything looked cloudy. What was buzzing?

A fog of flies covered his face crawling in and out of his nostrils. He flayed his good arm to beat them away. A rotten foul odor filled his consciousness. He looked to his left. His legs and left arm were pinned under a horse. The eviscerated belly of the animal spilled horseshit, blood and intestines from its body cavity. The smell of rotting flesh and death gagged him.

Consciousness faded then returned, his mind racing. What was he doing here? What was his name? He struggled to remember. He was Tom, Tom Pruit from Texas. He remembered a hot sticky day in early May of 1861, a man congratulating him for joining the Confederacy. He was in Athens, Texas, the County seat of Henderson County. He was nineteen and his brother Jim, three years older, joined at the same time. Where was Jim? Where were Captain Martin and the rest of their company?

A vision flashed of hundreds of cheering young men in celebration of going to war. Flasks of whiskey consumed as if it was water. Generous helpings of barbecue contributed to the atmosphere. A Confederate flag flew high on a long pole made of spliced pine saplings bound together. A man played the fife and another kept beat with a homemade drum. The Captain stood on a large sawed off tree stump under a shade tree. Speaking eloquently and forcefully, he assured everyone present that one Southerner could whip ten Yankees. Tom knew now that was just rhetoric, part of the big lie that war was glorious. He had seen plenty of Yankee soldiers that fought bravely and were willing to die for their cause every bit as much as Southerners were. In his mind, living for a cause was better than dying for one, especially a flawed one.

Tom's inward eye saw Captain Martin on the battlefield in Virginia. The officer, vigorously waving, hat in hand, yelled a hearty "Howdy General" to General Lee. Martin's unorthodox salute of "Howdy" stuck for the entire war. Tom's unconscious mind flooded with scenes of the Calvary charge. Cannon shells fell like hailstones. Bullets whistled through the air. Men died all around him.

He returned to the present. His head ached. He touched a deep furrow on his scalp cringing in pain. He slowly became aware of his surroundings. He lay in a slight depression at the edge of a small creek, which probably saved him from his mount crushing him.

Challenger, a gift from his father, a big black gelding was an impressive animal. A white blaze forehead and three white stockings made a dramatic statement. Challenger stood almost seventeen hands. The first time he sat astride the magnificent animal he felt a spiritual essence, almost all-powerful, but now the horse lay dead and he nearly so. A sense of urgency came over him.

Tom needed to extricate himself or die too. He wiggled his body little by little and tried to slip out from under the dead animal. It was exhausting. He stretched out his arms and clawed into the dirt. He strained, he twisted, he rolled, he pleaded with God then cursed him. In shame, he begged forgiveness.

He rested and began to pick at his other eye. Slowly he realized it was dried blood sealing his eye. A soldier's boot lay near him. He reached for it. It was heavy. He soon realized the former owner's lower leg and foot were still in the boot. He shuddered and threw the boot away. He had no sense of time as twilight cast long shadows.

His Cavalry unit had gathered the morning of the battle before sunup behind a shallow creek berm and quietly dismounted. They led their horses through a thicket of small oak trees. They kept a hand over their horse's nostrils to muffle any whinny that might give their position away prior to the attack. Their orders were to launch a surprise attack on the left flank of the enemy after the main frontal attack started. Was that today? He had no way to know.

Tom was extremely thirsty and had no spittle. His mouth so dry his tongue stuck to the roof of his mouth. He could hear the sound of a stream trickling over rocks, which made his thirst even more intense. Darkness was falling rapidly. He became aware of sounds from the meadow of muffled moans from mortally wounded men and animals soon to die. The putrid smell of death from the killing field drifted in the air and filled his nostrils.

Sleep fell upon him and then the nightmares came. He dreamed of himself standing to the side of a long line of soldiers, both Union and Confederate. They walked slowly in formation along a mound of earth. An unseen officer ordered them to stop and do a left face. A firing squad appeared and slowly lifted their rifles to their shoulders. Everyone in the line was crying out in protest. Their eyes full of terror.

Suddenly a puff of smoke, but no sound, just the visual impact of the bullets hitting their mark. His comrades pitched backward into the ditch. He saw himself lying with the others. He turned to look at the lifeless man next to him; no hint of life, only a vacant look of the dead stared back at him. Tom turned his eyes away and saw a figure floating above the mass grave. It was dressed in long flowing robes reflecting the sun as if they were rays of gold. The figure's eyes possessed all-encompassing love, piercing Tom's soul. A voice said, "Do not fear for I am with you. Put your hand in mine, rise and follow me and I will keep you free from harm and without pain."

He awakened to the sound of chirping birds singing happily. A sunny bright blue sky greeted him. The sound of a creek gurgling made him think he was home on the banks of Caddo Creek. Ordinarily he would eat a breakfast of biscuits, sowbelly and eggs. He imagined the taste and the smell. He felt stronger this morning. He remembered the dream earlier and the image of a loving being speaking to him. He knew his life was not over.

Tom tried again to try to free himself from under his horse. He lay with his head downhill and his boots felt less tight. He wiggled his toes. The thought of waiting for death pinned under his prize horse precipitated a super human burst of strength. He jerked his legs and feet out of his boots and slowly worked them down into the depression where he had room to maneuver. It was excruciating. Repeatedly he pulled his body until little by little he was free!

Too weak to stand, he knew that unless he was able to get to the stream for life preserving water, death was imminent. He crawled, stretching his arms out, dragging himself downhill to the precious water. The sweetness of the first taste was heavenly. Thirst quenched; he washed the blood from his eyes. He ran his finger through a long furrow on the side of his head. The pain caused him to black out and the haunting nightmares came again.

When he regained consciousness, his breathing was a series of deep gasps as though he was drowning. He knew the bullet had missed its mark by a fraction of an inch. He was exhausted. The sun high overhead shined warmly on his face. It took a few moments for him to realize he was on a battlefield on the outskirts of Franklin, Tennessee.

He was having trouble dealing with the reality of his situation. He thought of Mary Ellen, her voice as clear as if he were holding her in his arms. He clearly remembered the smell of her rich dark hair and the taste of her breath as he kissed her. She laughed and her almost black, brown eyes sparkled with delight in seeing him longing for her. Noises coming from the battlefield interrupted his fantasy.

He cautiously dragged himself back up the incline from which he had descended earlier. What he saw was a cataclysmic change. A beautiful meadow full of wildflowers, bees and birds a few hours before now yielded only the futile moans and cries of the dying. The landscape littered with thousands of dead or dying soldiers and horses lay in grotesque death poses. People, whose life meant something, snuffed out. Why? For what? Wasted lives, wasted families, wasted futures, wasted love, wasted dreams, brothers killing brothers, sons killing fathers, neighbors killing former best friends; none of it made sense.

He began to cry. At first he emitted a low guttural sound and then it became a shrill wailing, an almost inhuman sound. His hysteria became total. His lungs finally did not have the air to continue. Fatigue and fear made him unable to think. Consciousness left him.

Awake again he had trouble discerning reality from his dreams. The nightmares and the demonic horror of his unconsciousness still floated through his thoughts. A sound broke the silence of the battlefield. He carefully raised himself up to gain a higher vantage point and immediately fell back. The sound of voices drifted across the open plain where the two armies had confronted each other. What was it? His ears played tricks with his mind.

Singing? Singing? It was singing, a slow sad melodic chorus of voices.

Horse drawn wagons surrounded by black men and women came into view. A burial detail collecting the mangled refuse of humanity lying dead in a beautiful meadow of wildflowers; was such an irreconcilable contrast of death and nature. Some of the black men wore the blue tunics of the Yankee army. Others wore ragged cotton clothes. Fearful of capture, he slid along the dark fertile soil down to where his horse lay.

He was not sure how much time had passed since the battle. He needed a plan of escape and a plan of survival. His mind raced. He knew capture and prisoner of war camp was potentially a death sentence. He knew of the wretched conditions the Yankees provided to their prisoners. He also had seen how the Johnny Rebs kept their Yankee prisoners and it was no better. It was not so much intentional brutality, as it was the war itself. Everything was in short supply and both armies fed their own men first.

He was safe for the moment but time was not in his favor. His mind spinning, thoughts flashed back in his brain to the battle; his Cavalry unit thrown into frontal attacks against a superior Yankee force armed with repeating rifles. The Confederates charged at least three times. The Confederates attacked across a wide, open area that soon became a killing ground. The Union forces fired repeatedly from earthen breastworks into charging waves of soldiers cutting the Rebels down like sheaves of wheat.

Before he incurred his injury, he saw most of his fellow Texas Volunteers cut down in a bloodbath of gigantic proportions. He lived through several earlier battles but nothing like the carnage of men, animals and equipment that now lay in the battlefield just beyond the tree line. The wounded and several thousand dead would keep the Yanks busy for a while but he also needed a plan to evade potential search parties. He slowly began to assess his circumstances. He needed boots. He scoured the area around his dead mount.

Tom found his pistol lying close to where he first awakened. His Sharps rifle was a short distance away but the stock was broken. He made a mental note that he could repair it given enough time.

The Sharps possessed a kill range of upwards of five hundred yards. He had seen a skilled sniper use the gun to hit targets at nine hundred to a thousand yards. It shot a big 50 Caliber bullet. It put a hole in a man big enough to kill anyone instantly if it struck within a twelve-inch circle of the lungs and heart. The powerful gun was a single shot breechloader but no match for the rapid firing Spencer repeating rifles the Yankees possessed. Tom He carried an extremely sharp sheath knife in addition to a bayonet. He wore two bandoliers of cartridges, the first for the rifle and the other for his pistol, a Colt 44 caliber single action revolver. A single action required drawing the hammer back each time to fire. He counted his cartridges, eight for the pistol and twelve for the Sharps. He found his percussion caps, which were in his bandolier. The cartridges made of paper contained a premeasured supply of black powder with a round conical ball bullet but needed percussion caps to ignite the powder.

He and Jim practiced for many days before leaving Texas and both men became quite proficient with the Colt. Their Mother did not like guns so Tom and Jim would cross Caddo Creek and ride about a mile upstream to practice. They practiced drawing the pistol from its scabbard. Jim stood with his hands about eighteen inches apart, palms open and trying to clap his hands before Tom could draw the gun pointing it at his brother. Jim seldom fast enough always seemed to have the gun between his hands.

The saddle pinned under the horse still carried his rain poncho and a blanket that he removed. His saddlebags held some hard biscuits, jerky and coffee. Tom so wanted a cup of hot coffee but he dared not build a fire. He decided he would slip out into the exposed field to find a pair of boots that a dead comrade no longer needed as soon as it was dark.

While he waited for the sun to set and for darkness to fall, he began to gather his equipment and move everything further back into a clump of trees. He found a downed tree of fair size that could provide shelter and a hiding place until he could make his getaway. Tom wrapped himself in his blanket and poncho wiggled down behind the fallen tree and put a piece of jerky in his mouth. The jerky tasted salty. He relished it and waited.

Sleep evaded him. The thought that his brother Jim could be one of the dead lying in the meadow caused him to cry. Jim had been the pillar of strength that Tom had relied upon his entire life. Jim was not just his older brother he was his best friend

He prayed but the only words he could utter were, "God please let my brother be alive. If you need to take one of us let it be me. Why, why Lord did you spare me when so many lay dead in the meadow?" He could not understand and would never understand the rest of his days. Finally, he gave thanks that he was alive. A second chance at life; a gift so many did not receive was not to be squandered. He made a promise to God to make a difference in the world and not waste his life. Tom's family stridently believed in a life hereafter and what he had seen or thought he had seen in his vision definitely had the possibility of an interaction with God.

Tom realized that he was just a cog in the wheel of war. He charged alongside the other men sucked along in the vortex of violence simply because he did not want to be seen a coward. He witnessed many individual acts of heroism never thinking his own contributions significant.

He missed the voices of his fellow soldiers. Their laughter and joking playfulness replaced by a loneliness that was overwhelming. He had spent the last three years surrounded by the men of his company. Most of them young, some even younger than himself. All expert horsemen and frontiersmen they could shoot the eye out of a squirrel at a hundred paces, track a coon across a river, up a tree and follow him home.

Jim had never been far away and it gave him comfort knowing his older brother was with him. Jim was a stout strong man whereas Tom, tall and lithe, possessed the ability to out run his older brother. Jim might have been slower but he was the most courageous man Tom ever knew, not a crazy, reckless kind of courage but a man who could analyze circumstances and situations and use them to his best advantage.

Now Tom feared his brother was one of the mass of casualties in the meadow. Tom sobbed and stifled a second wail of grief and despair lest someone hear him. He had not felt such terror since he last saw Mary Ellen's Brother Elijah. The last time he saw the young soldier he was propped against a tree. Elijah looked at them through hollow eyes, too weak and delirious from dysentery and malaria to mount his horse. The memory brought a shroud of grief over him. Tom began to cry, the tears forcing their way through against his will.

His thoughts turned to home. Oh, how he wanted to be in his mother's kitchen with her making biscuits and gravy but most of all he wanted to be in the embrace of Mary Ellen. He could feel the softness of her skin and hear her voice. She was a tiny little thing with long black hair. He remembered the feel of her in his arms when he would squeeze her around the waist and sweep her up to kiss her lips.

Tom could read and write but he pretended to need her help as an excuse to spend time with her. He had actually finished six of the "McGuffey" readers. He also read Poor Richards Almanac, a popular publication of Ben Franklin. His favorite memory of Mary Ellen was of her reading to him as they sat in the shade of a large oak tree in front of her parent's home. Kissing was a rare blessing as Mary Ellen's folks were always within earshot. Whenever Mary Ellen paused, her mother would urge her, "Keep reading sweetheart" creating an impossible scenario for romance.

The memories brought on another feeling of despair. He prayed to God to sweep him up and carry him home away from this hellhole of death. Both Tom and Jim had been faithful to the Confederacy. Now after witnessing what to him was the apocalypse, he just wanted to be in the loving arms of his family. Three long years of mind numbing battles with little food, little rest and constant harassment by Union troops was a burden he no longer wanted to carry. He tried to sleep but his mind was racing. He contemplated desertion.

When they left Texas, his uniform consisted of a gray tunic with brass buttons, butternut gold braid on the collar and light blue trousers with a yellow waist sash trimmed in gray and a broad brimmed hat turned up on the left side with a feather. He looked quite the dashing young soldier. After more than three years of living in the field with scant opportunity to launder or mend his clothes, they were half-full of holes. Now the sweat, dust and mud embedded in the cloth covered with blood, animal excrement and death made the smell overwhelming.

The darkness of night fell over the meadow. He made a mental inventory of needed items; boots of course, but also ammunition, food and a warm coat as the weather threatened an ice storm. He ventured out just as a small thumbnail of a moon crept out from behind a cloud. He welcomed the light and moved stealthily into the field. An hour later, he returned safely to his hiding spot.

He was exhausted again but hopeful, because he possessed a bounty taken from his dead comrades. Boots with spurs, a rifle with an intact stock with more bandoliers of ammunition and a collection of various articles of clothing were now in his possession. He also scrounged more jerky, salt and coffee from saddlebags and some sugar, which was like a gift from God. He immediately stuck his tongue into the sugar stash and wondered how anything could taste so good. He even found two small flasks of whiskey of which he only whiffed a smell before putting them inside his breast pocket.

Tom recognized the fallen men and grieved their deaths intensely. His relief not to find his brother among the dead gave him hope. He slept a fitful sleep. The demons from the battlefield filled his mind and he awoke screaming. In the nightmare, he and his squad were reforming for the second charge. They were waiting for the Captain to lift his sword and signal their advance. He heard a slap to his right. A bullet struck the chest of the Calvary man next to him. He heard it distinctly because all other firing stopped. He was looking directly at the man and a single shudder rippled through the man's body. What had been a brave soldier suddenly collapsed off his mount into a lifeless heap on the ground never to speak, or love or hate again. He saw men fall repetitively and heard the bullet impacts. All of the man's hopes and dreams evaporated in an instant. He forced himself to think about his family and Mary Ellen until dawn to push the nightmare lying in the field not fifty feet away out of his consciousness. A loud growling, snarling, violent physical struggle during the night startled him. He assumed it to be between coyotes feeding on the dead horses or possibly on human flesh, which terrified him.

The rising sun streaked the sky with rose and yellow colored rays of light. He had slept little. He quickly gathered his cache of gear. Tom needed to pace himself until his strength returned but leaving now was necessary to avoid capture. The stream bottom provided cover and he decided to follow it for as long as possible.

Ten hours later, he estimated his position to be six miles south and west of the battlefield. While the night had been cold, he was grateful for the warmth of the sun. His swollen bruised foot and leg required that he rest frequently. A broken tree limb lying near the stream became his crutch. Tom left the cover of the streambed when it veered off to the north and continued southwest into a forest of loblolly pine trees mixed with occasional stands of poplar trees. A recent windy rain caused most of the leaves to fall from the poplar trees and together with the pine needles provided a soft quiet cushion for walking. Occasional thickets provided a place to hide in the event he encountered strangers.

As Tom walked, he realized desertion was no longer just a thought but a firm plan. If discovered by the Yanks he would spend the rest of the war in a prison camp. If caught by the Confederates he had a high probability of being considered a deserter and hanged. Neither was palatable. Under the best of conditions, he knew when healthy, he could walk 25 or thirty miles in a day. He also knew he would need to travel at night and skirt wide of towns and villages, which would slow him down. Tom estimated it would take him at least six weeks to walk to Jefferson in Texas and then another ten days southwest to his family and loved ones in Fincastle in Henderson County.

That night he tried to eat one of the hardtack biscuits. It was so hard that he placed it on a rock and hit it with his pistol butt to break it up. He gathered the crumbling pieces, put them in a small cup along with some of his sugar cache, poured some whiskey over the crumbs and made a mush so delicious he had to have a second helping.

As he lay in his makeshift bed of pine needles, he saw a star fall from the heavens followed by a stream of fireflies. He wondered if Mary Ellen had seen it too.

Chapter 2

Camp Douglas

Across the battlefield, Jim's awareness slowly lifted the fog of his dazed senses. He thought he must be at the gates of heaven. He heard voices singing gospel. Surely, he was dead. Expectantly he groggily opened his eyes and saw the sun was midway in its arc across the sky. If this was heaven, it was curiously familiar and unlike the vision painted by the preacher at Sunday go to meetings. The singing became louder.

Where was Tom? Slowly consciousness returned. The sound of battle and screaming men uttering dying epithets swept heaven away. How much time had passed since he charged across the meadow? He tried to stand up but a dead soldier lay across his body. As the voices approached, he tried to crawl away.

"Hey, dis here's another one dats alive" said a strapping big black man dressed in Yankee blue. He grabbed Jim and lifted him to a standing position. Jim struggled, trying to get away but the former slave was strong, stronger than he was for sure.

"Look like you done been shot in the leg Reb." Jim looked at the Negro but said nothing.

"Bring the wagon over here. No, not the dead wagon, the live wagon."

Another black man dressed in a blue uniform snapped the reins of a four horse team and stopped the wagon next to where Jim lay. Five or six other Confederate soldiers with various wounds sat or lay in the wagon. All of them had the glazed eyes look of terror on their face. A large Negro woman with a bandana around her head carrying a small satchel of bandages cut Jim's pants leg off and began to clean his wound, wrapping it in bandages.

"Water, have you got some water?" Jim's mouth was so dry he had trouble forming the words.

"Bring a cup of water over here for this man", the black woman said to a black boy who looked to be about ten years old. The boy handed him a cup of water and Jim washed it down in one swallow.

"More, can I have more?"

"No, Soldier boy, that is enough for right now. I got to stop your bleeding and if I don't, you won't need any more water."

Jim blacked out. When he awakened, it was pitch black. All around him, men were moaning and crying out in pain. Squeezed into a boxcar on a train with dozens of other prisoners he could barely breathe. Every time the train went clicking along from one rail to another, the men in unison gave out a yell of pain.

Most of the men lacked warm weather uniforms. That night the only thing that kept them from freezing to death was the body heat from the other prisoners. Jim tried to see if his brother Tom was among the crowded mass of men.

Jim yelled "Tom Pruit! Tom Pruit! Anybody know Tom Pruit?"

A lone weak voice cried in response "Yeah, I know him, but I ain't seen him since yesterday morning. Who wants to know?"

Jim could not make out who had answered. He yelled "Jim Pruit, his brother. Who are you?"

"Jim, this is Claudy Thompson. Claudy was an old friend from Poynor, Texas."

"Claudy, do you know if he is alive?"

"No pard, I don't, but I never saw him take a bullet either."

Claudy's news gave Jim the hope he so badly needed that Tom was still alive.

☆ ☆ ☆ ☆ ☆

Jim was uncertain as to whether it was hours or days he was on the train. The enclosed boxcar made it impossible to see

19

the sun and let little fresh air in. The stench of excrement mixed with the smell urine, sweat, blood and death was overwhelming. The men cleared a corner in each end of the boxcar for an area to defecate. The time seemed to stretch into an eternity before the train pulled into its final stop, Camp Douglas just outside of Chicago, Illinois.

It was dark and miserably cold. Yankee soldiers standing around large bonfires barked orders to form groups of ten men. Jim could hardly walk. He had to be helped to stand and another soldier half-carried Jim down a wooden ramp slick with snow.

The rag-tag group of dirty, bloody men hobbled along as best they could. Cold as it was though, he was happy to get off the train. Coming down the wooden ramp, he saw Claudy Thompson lying on the ground outside the boxcar. Jim pleaded with the man helping him to go over to where Claudy lay. Jim knelt by his friend despite a guard punching him in the ribs with a rifle butt.

The shock that Claudy was dead did not deter Jim from taking his dead friend's coat off his lifeless body. Claudy didn't need it any longer and he did. A guard threatened to club Jim if he didn't move along. As they marched toward the prison camp Jim glanced back at his now dead friend lying pathetically beside the train tracks.

Entering the stockade, orders to form up for inspection were shouted. A Union Captain next told them to strip down to their underwear. Jim soon realized this was all just a ruse to rob the prisoners. The guards went through their belongings taking everything of value such as watches, rings and gold coins. The wounded separated from the able bodied were then separated again by severity of injury.

Jim was admitted to the post hospital. Surprisingly both Union and Confederate soldiers shared quarters and no guards were posted. The food was decent and the doctors and nurses seemed to have a genuine interest in treating the patients. Jim learned later as he met other prisoners who had been at Camp Douglas for several months that prison conditions were not nearly

20

as good as at the hospital. Open sewers and filthy drinking water caused dysentery killing indiscriminately. Food shortages led many to starve while smallpox and pneumonia killed thousands.

Five days after his arrival, the weather improved. Jim and some of the other prisoners allowed on a porch facing the afternoon sun basked in its warmth. It was a huge complex consisting of over a hundred buildings and seven or eight thousand prisoners. Jim noticed a prisoner standing in plain sight in the middle of a large open area. The prisoner walked over to a fence that separated the prison yard from the post commandant's headquarters. As Jim watched the prisoner, he unbuttoned his breeches and began to piss. Suddenly a rifle shot rang out and the prisoner crumpled to the ground no warning given, just a bullet in the back.

Jim screamed, "You bastards! You dirty bastards!"

He hobbled off the porch trying to go to where the now dead soldier lay but other patients quickly grabbed him saying, "You go out there, you're a dead man!"

Jim heard later that an inquiry ruled the shooting was justified as the soldier had committed a nuisance. Jim concluded that if a nuisance could get you shot he needed to be very careful.

Jim also learned from another patient, "The smallpox patients live there in two buildings separated from the rest of the compound by a wire fence. I suggest you steer clear of them."

Jim responded, "Thanks for telling me."

In the middle of January, Jim was released from the hospital and moved to a barracks housing other Texas Volunteers. He was glad to be back with familiar faces despite the wretched conditions in the prisoner barracks compared to the hospital. His former Captain suggested Jim deal with his despair and melancholy by trying to help his fellow prisoners who were sick and feeble from starvation.

Week after week, month after month he nursed men who despite his efforts starved to death. He scrounged, begged and stole food throughout the camp. Every barracks had its own kitchen and Jim befriended the cooks. He bartered alcohol stolen from a secret still operated by some prisoners from Tennessee for meat scraps from the Georgia barracks and bread from the Alabama boys.

He made a clandestine visit one night to a barracks housing men from Florida. He took his mess kit and got in line as they were ladled a meager portion of potato soup. As he made his way through the food line, someone recognized him as a Texan. To say they were not happy to share was an understatement. A small riot erupted and Jim had to quickly dive under the edge of the tent and run for his life. Fortunately, he was able to fade into the thousands of other prisoners and elude his pursuers

It was a competitive environment where it was scratch, root hog or die. Several men in the kitchens knew of Jim's feeding the most helpless and they took pity saving him left over bread, most of which was green with mold along with the pitiful dregs of the soup pot.

In the middle of February of 1865, the Yankees began furloughing prisoners if they signed a loyalty oath. The Federals also made offers to their former enemy combatants of enlistment in the Union Army and full pardons if prisoners would agree to fight in the Indian wars out West. Something like ten companies of Confederates of approximately 200 men each signed up.

The Confederate surrender April 9, 1865 met with mixed emotions by Rebel prisoners. Most were war weary and tired of existing in the hellhole of a Camp Douglas and were happy to go home. Others, such as strident slave supporters were devastated. The news of Lincoln's assassination less than a week later was shocking to both Armies with the range of emotions running the gamut of surprise and horror to elation with some Rebel soldiers thinking that they were seeing an overthrow of the Lincoln government.

Jim just wanted to go home. He had enough of the Confederate Army, let alone the Union Army and agreed to sign the loyalty oath. It was a long wait, as he did not receive furlough orders until May 1, 1865. After the loyalty oaths, each man received clean but ill-fitting clothes and a train ticket home. They marched him and several hundred others down to the train station and shipped them south in boxcars.

In Nashville Jim transferred to a different train going to Memphis. In Memphis, he was to wait for a paddle wheeler that would take him downstream to Vicksburg in approximately a week. The departure day came and went. Jim checked in every day. Finally, he learned that the only transport available was a barge that would take him across the Mississippi River to Arkansas; from there he would walk home.

The barge taking him across the Mississippi was loaded with probably two hundred men. As they unloaded and began to split up to go their separate ways Jim saw a familiar face. It was Lew Rapier from his Frontier Battalion.

Jim called out "Lew, Lew! Hey, Its Jim Pruit from Henderson County."

The man turned and a look of recognition washed across his face. Rapier walked briskly across the wooden dock saying, "You are a sight for sore eyes."

Jim held out his hand for a handshake before he realized that Lew's right arm below the elbow was gone. Lew saw his look of surprise and quickly said, "Took a bullet to my lower arm and got lead poisoning so they had to take it off. Other than that I made it through without a scratch."

Jim was so happy to see another man from home that he began to cry. He wiped the tears from his eyes with the sleeve of his coat and said, "Lew, it is so good to see you, but I need to know if you know anything about my brother Tom?"

"No pard, I ain't seen him since Franklin."

Jim swallowed hard and told himself not to give into the despair he had felt while in the hospital in Illinois.

Lew saw what Jim was feeling and said "Pard, he's probably sitting at home in Texas sweet talking some pretty gal and not worried about either of us right now."

23

Jim with melancholy in his voice said, "I can only pray you are right."

Chapter 3

Shadrick Frater

Tom spent the day hobbling along using a stick for a cane. Night was falling as he found a depression next to the base of a big loblolly pine. It would offer some protection from the weather and a comfortable place to sleep. He scooped up several armfuls of pine needles for a bed and arranged his slicker over a low branch to make an improvised tent. He hunkered down drawing a ragged blanket up around his head and neck.

He suffered from nightmares frequently since the battle and tonight he resisted slipping into sleep. He wanted to think of pleasant events of home and family. A memory of a trip to Jefferson, Texas came to mind when he and his father were delivering cotton for shipment down to New Orleans. Jefferson was located on the Red River and the trip from their home on the Naches River near Fincastle, Texas took several days. Oxen teams pulled their load of cotton on homemade wagons with wooden wheels. They used pine tar to grease the wheels every morning, which would only last for a few hours. By the end of each day, the shrill screeching of the wheel on the axle carried a mile away.

On one such trip to Jefferson when Tom was about twelve, he and his father went to a big slave auction held on a wharf at the port there. A paddle wheeler steamed up from the big slave trading area of Natchez on the Mississippi River with its human cargo. Tom and his father watched as at least two hundred prospective buyers gathered around the auction block. After the boat docked, slaves were marched into a long shed standing next to the wharf. They stayed there until the auction was over. The slaves brought out in groups of six walked in a circle surrounded by wooden benches where the prospective buyers sat to view them. The slaves were required to climb up and down a set of steps to prove their agility. They were required to lift barrels of various sizes and weights to demonstrate their strength.

One of the Negros, a young black male about the age of Tom, walked with a significant limp. He was the victim of derisive catcalls from some of the buyers concerning his disability. Tom saw a look of desperation on the boy's face. Every few minutes, a new group of slaves, marched out for viewing. The young Negro soon returned into the slave shed.

Tom asked his Father "Papa, let's go over to the shed and look at him up close."

They made their way back among the crowd of buyers to the slave quarters. They found the young black boy crouched down against a wall with his head in his hands sobbing. Tom started to go back to the boy but one of the slave traders called out and stepped in front of Tom saying, "Ya can't go back there boy."

Tom said, "I want to talk with him."

"You got no business talking to him. Only qualified buyers are allowed to go into the slave area."

Tom's father stepped forward and said, "The boy is with me."

The slave trader quickly turned to see Tom's father and stepped aside.

Tom walked over to the black boy, knelt down and asked, "What's your name?"

The boy looked up and wiped away the tears and snot from his cheeks and nose with the sleeve of his ragged shirt. "Massa, my name is Shadrick, Shadrick Frater but mos folks jus calls me Shad."

"Why are you crying?"

"Well Massa I's dun been taken away from my mami and my papi an I's don know where they dun gone. I's so fraid dat I's gonna get sold to a mean man."

"When did you last see your folks?"

"Mos of six weeks ago Massa before we dun left Savannah on de boat. Every time de boat stop and they sell some of us slaves but nobody dun buy me."

Tom's father asked, "Tell me about your foot."

"Well Massa when I's wuz a little boy I's wuz run over by a wagon and ever since I's been like this."

"Let us see your leg." The young black boy pulled his pants leg up to reveal an injury long healed that had left a curvature in the lower leg bones.

"Do you have pain in your leg?"

"No Massa. I's jus walk funny and not as fas as mos folks able to walk."

Tom looked up to his father and said, "Papa, let's buy him. He looks to be about my age."

Tom's Father replied, "Tom, the boy won't be able to help us. He most likely will be hard pressed to be sold here today, to anybody. Best for us to let him be."

"Well that means you wouldn't have to pay a lot for him then."

Tom's Father looked at Tom, "We are not running a home for disabled blacks."

"I will use my own money from my trap line to buy him then!" Tom spent every morning checking his line and saved the money for special things for himself when they visited Hawkin's Store.

"Tom, you are not old enough to buy a slave."

"Papa, please! I can't stand the thought of what is gonna happen to him if he doesn't sell to someone who has some caring about him!

Shadrick, bewildered by the conversation simply sat quietly with frightened eyes flitting between Tom and his father.

"Just what do you think is gonna happen to him?"

"I don't know but nobody is gonna take care of him like you and Momma and I will."

Tom's father had looked at him sternly and said, "How much do you have saved?"

"I've got nearly thirty dollars."

"Tom's father said, "Go talk to the trader and see if he will take what you got to offer."

His father's words brought a tremendous sense of elation. He jumped to his feet and ran over to where the trader was standing. "Mister I want to buy this boy and I will pay you thirty dollars in gold."

The trader who stood over six feet tall and weighed over two hundred pounds started laughing so hard Tom thought he was going to fall down. When the trader quit guffawing he looked first at Tom and then at the slave boy and said, "Why in hell do you want to buy a cripple?"

Tom stood up as tall as he could and said in his strongest voice, "Ain't none of your business!"

The trader started laughing again saying, "Why if you ain't a hot one. Now boy, I ain't selling him for less than two hundred and fifty dollars."

Tom's father chimed in at that point saying, "Mister, I'll give you a hundred and a half"

The trader paused for a few moments as if calculating the value of a human being came to him as easily as buying or selling a horse. He finally responded, "Mister ya drive a hard bargain but ya gotta deal."

Tom could hardly believe what he heard but he was ecstatic that he had saved this young black from some anticipated but unknown horrible fate. Shad at the same time broke out into a toothy grin and said, "Thank ya Massa. Thank ya Massa for taking me home wid ya."

From that moment, Tom and Shad became fast friends. They did chores together. They ate together and on many nights, Tom slipped out of the main house after everybody was in bed and slept in Shad's room down at the barn with him. They went fishing every chance they got and explored all of the woods around the family farm.

There were things that Shad took longer to accomplish than it took Tom but Shad proved to be a reliable worker and always did his chores. He was always polite to Tom's mother and offered to do extra work for her after an especially delectable fruit pie she made for the two boys. Tom, on the other hand, took the delicacies for granted but now after four long years of war he longed to be with his loved ones and to smell and taste that fruit pie again.

Tom's father played both the banjo and the fiddle and he taught Shad how to play the banjo. Shad faithfully practiced and quickly became nearly as good as his teacher. Many evenings the two of them entertained family and friends while playing such happy tunes as Camp Town Races and Ol' Dan Tucker. Tom remembered some of the humorous lyrics from Ol' Dan Tucker and he found himself humming the tune and lowly singing the lyrics.

> I come to town de udder night,
>
> I hear de noise an saw de fight,
>
> De watchman was runnin roun,
>
> Cryin Ol Dan Tucker's come to town.
>
> So get out de way! Get out de way!
>
> Get out de way! Ol Dan Tucker.
>
> You're too late to come to supper.
>
> Tucker was a hardened sinner,
>
> He nebber said his grace at dinner;
>
> De ole sow squeel, de pigs did squall
>
> He ate de 'hole hog wid de tail and all.
>
> Old Dan Tucker wuz a mighty man,
>
> He washed his face in a fryin' pan;
>
> Combed his head wid a wagon wheel
>
> And he died wid de toofache in his heel.

Chapter 4

Orange

When the Texas Volunteers left Texas from Jefferson to join in the fighting they boarded paddle wheelers bound for Memphis. The riverboats were loaded to the point of sinking with men, horses and war supplies. They traversed Big Cypress Bayou to Caddo Lake down to the Red River's confluence with the Mississippi, which made for a leisurely trip quite unlike going to war. Under his current circumstances that would be impossible as the Yankees almost certainly controlled both Memphis and Vicksburg and the Mississippi River all the way South to New Orleans and north of Memphis to Ohio. He faced a predicament that possibly afforded no escape.

Tom limped along favoring his leg and foot for two more days always walking toward the setting sun . He estimated that he had covered perhaps fifty to sixty miles. His foot was better but still sore and it hindered and slowed his pace. The jerky supply was dwindling and he decided that he needed to try to kill one of the plentiful rabbits or grouse he flushed from the undergrowth. Using a gun was not an option since he feared discovery; so he had begun practicing throwing stones. When he was younger, he had been quite deadly with his aim chunking rocks at all sorts of wild game. He practiced flinging a few stones during one of his rest breaks. His rumbling stomach was determined to get something to eat.

Tom armed himself with a pocket full of round stones from the bank of a small stream. He proceeded along the edge of a thicket and soon enough he startled a young cottontail. He missed with his first throw but stunned it with his second. He quickly skinned the little rabbit and ate half of it raw with the ferocity of one of his pet dogs. He ran a stick through the rest to make carrying it easier until he stopped for the day. Building a fire was out of the question since the smoke could be seen and he did not want company. After eating, he decided raw rabbit with a little salt was not all bad. Normally raw rabbit would not be part of his diet but hunger had a way of making it palatable. The following day he knocked down two more little rabbits, which gave his confidence a boost.

Over the next several days, Tom's foot slowly returned to normal and he was able to discard his crutch. The swelling went down and he felt lucky that it had not been broken. He estimated that he had walked a little over a hundred fifty miles since he left the battlefield. Twice he encountered different groups. The first occurred when he nearly walked into an encampment of a small detachment of Union soldiers. They were laughing and recounting their capture of some Confederates. He could see a guard watching their horses picketed in a grassy area just a few feet from where the main camp was located. Tom was tempted to slip in under the cover of darkness and steal a horse but he knew the sound of nervous horses would alert the soldiers. As tempting, as it was to obtain a horse, discretion required he detour far enough away so as not to be detected.

A smaller, second group moved quietly along the edge of the tree line. The soldiers rode directly toward him. Tom panicked. He dove into a large bramble of blackberry bushes with long thorns. He paid no mind to the sticker thorns and laid still as a mouse. The Union riders skirted wide of the bushes saving Tom from discovery. The lack of ripe berries probably kept him safe.

Tom began walking some at night during the light of the moon. Darkness afforded him more opportunity to avoid detection, as stealth was vitally important to his avoiding capture day or night. If the Calvary group he saw was looking for Confederate stragglers that meant that there were other men trying to escape but he had no way to confirm his premise. He still ate mostly rabbits that he killed with a stone although he occasionally scored a squirrel.

He passed several farms, which appeared to be deserted, but he decided to stay away from any place affording someone else the element of surprise. In the late afternoon dark low-lying clouds boiled angrily in the sky as he approached another deserted homestead. He laid quietly for a time in the midst of a copse of trees and watched. Not seeing any activity, he circled around to the far side to see what if anything or anybody was present.

He slipped closer, crawling through deep grass and ran crouching to the back of the barn. A squall was moving through and the barn doors were open and swinging in the breeze. He could see inside and there was no evidence of anything or anybody. No chickens or other domestic animals were present. He assumed one or both of the armies passing through the area had appropriated everything. The door of the house lay broken in half from a battering and the shutters on the windows hung haphazardly keeping out little inclement weather.

The velocity of the wind increased, driving sleet with such intensity that it felt like pebbles striking his face. The protection offered by the house was so tempting he decided he would take shelter in it for the night. As he turned to retrieve his equipment, two figures appeared out of the storm to his left. They walked heads down pushing against the cold wind, faces covered and collars up trying to shield themselves. He dropped instantly trying to pull himself into the ground like a gopher going down his hole.

He laid there for only seconds; self-preservation overcame his desire for shelter. His intuition told him to slip away and conceal himself. He slithered on his belly until he reached his gear in the cover of the trees. He retreated further into the tree thickets and decided to move on. An hour later, he stopped for the night. It was a cold, miserable, sleepless night. He felt remorse for not challenging the men but the odds of two against one were not in his favor.

The next morning Tom awakened to voices. The sunrise brought a strong gusting wind and with each gust, the voices would get louder and then fade away as the breeze died down.

Slowly he grasped the butt of his pistol and opened his eyes. He lay completely still with all his senses at high alert. The sound wafted through the trees again. There were at least two voices; one gruff sounding and the other a higher pitched voice screaming in pain. Tom rose to a squat to try and better identify from what direction the sound emanated.

He slowly turned in the direction from which the wind was carrying the sound, carefully moving from one clump of vegetation or copse of trees to the next. He was startled to see an older white man with a full gray beard and dirty gray hair standing over a young black boy with a bloody face lying on the ground.

There did not appear to be any other persons present. The stranger grabbed the boy by the arm and jerked him to a standing position then slapped him hard in the face. Blood squirted from the boy's nose and he fell to the ground. The stranger reached down, grabbed the boy's arm again and jerked him back to his feet. The stranger drew his hand back once again but before he could finish the motion Tom spoke, "Hold on mister, what's going on here?"

The stranger whirled to face Tom. The boy's face contorted in fear. The stranger snarled, "This little black bastard tried to steal some of my food. What the hell is it to you anyway?"

"Mister it seems to me that you have got the best of him so why don't you ease up a little."

Tom looked at the boy and said, "Were you trying to steal his food?"

"Yessa, I's hungry. I' ain't had nuthin' to eat for almos' a week."

Tom looked at the stranger. The man's eyes exposed a sinister meanness. Tom asked, "What did he try to steal?"

"He had his hand in my grub sack when I caught him. Don't matter what he was trying to steal."

Tom pointed at a canvas bag sitting on the ground. "Is this your grub sack?"

The stranger nodded in affirmation as Tom bent to pick up the disputed object. Tom opened the sack and saw it contained an ample supply of jerky and dried fruit.

"Looks like you got enough to share with a small boy."

"Mister, I ain't sharing with him or nobody else; so why don't you mind your own business and get the hell out of my camp."

The man drew a knife from his belt and held it to the boy's throat.

"You come into my camp uninvited and try to tell me how to handle my business. Mister, I'm gonna cut this here boy's head plumb off and hang his head on a stick."

Tom's eyes never left the stranger. He swiftly raised his pistol and fired. The bullet struck the stranger in the left eye and his brain exploded out the back of his head. The man's face went slack; his body collapsed like a rag doll on the ground. The boy did not make a sound. His eyes revealed his terror, he said nothing nor did Tom. They just looked at each other for several seconds. Tom's eyes swept across the area to see if anyone else was near but saw no one. Tom was first to speak but did not stick his pistol back in the holster.

"Is there anyone else here?"

"No massa. Nobody."

"Who are you boy?"

"Orange."

"I mean what is your name."

"Orange."

"Orange is your name?"

"Yessa."

"Who's with you?"

"Nobody."

Tom stood now and looked all around and asked ,"What ya' doing here?"

"Jus tryin to find somptin to eat."

Tom was skeptical and asked him "Where are your people."

"Dun got none. My papi got hisself sold by Massa Jefferies after he wuz crippled up so I don know where he is and my mammi's dead. She dun got sick after being out in a snow storm when we got caught between the Yanks and the Rebs durin a fight there at Memphis. My sista dun got married and moved a long way off last year."

"You mean to tell me that you are out here all alone?"

"Yessa."

Tom rose to a crouch saying, "Let's get out of here before someone comes to find out what that gunshot was all about. We need to get my gear and put some distance between this dead fella and us. Here take the old man's grub sack. I will get the rest of his equipment." He took the boy by the arm and led him back to his camp asking, "How old are you?"

"I's fifteen maybe."

The boy looked much younger. He was short for fifteen and terribly thin. Never the less Tom was angry with himself for letting someone push him into discharging his pistol. The old man needed killing, Tom was certain of that. The boy seemed harmless enough. His clothes were nothing more than a collection of rags. Covered in dirt and his hair matted into a cluster of unruly puffs the boy was a wretched example of humanity.

Once they were back in camp Tom reached into the dead man's grub sack and pulled a hunk of jerky out and offered the boy some asking, "Are you still hungry"?

The boy's head bobbed up and down in affirmation, "Yessa, I shore is."

"Well, we are gonna eat this ol' boys jerky that he so generously wanted to keep for just himself."

Tom looked through the grub sack and smiling said, "We are in luck, "Not only is there jerky, he had coffee, sugar and whiskey too." Handing the boy some of the jerky he said, "Where did you and your mother live before the war?"

"I don remembers but my mammi dun tol me she came on de ship to Georgia an wuz sold on the dock to Massa Johnson. Den she gets married to my Papi and they has me and my sis, Esther, who wuz two years older den me. My mammi and papi lives wit Massa Johnson for almos' nine years. Den Massa Johnson gets sick and die. His missus puts us back on the dock and then wees sold to Massa Jefferies. Massa Jefferies wuz needing rice planters and my papi wuz the bessst rice planter on the plantation an he tol Massa Jefferies mama wuz a good cook and servant fur de house too. So we wuz lucky and got sold as a family and he dun made us to walk out to Vicksburg. All the men and women wuz chained together hand and foot and we walk for days and days. Us chiluns had to try and keep up the best we could. Why, when the men and womens had to go mavi de still all chained up"

"Mavi, what's that?"

"What you's call shit. At night Massa Jefferies lock us roun a tree so we don run off. Massa Jefferies tol us that ifn we wuv to run off he'd sic the dogs on us. Dem big dogs had lots of sharp teeth."

Tom listened to this young Negro with a sense of morbid fascination. He knew some slaveholders treated their slaves horribly but his Father always dealt humanly with theirs. He inquired, "How many slaves did your Master bring here with him?"

"Well I's don rightly know. We starts wit a lot but long the way Massa Jefferies sell some to de folks in towns we pass through. Once one of my mammi's sisters took sick and died. They wuz all chained together so Massa Jefferies took an ax and chopped her arms and legs off to get her free from de chains and we jus left her there by the road. My mammi jus cry and cry but it don do no good."

"Georgia to Vicksburg is a long way; especially, in those conditions. How old were you then?"

"I's not fur sure, bout five I's think."

"How many years did you live with Jefferies?"

"I's don know fur sur but we wuz wit him until Vicksburg got captured by the blue coats and den Massa Jefferies tells us we got to go to Memphis. He dun make all us slaves walk to Memphis"

"What happened to Jefferies?"

"Well suh durin the blue coats big fight in Memphis with de Rebs he don got on his horse and ride outta town and left me and my mammi an the rest o' us slaves wit nothing to eat and no money."

Tom was struck by the resemblance of this young Negro to Shad. They both had the same sad story, which only confirmed Tom's rising consciousness of his distaste for the slave trade. The physical resemblance between the two boys was almost like it was Shad talking to him.

"You know where we are?"

"Yessa I knows. We's jus bout five mile to Memphis."

"When did you leave Memphis?"

"Coupla days ago."

"Which Army controls the town?"

Orange replied, "The blue coats."

Tom could hardly get his lips to pronounce the next question. "Do they control the river too?"

"Yessa, when the Rebs left they wuz runnin fast trying to get outa town quick. Some of dem didn't even take their guns."

Tom realized that his situation was dire. He needed to think about how to continue. He had listened to the excited reports of the South's surrender of Vicksburg that occurred several months previously never thinking that he would be in his current predicament. Now his escape route was much more dangerous than he imagined. Apparently, Union troops controlled everything to the west of his current location and everything to the east. If Union forces controlled the Mississippi River from New Orleans to Memphis, he was completely isolated. He needed a way to cross the river undetected and that called for a raft or a boat.

Tom asked the boy if he liked the jerky and offered more of the dead man's jerky. Tom needed help and this boy just might be

39

able to give it to him. He offered another piece that was accepted enthusiastically.

While Orange chewed the jerky, Tom posed a question to him. "Could you show me a way to get through the Yanks defensive lines at Memphis to the river?"

Orange answered, "I's can shows you how I's got out and we's can mos likely get back in that way, but we's need to do it in da dark and ya gotta promise me that ya will take me wid ya."

Tom was startled that the boy expected to go with him. He looked at the boy and tried to discern from the boy's face if this was a serious request.

"I can't take you with me. I'm going to Texas."

Orange did not blink an eye saying, "Wid my Mammi kilt I's got no mo people who cares bout me. I's been sneaking roun stealin food ever since the blue coats dun took over. They sho don't cares bout me and neither do the Rebs. You's da first man dun give me anything to eat an ya dun it wit out me begging. I's can tell you's a good man an you's need me an I's sho need *you's*. I's strong and can run fast and being small I's can get places ya can't."

Tom digested what the boy said. The kid just might be of some help, besides what choice did he have. Tom cleared a patch of ground so they could scratch out a map. He gave a stick to the boy to begin drawing. Tom tried to memorize the sparse information the boy related concerning the path through the Yankee lines to the river. He made it clear to the boy that he needed to get a boat. Nodding in affirmative response the boy said he knew exactly where and what Tom required, and how to get it.

Tom took the boy back to his camp and packed. He decided it would be a good idea to leave the immediate vicinity just in case the dead man had friends in the area. They walked in the direction of Memphis and after an hour spent the rest of the day resting. Tom reflected that evening on what this young black told him about his past and knew how lucky he was to have been born white.

Chapter 5

Down the Mississippi

They left as full darkness fell over the area. Tom kept the lad within arm's length in the event the boy tried to escape or give an alarm. Not fully trusting the boy was not leading him into an ambush, he had few alternatives. About midnight they passed through a thicket and Tom could see lights of a settlement. He was anxious to get to the river but he realized that caution was paramount, so he tempered his desire to plunge ahead. They moved slowly and quietly as possible to a vantage point where he could actually see the river's edge which was less than a half mile away. The boy tried to point out where there was a pier of sorts but it was a moonless night and Tom could not see anything to indicate the presence of any boats. He decided that they would wait for early dawn. With luck, he could find a craft that would be suitable for the two of them to navigate the big river.

They stayed next to a rock shelf in the midst of a thicket of brush concealing them from any one coming through the area. Tom, unable to sleep due to the adrenaline pumping through his body, laid awake with his mind racing. He was so close and yet so far from his goal to cross to the West side of the enormous river that it felt as if home was just over there. Thoughts of home brought memories of Mary Ellen and he wondered if she missed him.

She was just a slip of a girl of fourteen but mature for one so young. She announced one day at a Sunday dinner for family and friends that she was going to marry him. Her declaration embarrassed Tom and he could feel the crimson fire etched on his face. He had always been shy around the female sex to the degree that words seemed to jumble up when he tried to speak. She had given him his first real kiss the day he left to go to war telling him she would be waiting. The embrace shocked and aroused him. She had thrown her arms around his neck, her lips open and full against his while pressing her firm breasts on his chest. That cherished memory helped keep the demons at bay.

At the first hint of daybreak, Tom was startled from his dream by someone playing reveille. The hair on his body stood on end knowing he was in the midst of enemy soldiers. He crept out of their hiding place. Using his spyglass to scan the area where Orange said there were possible boats to steal, he saw several nondescript small fishing boats tied to a pier. After studying the different boats, he surveyed the walking paths leading to the pier.

The closest building was about a hundred yards up a slope that lay along a rising cliff line where the path continued into the town. About two hours after sunrise two men walked down that same path to the pier. They proceeded to untie a small skiff and rowed upstream. Late that afternoon the same two men rowed the little boat back and tied up at the pier. The only other people he saw during that time were two Negro women who came to do their laundry. Activity on the river was limited to a couple of paddle wheelers going upstream and one going downstream.

Two hours after full darkness, Tom and Orange began to make their way down to the pier. It was a fingernail moon and anyone would have great difficulty seeing them approach the pier. The first boat tied closest to the river's edge had no oars. As they crept low along the pier, Tom decided to take the boat the two men used earlier. He and the boy quietly untied the boat loaded their stash of supplies and shoved themselves out into the river. The current soon took them downstream. Orange huddled in the bow and Tom handled the oars. The river was more than a mile across at this point. Tom felt that they needed to use the current to help push them down the river. He tried to be as quiet as possible taking only occasional dips with his oars to help steer them down the river as it meandered along.

Tom planned to use the boat for several nights drifting ever further downstream. They would hide out during the day in one of the many thickets growing along the bank. The river current cooperated in taking them silently downstream. In the wee hours of the first night, they rounded a bend, which formed a large horseshoe. Suddenly they ran almost up on top of an anchored paddle wheeler sitting in a calm eddy of the river. Tom had forgotten that the big riverboats would not be moving during the dark of the moon as they would likely run aground or hit a log that could sink them. Tom immediately lifted the oars out of the water and got down in the bottom of the skiff. They drifted by without anyone raising an alarm. He knew they had been lucky and was determined not to let it happen again.

Orange proved his value the next morning by spearing several catfish with a sharpened willow branch. Using Tom's long knife he cleaned and fileted the fish. He weaved a grid of green willow branches to lay the filets on while they cooked. They built a small fire and Tom had his first cooked food in over a month. He sprinkled salt over the fish as it cooked. When the meal was over Tom dipped his hat in the river and doused the fire. They made sure to cover the skiff with dead branches and river trash to conceal it from the most prying eye. They then crawled into the brush to sleep.

As the afternoon sun began to set in the west, the sound of a paddle wheeler horn blowing from the direction of the river awakened them. They saw a column of smoke and then could hear the splash of the paddles making their circle pushing a large boat upstream towards Memphis. As the riverboat disappeared around the horseshoe, they began their second night on the river.

Tom felt rested after his daytime nap, as did Orange. Orange asked if they could talk and Tom agreed if they kept their voices low.

Orange asked, "What's it like in Texas?"

"Well it's not a lot different than here where I live. We have lots of tall pines but a lot less water."

"Are there lots of slaves there?"

"Yes."

"Do's you own slaves?"

"Well, I don't personally own any slaves but my father does."

"Do's you's have a wife?"

"Nope, not right now. But I aim to as soon as I get home. That is if she will still have me."

The boy had a quizzical look on his face and said "Well why wouldn't she still want you's?"

"Well I've been gone for almost four years."

"I's bet she misses you just as much as you's miss her."

Tom reflected on what this little black boy said. He wondered how a child could possess such hopeful wisdom. He began to talk about his own hopes and dreams for the future with Mary Ellen. He imagined how perfect life would be in her embrace. Her face always radiated a beautiful smile and her clothes could not hide her womanly figure. He continued reminiscing aloud for several minutes until he noticed Orange had gone to sleep. Tom was glad to just have the silence and let his mind wander back to the family farm and the love of his life. A dim light appeared on the West bank ahead. Tom had been charting a course a short distance off the bank but now he worked the oars to take them out into the middle of the river.

As they approached the light, he could hear voices and see figures around a bonfire. Tom reclined in the bottom of the skiff with Orange and let the river current slowly glide them past the camp. He hoped the fingernail moon did not cast enough light to give them away.

Suddenly, the skiff hit an unseen log. The boat rocked violently to the left throwing Orange into the dark murky river. The sound of the splash rolling across the surface of the river seemed to be as loud as a gunshot to Tom. The men in the river camp yelled, further startling Tom. The skiff was sweeping along in the current faster than Orange and he would be out of sight in seconds.

Tom quickly began rowing back to Orange. The boy floundered, going under several times hollering for help. Tom threw a rope to the boy. The first time Orange did not catch hold of it. On the second throw, the boy got a firm hold and Tom drew him to the skiff. He quickly hoisted the boy aboard. Orange was unhurt but soaked and chilled to the bone. Tom began to row hard downstream to get out of range of any possible gunshots.

Tom hoped the darkness obscured them from anyone on shore. A lantern's light abruptly penetrated the dark reflecting a man standing in a boat searching for them. Tom and Orange had the advantage of knowing where the boat in pursuit was whereas the darkness concealed them from sight. Thirty minutes later Tom, clearly exhausted, let Orange row. Morning found them hidden in an estuary of the river. They were too tired to be hungry and fell asleep almost immediately.

The spring runoff increased the flow and speed of the river current. They watched it build for several days. With an increase in the water level, more logs and tree branches were present which increased the danger to their small boat. If they hit something and capsized, Orange would almost certainly drown since he did not swim. Tom spent considerable time discussing with Orange what he needed to do if they capsized in the fast moving current. He advised the boy to hang onto anything floating in the water until Tom could swim to him and give him a hand.

Over the next few days, Tom developed empathy for the pitiful circumstances experienced by the young black boy. He appreciated the banter they exchanged as they floated down the river and frankly, the boy was proving indispensable along the way. He willingly gathered firewood without complaint and his spear fishing skills fed them several times.

Tom learned that Orange was one of many slaves liberated in Memphis by the Union forces. Unfortunately, freedom meant little food and no place to call home. He and his mother lived in a makeshift shelter on the outskirts of Memphis until she died from consumption. It was an atmosphere of self-preservation for most and none had time or interest in trying to help a small black child. The black men conscripted by the union forces cut firewood, dug trenches, built breastworks or trained to fight in the war. The women cooked in large outdoor field kitchens for the Union forces and the captive Confederates. Their pay was to eat the leftovers, which were scant if any at all.

Tom found Orange to be intelligent with a winning personality and quick quip to lighten most difficult situations and a valuable traveling companion. His ragged clothes and bare feet were little defense from the cool night air so Tom made him some sandals out of the upper portion of his boots. He cut the sleeves of a tunic down short enough for him and with the rest of the leftover sleeve, he fashioned leggings for the boy to wear. He was a funny looking thing dressed in the gray cloth and yellow stripes of a Confederate.

Prior to the battle at Franklin it had become evident that the South was losing the war. Rampant talk permeated Tom's unit. Food and ammunition had become scarce if available at all. The only reason they continued to fight was stubborn pride. Tom and his brother joked about not letting pride shoot your ass off. All the men of their unit separated from family for over three years were hungry, home sick and war weary.

Tom made the decision to desert with reservation, but after seeing the bloodshed of four years of war Tom did not have the deep conviction of fighting for a cause that he saw as flawed. His father owned slaves but treated them with respect and benevolence. When slaves were sick, his family nursed them back to health. They ate the same food as Tom's family. Tom's father made trades with other slave owners to acquire wives or husbands and never broke up their slave families. He never saw his father beat a slave. His father had always said you get more flies with honey than with vinegar. Yes, they owned slaves who had little rights outside of the shadow of his father but his entire family tried to deal with their slaves with humane respect.

In Tom's memory, only one black man ever ran away, Big Jake. His father said that he would not go after him because if he ran off once he would do it again. A few weeks later Big Jake was brought home at the end of a rope behind a mule. Whipped and beaten by white men he begged them to take him to the Pruit farm. Big Jake frequently told the other slaves that Massa Pruit was a good man.

One afternoon Tom asked Orange, "How does it feel to be a freedman?"

"I's not free. I's belong to you now. You's my new massa now."

"Whoa. Whoa. Whoa." Tom countered. "I am not your master. I am your friend and you are my friend. The Union soldiers made you free. When we get to Texas you can stay with me but only if you want to. You can work for me but most likely it would be for just room and board cause I got no money to pay you."

Tom saw a perplexed expression on Orange's face as he contemplated exactly what Tom was telling him. He had no immediate response. For a long time he sat quietly in the bow of the skiff trying to wrap his mind around his new circumstances.

The next day just before sunrise, they came to the confluence of the Arkansas River with the Mississippi. They could discern the outline of several structures on the West side of the big river and on the Northern bank of the Arkansas. It looked as though whoever lived there was still sleeping as they saw no activity. Tom was tempted to take the Arkansas upstream but decided to continue with his original plan, which was to stay on the Mississippi until they got to Vicksburg. He knew that home was due west of Vicksburg and that knowledge would help him to walk towards the setting sun. A railroad track led from the Mississippi due West toward Monroe, Louisiana. He hoped to follow the railroad track and use the bridges to ford some of the rivers that crossed the area.

Floating down the river was a luxurious way to travel, compared to what they would face traversing open country on foot. They were still moving only at night. They were aware that traffic on the river had increased during the day. They could hear the steam engines and see the smoke stack plumes of the big riverboats from their hiding places during the day. As the moon progressed from fingernail to approximately three quarters, they began to see paddle wheelers navigating the river at night. A continuous lookout for the big riverboats was required to avoid a collision or turbulence from the wake as they passed. Plantation homes along the riverbanks were unequaled for size and beauty with anything Tom had seen in Texas.

It was becoming increasingly difficult to avoid discovery. Several times passing paddle wheeler passengers waved to them and Tom and Orange waved back. Each night the increased light cast by the moon's glow made concealment more difficult. Tom estimated that they would get to Vicksburg within the next two to three days. As soon as they saw the lights of the settlement, he intended to pull into a suitable area on the bank and strike west along the old Vicksburg to Shreveport rail line.

Tom was not sure of the day or the month but the days had become warm. He luxuriated in letting the sun remove the evening chill every morning after a night on the river. The Mississippi was meandering in a lazy curving path as it flowed south. The water was a murky brown everywhere except in the protected little eddies of the oxbows on the river. That was the best place for Orange to spear fish. He provided them with a plentiful supply of fish, however fish became tiresome to Tom. He yearned for some good beefsteak or pork sausage with biscuits and gravy. Frog legs had also become a staple, which the boy caught and was a welcome change. They became comfortable building a small fire back off the river in dense undergrowth to cook their food. When they were

49

finished cooking Tom made a habit of putting the flames out quickly so their smoke would not draw attention.

This particular evening they could see a large plantation home and several outbuildings come into view on the East bank of the river. What looked like a smoke house was close to the river's edge. Tom decided that he wanted to see if it contained any meat. He doubted that there would be anything worthwhile in the building as Union troops generally stripped most plantations of anything valuable.

He maneuvered the skiff close to the shore and just upstream from the smokehouse he put into the bank. He told Orange to keep a sharp lookout and to shove off into the river current if anything went wrong. Tom quietly approached the building and opened the door. It was not a large building, probably fifteen feet long and ten feet wide.

Two surprises awaited him. The building actually contained several hams and turkeys hanging from the rafters. As he cut one of the hams down, he heard a noise. The building was too dark to see all the way to the rear of the building. He sensed someone else was inside with him. He assumed a crouched defensive posture with his bayonet at the ready calling quietly, "Who's there?"

He was able to make out a small young black boy huddled in a corner behind a pile of burlap bags. The boy did not answer immediately. Tom slowly approached the boy and said, "What's your name?"

The boy said, "Massa I's don' mean no harm. I's jus' hungry."

Tom again asked, "What's your name?"

"Moses."

Tom stood to his full height and asked, "Are you alone?"

"Yessa Massa, I's alone".

Tom got the youngster by the arm and made him stand. He determined the boy was unarmed and did not present an immediate threat. Tom finished cutting the ham down and then a turkey. He then turned his attention to Moses once again.

"Do you live here Moses?"

"No sa, I's jus' hidin' here."

"Moses I am going to step back out the door and I want you to sit down back in the corner where you were earlier. Ok? Don't make any noise or I will stick my knife clear through you. Understand?"

The boy's eyes seemed to fill his whole face said, "Yessa Massa, Moses will sit. Moses be quiet."

After loading the ham and the turkey in the stern of the skiff, Tom shoved the boat off into the current and promptly stepped into a deep hole causing a splash. His struggle to get back in the boat caused more splashing. Dogs began to bark. A man with a lantern rushed from the plantation house toward the smoke house led by a pack of howling dogs.

When the man approached the smoke house, he called out telling anyone inside to come out. Shortly, there was the sound of a scuffle with men's voices, dogs barking and snarling and Moses screaming. Tom and Orange lay silent in the skiff listening to the horrible beating delivered at the smoke house while the plantation slowly disappeared into the darkness. Tom knew that they were extremely lucky to have gotten away.

Tom began to feel guilty that he had not prevented Moses' capture. For a moment, he thought that they could have brought the boy along with them. He also knew that the skiff would not carry any more weight without taking water on in some of the paddleboat wakes they crossed. Orange was crying quietly knowing the screams could have been his. After a long night on the river, they finally set up a camp where they gorged themselves on the smoked meat and immediately fell asleep.

Chapter 6

The Trade

They floated in silence the next night, still thinking of the heartrending screams of a young black boy they did not even know. Not more than a quarter hour before full sunrise, the skiff rounded a long oxbow meander of the river when they saw the lights of Vicksburg. Tom was rowing toward the West bank when a man standing on the shore began waving at them.

The man cupped his hands around his mouth and yelled that he needed to get to the other side of the big river. A horse was tied to a tree slightly behind the man. The man was offering to pay them to take him across the river. Tom cautiously worked his way into a quiet eddy near the man. He kept the skiff far enough out that he felt the man could not approach them without them escaping back into the faster current.

Tom quietly told Orange, "Get my pistol out of my saddle bags and hand it to me."

He covertly slipped the gun into his belt. The man wore the remnants of a Confederate uniform. His breeches originally Confederate gray looked a splotchy brown. His hat had a large rip in the crown. Tom felt sorry for the man he looked so bedraggled but realized he looked just like him or worse.

The man called out, "My family and farm are in Mississippi and I need to cross the river. Can you give me a ride across? I have some money and can pay you for the trouble."

"How many of you are there?"

"I'm by myself."

Tom was hesitant to take the skiff out of the deep eddy into the bank of the river. He was scanning up and down the area both left and right of where the man stood.

Finally, Tom asked, "Is that your horse?"

"Yes sir, that's my hoss. He's a Tennessee Walker and has the easiest gait I ever sat upon," the man responded.

"Are ya willing to trade the mount and saddle for the boat?"

"Mister, I got no use for my hoss if I got a boat an I shor couldn't swim that hoss across this big river."

The temptation was too great for Tom. The thought of riding rather than walking to Texas was too attractive. He rowed the skiff to the shore. The man helped drag the craft ashore to an area hidden from sight of anyone on the river. Tom maintained a wary eye and told Orange to do the same.

Without giving a lot of information concerning his own unit, Tom engaged the man in conversation trying to learn which unit and in which campaigns he participated. The man gave his name as Fred Simpkins and said he was from Crystal Springs, Mississippi, and a private in Company C of the 16th Mississippi Infantry. He had been part of the Trans-Mississippi Department. His unit defeated the Yankees coming down from Little Rock and prevented them gaining control of the Red River but not without great cost of both men and equipment.

Simpkins told Tom that the rail line was inoperable due to the Confederates sabotaging the engines so that they could not hold steam. They dismantled several working parts and hid them by burying them in the bayous. Surprisingly the Yankees had not bothered to damage the engines or rail cars. Fred also told of the hardships that the Confederate forces faced including hunger, dysentery, malaria and smallpox.

Tom and Orange shared their bounty of smoked turkey and ham with their new friend. He was skin and bones and amazingly looked much like the South's nemesis, Abraham Lincoln.

Tom asked if Simpkins had seen or heard of his brother but the dirty haggard man knew nothing. The conversation continued for a short while when Tom asked, "Fred, if you are infantry how did you come to be riding a cavalry horse?"

Simpkins looked up and with a wry smile said, "Well pard, I figured Ol' Jeff Davis owed me a ride home since I had walked all over Arkansas, Mississippi and Louisiana for him. Since Lee surrendered at Appomattox, three days ago, everybody's going home. So, I helped myself to this fine steed from the corral behind the General's tent."

Tom jumped to his feet shouting, "Lee surrendered?"

"Yes sir, the war is over! The news came in over the telegraph. April 9th will be a day to remember. We were all relieved of duty and allowed to return home. We supposed to go back and get paroled from the Yanks in a few weeks but I don't think many of the men in my unit will go back to get no piece of paper."

Tom immediately began to dance a jig round and round their beach. After a few minutes of revelry, Tom tried to absorb the news but could not believe it. His pulse was racing and he felt light headed with the news rolling around in his brain. Suddenly, the reality of going home brought him to tears. He sat down and cried openly for several minutes. Simpkins and Orange sat and watched. The emotional impact not lost on them either.

Finally, Simpkins said, "I just want to go home to my family. I ain't seen 'em for two years and I just hope they are still alive. I shor need that there boat to get myself across this river and if you want the horse we got ourselves a deal."

Tom stood and walked to the disheveled starving soldier who sat cross-legged on the sandy shore and held out his hand. Tom had lost track of time since the Battle of Franklin. The realization that it had been over three months since the carnage of the battle in Tennessee made him realize that it was still a long way home.

The adrenaline flowing through Tom's body put the need for sleep at bay with the thought of home. He decided to leave immediately for Texas. The horse, a fine animal standing sixteen hands, was a black gelding with a blaze on its face. While the horse was spirited, it responded to rein commands without resistance. The horse had an easy gait and a lengthy stride that would cover many miles in a day. Tom estimated that they could be home in a two weeks or less. He planned to follow the rail line to Monroe, which offered a cleared right of way for the most part.

As they rode along Orange said, "Massa Tom, this horse needs a name."

Tom thought a moment and then said, "You're right. How about we call him Walker since he's a Tennessee walking horse and we ain't having to walk ourselves anymore?"

"I like that name, Mr. Tom. His name is Walker!"

They skirted a marsh, which required riding several miles out of their way to avoid numerous alligators. The afternoon temperatures became hot and caused perspiration to run down into their eyes. They began to miss the cool breezes that the river had afforded them earlier. Large thunderheads began to build in the sky to the southwest and rain started to fall late in the afternoon. Lightning flashed across the sky and the wind became increasingly strong so Tom decided they needed to take shelter in a stand of oak trees.

Tom hobbled the gelding and tied a lead rope from the horse to his waist as further protection from the horse possibly getting away. He and Orange gathered some large broken down branches to try and make a shelter but it was going to be a wet miserable night as Tom's poncho didn't cover them both completely. They ate what was left of the smoked ham from the plantation house and hunkered down trying to gain shelter from the storm.

They welcomed the sun as they awakened wet and chilled to the bone. With Walker saddled, Tom stepped into the stirrup and held a hand down to Orange who swung up behind him.

As they approached the western edge of the bayou, the land gently rose until they were riding in tall loblolly pines. They were able to make good time now with the stormy night behind them. Late in the afternoon, they came upon two former Rebel soldiers walking east. They exchanged pleasantries and briefly spoke about Lee's surrender. The men also were curious as to why Tom was riding with a black slave boy. Tom's reply was that the boy had helped him out of a tight spot and he was merely returning the favor.

As they parted company one of the men said, "That's mighty fine horse flesh ya' got there."

Tom simply acknowledged with a tip of his hat and replied "Thank you."

After the men were out of sight Tom said to Orange, "Those men are trouble and we need to be watching our back. So keep a sharp eye out."

As dusk approached, a small white tailed buck startled them when it broke through a small thicket and ran a short distance before stopping. Tom took his Sharpes from his saddle scabbard and fired one shot dropping the little deer where it stood. Tom gave Orange his long knife and the deer was quickly gutted. They took the two rear quarters to cook for their only meal of fresh meat other than rabbit and squirrels in several weeks. They had a smoky fire due to the rain the day before but it was hot enough to cook the two quarters of venison. What they did not eat that evening they would take with them for later.

Tom once again hobbled the gelding but this time he tied the lead rope to Orange's waist before bedding down for the night. Tom told Orange, "I'm uneasy about those two Rebs we met earlier today. That one fella was too interested in our horse. I want you to bed down here next to the fire."

Tom pointed to a large tree that had fallen across another tree making a small crevice partially covered by branches. "I am going to sleep under that big log over there."

Tom took the saddle and positioned it to help disguise the fact that only Orange was sleeping close to the fire.

"If you hear anything lay still. Wait for whoever is out there to expose themselves. Here is my pistol. I don't want you to use it until you are absolutely sure what and who you are shooting at. Ok?"

Orange nodded his understanding with big wide eyes and a worried look on his face.

"I want you to wrap up in the bedroll and lay with your face away from the fire to make it more difficult to see whether it is you or me." Orange again nodded his understanding.

Tom cleared a place next to and under the big pine log and piled pine needles on it to provide some comfort, warmth and concealment. He wrapped himself in his poncho and lay down. The wind was blowing and the pines were swaying in the moonlight as he looked up at the stars.

He thought of Mary Ellen. Oh, how sweet it was going to be to hold her in his arms once they got to Texas. The night sounds of crickets, owls and coyotes wailing in the distance became a comforting melody as he drifted into exhausted sleep.

Awakened by the sudden cessation of those comforting sounds, all his senses were on alert. Tom shifted his eyes to see the fire pit where Orange was sleeping. He saw nothing and heard nothing. He was ready to doze off again when the horse snorted and moved away from Orange drawing the rope tight that was tied to Orange's waist.

Orange sat up and said "Who dat'?"

A large man plunged out of the darkness. He hit Orange in the face knocking the young boy unconscious. Tom drew his bayonet and in one lunge pounced across the short distance to where the man who slapped Orange stood and shoved the knife into his lower ribs. He twisted the blade, pushed upward driving the blade deep into the man's body cavity. A second man emerged into the fire light. Tom instanly leveled his rifle at the second man. The flash of light and the explosion of sound from the discharge of the fifty-caliber rifle filled the entire camp.

The first man lay face down. He was still breathing. The other man laid spread eagle on his back not moving. Tom rolled the first man face up. The same man who complimented his horse earlier stared back and tried to speak, but his lungs were filling with blood and his breathing rattled with the gurgle of death. He died without saying a word.

Tom went to Orange who was slowly coming to his senses. He sat the boy up and got a good look at his face. Orange was going to have a purple shiner on his black cheek but other than not knowing what had hit him he seemed to be ok. Tom built up the fire and started a pot of coffee. The sun would be up in an hour or so and they would need to move on quickly. He was worried the gunshot was going to alert anyone within earshot and that the dead men may have friends nearby.

After the sun was up Tom pulled the two men over to the base of a large pine and sat them up beside each other. He took their pistols and ammunition stowing them in his saddlebags. He looked at the insignia of what was left of their uniforms and determined that they were from Louisiana. He assumed that they had friends in the area and it would be best if he and Orange high tailed it further West. Tom chose to take a path that was close to a bayou. Riding in shallow water for several miles, he wanted tracking them to be difficult for anyone following them.

The realization that fellow Confederate soldiers could be as dangerous as highwaymen required him to be extraordinarily cautious with everyone they would meet.

Chapter 7

La Fontaine

Tom and Orange crossed the Ouachita River west of Monroe, Louisiana, without encountering any further problems. They passed several large abandoned plantations during the morning with ornate mansions fronted by tall columns and large windows showing extensive fire damage. Cotton fields lay burned and everything left to the vagaries of war. A short distance west of the river, they came upon a farm with a modest house. The fences were in good shape and a milk cow was in a pen next to the barn.

There was an older man hoeing a garden. Upon seeing them, he waved and motioned for them to come closer. He introduced himself as Pierre La Fontaine and he appeared to be about 60 years old. Tom was relieved at the cordiality and introduced himself as Tom Pruit from Henderson County, Texas, and his friend Orange.

Lafontaine commented, "From the looks of you two it has been a while since you had a bath and a good meal, so step down and put your horse over in the barn. There is grain in the barrel beside the stall. Then go to the well and wash up. There is a big trough, which you are free to fill with water and get a real bath. There is soap by the well."

"Much obliged Mr. La Fontaine, we sure appreciate your hospitality," Tom replied.

Tom unsaddled Walker and placed him in a stall while Orange got a ration of oats out of a storage bin and fed the horse. At the well, Tom pumped water for Orange into a wooden trough about six feet long. Orange undressed, submerged himself in the clean water and began to scrub himself. When Orange finished Tom pulled a wooden plug and the trough drained. Orange pumped fresh water for Tom while singing a gospel song. The words were "Sometimes I feel like a motherless child" and the tune was slow and mournful. Tom said, "Where did you learn that song?"

"My Momma dun sung it to me."

"What is it called?"

"Like a Motherless Child."

"Well, I like it so keep singing it."

They had not bathed since leaving the river and the soap made this bath special as it removed the stench of sweat, dirt and campfire smoke. They both enjoyed the luxury of washing the grime and dirt away.

La Fontaine appeared from the house saying, "I think you both need a change of clothes."

He handed Tom a shirt, trousers and a wide brimmed hat. Motioning to Orange he said, "Now for you, my young friend, I have cut the sleeves short on a shirt that should fit and I think that you can probably wear these boots. They were my nephew's but he has outgrown them and besides he has not been here in over three years. After you get your clothes changed we will eat."

As Tom and Orange got into their new clothes, Orange remarked, "I ain't never had no boots this good in all my life."

When they were finished, they walked over to the front porch of the house but Tom was hesitant to enter.

Tom called out "Mr. La Fontaine."

La Fontaine called back, "Come around back to the cook-house and you can share what I have."

Tom and Orange walked around the corner. The cookhouse held large brick ovens where Lafontaine was carving pieces of meat from a big pig on a spit over a fire pit.

La Fontaine said, "I shot this old boar yesterday while he was rooting my garden and I think you will find him to be quite tasty. He has been over the fire since yesterday afternoon."

A large magnolia tree provided a canopy of shade over a long wooden table placed between the cookhouse and the main house with log stumps along both sides to sit on.

"Please, please sit down and eat. There are onions and potatoes from last year's harvest as well as the loin on the platter," said La Fontaine gesturing for them to go to the table. La Fontaine proudly offered each a glass of wine that he said was from his family's vineyard in France.

As they ate, Tom asked La Fontaine, "How did you escape being ravaged by the Yanks who obviously burned the surrounding plantations?"

La Fontaine replied, "The Yanks didn't do it. When the Yankee expeditionary force came through, the Southern Loyalist landowners in a scorched earth action burned their own cotton fields and homes. The Blue coats were more interested in the railroad and performed very few acts of vandalism to individual plantations."

He went on to say that he had seen the trouble of war coming and decided to sell all of his slaves and a much larger piece of land with a grand mansion and move to this location to finish out his life after his wife died.

La Fontaine provided Tom with news and his perspective on the war. Confederate forces conscripted all of his horses and wagons and few if any wagons or carts were still in Louisiana or East Texas. Even the church bells had been taken and forged into cannons. In his opinion, the South was destitute, the proud gentry reduced to paupers and everything of value given up for a war that could not be won.

Shreveport had been a central shipping point for goods coming out of Texas and traffic on the Red River had been quite prolific. Cotton, sugar and cattle had been loaded on steamboats and sent to New Orleans until the Union blockade made it impossible.

La Fontaine asked Tom, "I am curious as to why a Confederate soldier is traveling with a black boy as a companion. Is the boy your slave?"

"No sir, the boy is not my slave. He is my friend and we have made a long difficult trip from Tennessee to this point. This boy was freed by the Yanks at the battle of Memphis. We met after my regiment of Texas Volunteers was shot to pieces down to the last man at the battle of Franklin. I was wounded and escaped capture with Orange's help. We were able to get through the Yank lines to the Mississippi, where we stole a boat and made our way down river. The boy has lost his family to the war and has asked to come West with me."

La Fontaine absorbed what Tom had said for a few moments before responding. "You will need to take precautions as the people here do not relish black freedom, nor do they look kindly on black-white friendship. The Yankees may have won the war but they have yet to win the hearts of Southerners. You need to avoid towns as much as possible."

Tom nodded in agreement. Orange simply listened without any response.

The absolute comfort of sleeping in a down bed that night was something Tom had missed since he left Texas. Orange would not leave Tom to sleep in his own bed in the next room sleeping instead on a pallet on the floor close to Tom. Tom asked, "Orange, you are missing sleeping in a real bed. Don't you want to take advantage of the opportunity?"

Orange's fear of being left behind dictated his saying, "No Massa Tom. I be just fine right here."

"Well what if I get up during the night and step on you?"

"I jus roll over an go back to sleep."

The next morning after an evening spent with La Fontaine spinning one story after another about his family and France, Tom and Orange almost reluctantly left their new friend. La Fontaine generously provisioned them with food for several days for which

63

they profusely thanked him and pledged that one day they would return the kindness if they crossed paths in the future.

The rail line right of way they followed ended at Monroe. They would now follow a telegraph line along a narrow dirt road leading west to Bossier Parrish, which was across the Red River from Shreveport. They circled several miles to the North of the small Monroe community and only saw a few people walking to and from the town and then only at a distance too far for anyone to identify them.

During the night of the second day after they left Pierre La Fontaine's hospitality, Tom took sick. For the first time in many months, chills and fever from malaria made him so delirious he could not mount the horse.

Tom heard Orange say, "Massa Tom, you best rest here while I get you some remedy, I seen'em along the trail today." He retraced their tracks and scoured the area looking for flowering button willow shrubs with seed pods.

Once he gathered a sufficient supply of seedpods, he started a fire. He went to the swamp and looked for a pool of relatively clean water. Taking his hand, he swept away any water spiders, dipped Tom's metal coffee cup in the water and then sat the cup at the edge of the fire on some coals to boil. When the water was hot, Orange sprinkled some of the willow seeds in it and waited for the seeds to create a tea like mixture. Orange forced Tom to drink saying, "It tastes bad Massa Tom but it helps you's get well."

Orange repeated the process several times. Then Orange boiled water to put in their canteen. All he could do now was wait to see if Tom would need more tea. Chills, fever and delusional dreams followed by a fitful sleep continued throughout the next two days and nights before Tom began to get better.

As Tom recovered from malaria, the weather turned against them as well. High winds took down some of the tall pines around them as hail pelted them like buckshot. Lightning flashed, the air crackled all around, hitting so close that the hair on their heads stood on end. An acrid smell permeated the air. The best they could do was crouch behind some brush and wait for the storm to pass. Orange had tied their horse Walker beneath the outstretched branches of a large live oak tree.

During the storm, Tom saw a lightning strike hit the big oak breaking a large limb off. In horror, he watched it fall on Walker, trapping the horse beneath one of the large branches. The limb had a fork, which kept the weight of the largest portion of the trunk from crushing the horse. Tom enlisted Orange's help, "Come with me. I'm not sure I can do this by myself."

They slipped under and through the smaller branches of the downed limb. Upon reaching Walker, Tom stroked the horse to calm him saying, "Easy boy, Easy. Orange hold the lead rope."

Running his hands over the horse to see if he had broken a leg and not finding anything seriously wrong with the horse Tom was immensely relieved. He asked Orange to continue to comfort the horse and try to calm him down so that no further injury occurred struggling to get free. Tom saw a large limb he could use as a fulcrum to lift the big branch pinning the horse to the ground. He was able to find a lift point and pushing with his full strength under and up he was able to give Walker the space to get his back legs from underneath the tree trunk.

Once the horse was free, Tom was able to further examine the animal and found no broken bones. The horse apparently had miraculously only suffered a sprain in the left back fetlock. Walker would limp but would fully recover if they could rest him for a few days.

Chapter 8

The Loyalty Oath

April 19, 1865 Tom and Orange walked into Cane's Landing in Bossier Parrish on the Red River. Tom felt it was best not to stress the animal with the weight of carrying two riders even though Walker, was mostly recovered from his fetlock injury. Tom was familiar with Cane's Landing. This was where he had embarked on a steamboat for the war four years earlier. Prior to his departure a loyal benefactor of the Confederacy, Mary Cane hosted his entire unit to a grand party at her plantation. It was the most elaborate spread Tom had ever seen. Mrs. Cane, a widow, spared no expense for her "boys" as she called them.

Tom remembered a stable close to the waterfront. He spent several weeks hanging around the place while he was waiting for his regiment to ship out and became friendly with an old Frenchman called Boudreaux who owned the place. He realized it had been almost four years and he hoped that Boudreaux was still there and would remember him.

As Tom and Orange made their way through the outskirts of town, they saw dozens of Union soldiers both white and black lounging around several of the whiskey joints lining the dusty street. The sound of piano music and raucous laughter carried out into the street. Soiled doves with painted lips lounged seductively out on the porch of one of the saloons. They sat with crossed legs exposing thighs and wearing dresses that scarcely concealed their ample cleavage. They suggestively called to Tom as he and Orange walked by.

Orange said, "Massa Tom, Massa Tom. You's know dose ladies, Massa Tom?" Tom ignored him and just walked faster.

Orange continued "Massa Tom, dem ladies, dey talking to ya. Ain't you's going to answer dem?"

"No Orange, I don't know them and I'm not answering them. Now ignore them and stop bothering me."

"Well it shor seems they knows you's."

Tom was very nervous about being in the midst of his former enemies; however, no one paid much mind to two dirty individuals leading a lame horse.

Tom was relieved to see Boudreaux standing inside a corral feeding several horses. The old man turned and saw Tom approaching. In Tom's mind, he had not changed much since he had seen him. A little more stooped but just as lean. After a puzzled look, a glimmer of recognition became apparent. His gaping smile showed half his upper and lower teeth missing. He had a bulbous red nose protruding from a wrinkled face as evidence of drinking too much whiskey over the years. He exclaimed, "Well I'll be. I never thought I would see your ugly face again."

Tom's face broke into a big grin, "To tell you the truth I wasn't sure you would either. This is my sidekick Orange."

"I'm mighty glad to knows you's Massa Bou."

After Tom and Boudreaux shook hands and briefly exchanged information on Tom's war experience, Boudreaux lamented about the high number of casualties saying. "I sure am glad that you didn't catch a rifle ball during this bloody time."

"Me too, but I saw plenty of my friends killed and I don't know what happened to my brother Jim. I was hoping that he might have made it back through here and stopped to see you."

"Yes, I remember him but I haven't seen him. A fine man he was. He had a way with horses that I really admired. Speaking of horses, that is a fine looking animal you got here but he looks like he needs a little doctoring."

"Yeah, we had a tough time in a windstorm and a tree fell on him. Do you think it would it be possible for us to layup here with you for a few days? I have got a pistol and scabbard belt to offer in payment for our keep."

Boudreaux leading Walker into a stall said, "I don't need no pay for you staying here with me Tom but I will let your boy

Orange clean some stalls and feed the stock for a pallet of straw for you to sleep on in the barn. As I remember, you were good at breaking a bronc and I got a need for you to help break some for me. I have a contract to provide hosses to the Army and if you can help, I may even be able to pay you a little something. Might even be able to spare some vittles for you too. What are your plans?"

The thought of making money excited Tom. He reckoned he might as well put his time to good use.

"Well I was hoping to be able to lay up here with you for a few days and get this horse well. I might as well make a few dollars while I do that. Sure hope you have horse liniment for the leg."

"I got just the remedy that ought to help," said Boudreau as he went into the barn. He quickly returned with a mason jar that contained a murky looking thick solution and a handful of rags.

"Here, put a liberal amount up and down the leg and then wrap it tightly. We need to treat him morning an night for a few days."

Tom sniffed the concoction and wrinkled his nose in disgust.

"What is this stuff?"

Boudreaux laughed.

"My own private mixture. Just put it on the horse. It ain't for you to drink though it would work on your sore spots just as well. It's a concoction of arnica, witch hazel, camphor, pine tar, turpentine for the swelling and laudanum. The laudanum should help the pain. I use it on my own aches and pains."

Tom did as told smearing the concoction on the injured area. "I also need to arrange a way for us to get across the Red River and then we are going home to Texas."

Boudreaux looked at him and said. "You know the Yanks are in control of the river don't ya?"

"I assumed as much from what I could see of the troopers all around town."

"Have you got your parole papers? They won't let you on the boat without them."

"No. I didn't know I needed parole papers."

"Well you got to go down and see the Yank Colonel and register yourself in and sign a loyalty oath to the United States of America. Otherwise, you are going to be considered an outlaw. Come on let's get you and the boy something to eat and a dip in the horse trough to get some grime off your face. I've got a bar of soap that ought to do the trick. Tomorrow I'll take you down to the Yank office." Tom resented the necessity of allowing some Yankee to rub his nose in the defeat of his proud Confederacy but swallowed his pride just to be able to get home.

The next morning Boudreaux shared a breakfast of biscuits, bacon and coffee with his guests. When they were finished Boudreau went out to feed the horses boarded in the stable and Tom spent time removing the previous days wrap and massaging Walker's fetlock. It was still tender but the animal seemed to be improving.

Orange sat on his haunches in the middle of several fresh piles of horse droppings. A swarm of buzzing flies circled all around and his arms flailed continuously to keep them from alighting on his face. He asked, "How much longer till he's well?"

"Not sure. Get a shovel and clean up this corral before the flies cart us both off. I don't want to have them blow Walker's fetlock and fill it full of eggs."

Tom proceeded to slather more of Boudreaux's home concoction on Walker's leg and wrapped it again.

Boudreaux came into the stall, "Looks like you are about finished doctoring your horse so let's go down and let me introduce you to the Yank boss man. I know him. I helped him out with his own lame mount and he ain't near as disagreeable as some of the Carpetbaggers he brought to town with him."

Tom said, "Carpetbaggers, what the hell is a Carpetbagger?"

"Government appointees the Yanks have sent down to tell us how to run our life. Some of them are decent people but most of them are arrogant assholes. They like rubbin' it in that they won and we lost the war. You're gonna find that the boy has more say with them than you do."

Boudreaux accompanied Tom with Orange tagging along to the center of town. A black Union Army Captain sat at a desk on the porch of what was a grand hotel called the Inn on Milam Street. It was in the middle of the theater district that now housed the Central Command for Military Government in Louisiana. In addition to the offices, the majority of the upper floor was used to billet officers. The Captain, not much older than Tom, was impeccably attired in his crisp blue uniform.

He glanced up as the two men and the boy approached and acknowledged their presence saying, "How may I help you gentlemen?"

Boudreaux spoke up, "This here young man needs to see Colonel Crowell. He wants to sign the Loyalty Oath and get his pardon."

Tom was startled by the polished way this black soldier spoke in a clear educated manner. He had never seen a black person who did not speak in a pidgin accent. He wondered where a black man could have been educated to be able to read and speak with such clarity.

The Captain with a furrowed brow ran his eyes up and down Tom and said, "You are out of uniform soldier."

Tom thought, "*My God man, I just finished fighting a four year war!*" He could feel his face flushing in anger but managed to push his feelings down. He came to attention and snapped a salute, "Yes sir, my uniform rotted off my back sir, and I had to wear what I could find. Sir!"

"Very well, I am Captain Adams. I need to ask you for some information. I want your name, rank, and unit, date of birth and date and place of enlistment."

"Yes sir! My name is Samuel Thomas Pruit, Sergeant, Thirty-Second Regiment, Crumps Battalion, Texas Cavalry, Mounted Volunteers. I enlisted in May of 1862 in Jefferson, Texas. I was born in 1841, May the 28th.

"How tall are you Sergeant?"

"I am six feet, one inch. Sir!"

"What color are your eyes?"

"Brown. Sir!"

"I see that your hair is light brown."

"Yes sir!"

"What is your weight?"

"Before the war I weighed one hundred-seventy pounds but not sure today. Sir!"

The Captain gave an appraising look at Tom. "From the looks of you I would guess one hundred forty."

"All right, I will prepare the necessary document. You need to read the oath. You do read don't you?" The Captain haughtily handed Tom the printed document.

Again, Tom could feel his ire rising but managed a, "Yes Sir!"

Tom silently read the Oath. It said:

"I, _____ do solemnly swear, in the presence of Almighty God, that I will henceforward faithfully support, protect and defend the Constitution of the United States, and the Union of States thereunder, and that I will in like manner abide by and faithfully support all acts of Congress passed during the existing rebellion with reference to slaves, so long and so far as not yet repealed, modified or held void by Congress or by the Supreme Court, and that I will, in like manner, abide by and faithfully support all Proclamations of the President made during the existing rebellion, having reference to slaves so long and so far as not modified or declared void by decision of the Supreme Court, so help me God.

This Oath is taken and Pass accepted, with the full understanding that if the party receiving it be found hereafter in arms against the Government of the United States or aiding or abetting its enemies, the penalty is death."

While Tom was reading the Oath, Boudreau and Orange went into the Colonel's office. He could hear the good-natured conversation when the colonel said, "Boudreau, what brings you to see me? I did pay you for your veterinary work didn't I?"

"You did Colonel. I'm just accompanying a friend of mine who needs to sign his Loyalty Oath."

Chuckling, the Colonel looked at Orange and said, "I don't think he is old enough to require one. Do you?"

Boudreaux laughed and said, "No, it is for the young man outside with the Captain."

About that time, the Captain escorted Tom into the Colonel's office saying, "Colonel, this is Sergeant Pruit, and he is prepared to have you administer the Oath."

The Colonel seated at his desk did not stand. He was a gentile looking man with a neatly trimmed mustache and dark hair graying at the temples. His blue eyes scanned Tom up and down. The Colonel questioned him about his war experience. Tom related how he had been one of the few survivors of the Battle of Franklin. The Colonel remarked, "Yes that was a bloody day for both sides. The Union Army took almost three thousand casualties and the South had over seven thousand dead."

"I must ask you a couple of questions Sergeant. Do you own property valued at or greater than $20,000?"

"No sir."

"Do you own or have you owned slaves?"

"No sir."

"Then you will still be able to vote since you were not an officer. Do you think you can sign our Oath?"

Tom looked the Colonel in the eye and replied, "Colonel I am ready for this war to be over and go home and if that means that I have to sign this Oath then I will do so and give you my word that I do so freely."

As soon as the Colonel signed his pardon, the sense of relief that flooded over Tom was total. He soon became melancholy thinking about the last four years. What a waste of life and treasure, to the South and to the North. Tom vowed to himself that he would never again be trapped in such an event. His only goal was to go home and marry Mary Ellen.

As soon as they got back to the livery Boudreau pointing at a set of pens at the far back of his property called, "Com'ere boys and meet your new friends!"

Tom saw a dozen or so rawboned broncs huddled in the pens. They looked like they would stomp most men into the ground and be glad to do it. He climbed over the rail fence and slowly approached the horses as they backed away into a snorting, milling bunch. One particularly big bay had scars on his shoulders. He approached the horse saying more to himself than anyone else, "You must be a tough ol' bastard." It looked like someone wearing spurs with big sharp rawls had cut the horse nearly to pieces. Tom wondered how that fella looked after he finished riding him because the horse was still rank as a skunk. He turned to Boudreaux and saw the sly smile the old bugger had on his face.

Tom shook his head saying, "Boudreaux, I lived through a shooting war with the Yankees but I don't know if I will be able to walk after dealing with this bunch."

"Why, their looks belie the gentle spirits they are."

"Yeah, if they are so gentle why aren't you breaking them yourself?"

"My bones are too brittle at this stage of life."

"I'll likely have no bones at all after two minutes in the middle of this bunch."

The old man chortled, "Oh, I got lots of confidence in your horse sense. Why most of these horses will be gentle enough for the preachers' wife to ride to church after just a couple of rides by a wrangler like yurself."

"Yeah, she will probably be going to my funeral."

Tom called to Orange, "Go to the barn and get a lariat that is hanging on the wall by the door and the hackamore next to it. Bring an empty feed sack too."

Tom shook out a loop and walked toward the big bay with the scarred shoulders. The horse knew immediately as though

Tom had sent a telegram that he was the chosen one. The bay's eyes widened and his nostrils flared as he tried to duck behind some of his friends. The milling increased in pace as Tom calmly circled his prey. With the flick of his wrist, the loop flew out low to the ground and caught the right foreleg of the horse. Tom tightened the loop and set his heels in the dirt of the corral. When the big horse hit the end of the rope, it snapped taunt and the horse flipped with all four legs in the air landing on his back.

Surprise showed in the animal's eyes as he tried to suck back the breath knocked out of him by the impact with the ground. He rolled, got back to his feet and started running with the rest of the milling horses again. Tom spilled him again and the bay once again hit the ground wondering, what the hell, was going on. After several spills, the horse got to his feet shook his head and just stood there wild-eyed and trembling.

"Now that I got your attention, Mr. Hoss, we're gonna get acquainted."

Tom threw the loop over the bay's neck and the horse took off dragging Tom around the corral. What the horse did not realize was that every time there was any slack Tom was winding the rope round and round a snubbing post. Every time he made a circle, the rope shortened, until he was snugged up tight by the post.

"Orange, quick, give me the hackamore and the feed sack. Boudreaux, put the rest of the horses in the other corral."

After the hackamore was secure, Tom rubbed the feed sack down the bay's neck and back and the horse responded by rearing, snorting and kicking until finally he just gave up and stood by the snubbing post trembling. Tom worked the feed sack over the bay's head and threw a saddle blanket over his back followed by a saddle. Nothing much happened until the cinch tightened. Then the bay broke out into a new burst of kicking with both front and back feet.

"I'll climb on him and you cut him loose."

Tom put his left foot in the stirrup, the bay sidestepping the whole time with Tom jumping on one foot to stay with him. "As soon as my ass hits the saddle cut him loose."

Boudreaux yelled, "Take this quirt. You're gonna need it."

The quirt, a short whip of leather wrapped around a sock of lead shot, was designed to get an animal's attention in short order. The bay did not know he was free until Boudreaux let out a Rebel yell startling the horse, Tom and half the town. The horse crow hopped around the corral running into the corral corner posts nearly breaking through the fence rails. The bay was soon all out bucking and ran Tom up into the corner of the corral again.

"Use the quirt on his nose and get his attention," yelled Boudreaux.

Quirting seemed to penetrate the bay's brain. He backed off the fence corner but the sack came off at the same time. Round and round the corral they went until the horse tried to jump the fence. He almost made it but his front legs hung on the top rail causing him to fall back hitting the ground like a wagonload of bricks. Tom stepped clear and as soon as the bay was on his feet, Tom was on him again, tight in the saddle. Snorting, grunting, slobber flying off his snout the horse finally quit the stiff legged crow hopping and broke into a full gallop racing around the corral. The bay slowly tired until he could buck no more and stood wheezing and spread legged as if to keep from falling down.

Speaking to the bay Tom said, "That ought to be enough for today ol' hoss cause, it is damn sure nuff for me. We will let you go think about your lesson until tomorrow."

Boudreaux sitting on the top rail of the corral with a huge smile on his face said, "Well now cowboy, that thar hoss is gonna be as tame as Miss Finnegan's goat."

Tom looked at the old man saying, "You are the craziest loon in the swamp."

A big belly laugh rumbled across the corral from the cagey old man. "I'll betcha a twenty dollar gold piece against a three legged goat."

Two weeks later Boudreaux declared all horses broke and Walker well enough to continue their journey. Tom sold one of the dead Reb's pistols for enough to pay the fare on a ferry to the West bank of the Red River for himself, Orange and the horse. Just before Tom and Orange were to leave, Boudreau flipped Tom a twenty-dollar gold piece. Tom looked at the coin, "This is double what you owe me."

Boudreaux gave Tom a sly smile, "Think of it as a wedding present. Besides, I sold Miss Finnegan's goat."

Chapter 9

Home at Last

Mary Ellen awakened the morning of May 10, 1865 to the distressful bawling of their milk cow. She hurriedly dressed and rushed down to the barn to find Milk Cow giving birth. The about to be born calf's feet were sticking out past the fetlock of the front legs. Luckily, it was not a breach birth but Mary Ellen knew that she would need to have her father's assistance in birthing this calf. She yelled for Fate, one of their slaves, who she heard stirring in his house next to the barn. "Fate, go get my Papa! Milk Cow is birthing and she is in trouble!"

The little orange, tan and white Guernsey cow normally possessed a pleasant disposition. Everyone knew she was Mary Ellen's pet. She had bottle-fed the small Guernsey heifer after the calf's mother died giving birth. The calf followed her everywhere even trying to get in the house.

The Guernsey responded to Mary Ellen better than anyone else in the family especially at milking time. Mary Ellen took pains to wash each teat before and after every milking. The cow never hesitated to come when Mary Ellen called her name. The Guernsey never balked or kicked when milked by Mary Ellen unlike when her father's rough hand squeezed her teats.

Mary Ellen took great pride in churning the cream into the best butter in the community. She used just the right amount of salt and sugar to make it delectable, according to the county fair judges who awarded her First Place at the last County Fair.

She put a short rope around Milk Cow's neck and led the distressed creature into a squeeze alley used to doctor cows and horses. After securely tying the lead rope to a post in the alley, she got some sturdy logs to block the cow front and back in the lane.

She saw her father, Alexander, running to the corral and said, "Hurry Papa, she is struggling and I am afraid we are going to lose her."

Alexander quickly assessed the situation telling Fate, "Get me a pail of water from the well and a bar of soap."

Alexander stripped his shirt off and ran his experienced hand along the side of the cow's belly to see if he could feel anything. "I was afraid she was having twins but I don't feel more than one calf."

Fate brought the soap and water and Alexander quickly washed his arm up past his elbow once and then again a second time leaving the bubbly suds on his arm for lubrication. He worked his arm into the birth canal past the calf's protruding feet and legs. Milk Cow bellered loudly but stood still as if knowing she needed the help he was giving her.

"Mary Ellen, I can feel the head and I am trying to push the calf back but the cow is pushing towards me. I want you to try to sooth her by stroking her neck and talking to her. Once I get it turned, it should be quick."

Just then, Milk Cow moved her bowels and stinky loose diarrhea ran down Alexander's arm and chest in a river of greenish brown, covering his stomach and pants down to his boots.

Alexander wryly commented, "Well thank you very much Milk Cow. I hope that gives you room to let this baby be born."

The pressure lessened, Alexander was able to get everything in alignment. The mama cow did the rest of the work and birthed a fine baby heifer. A moment of panic washed over Mary Ellen. The calf looked dead. The eyes were glassy. The tongue, thick and swollen stuck out one side of the mouth. Mary Ellen cleared the newborn's nostrils and throat then gently pressed the rib cage to help it draw breath. The little heifer lay on the ground emitting a raspy sound in the effort to get air into her lungs. The calves' swollen tongue suddenly flicked. The glassy eyes fluttered and opened and then the legs began to twitch. In just a few minutes, the calf was standing on wobbly legs trying to suckle for her first meal.

"Oh Papa, isn't she beautiful! She looks just like her mama!"

By late morning after all chores were completed, Mary Ellen worked alongside Alexander repairing a pigpen their big boar destroyed. Normally one of the slaves would have been doing this work but Alexander learning of Lee's surrender at Appomattox, called the slaves together and made the announcement they were freemen. He explained that if they wanted to stay and work they would draw wages and continue to live on the farm. Alexander asked they stay until the cotton crop harvest was finished. He promised they would receive food and clothing in addition to wages. Most of them disappeared within a few days of learning the war was over with the exception of old Fate. Fate was born on the Curry farm living there his entire life. He said Mr. Curry had always treated him well and besides he did not know where else to go.

The Curry family farm was on the East bank of Caddo Creek just north of Fincastle. Prior to the war The Curry's were quite prosperous. They raised cotton and harvested over four hundred bales every year prior to the war. The farm only had about twenty-five head of range cattle whereas before the war they owned almost three hundred head. Remaining were a couple of milk cows and three yokes of oxen, thirty head of sheep, two mules, five horses, a boar hog, five sows and six young pigs left from over a hundred swine when the war began. They traded the cows, pigs and lambs one by one to get staples like flour, salt and sugar. Fortunately, the sows were pregnant and would soon produce another litter. Confederate Quartermaster beef requisitions had taken most of the beef cattle but the paper money they paid with was now worthless.

Mary Ellen had watched war years wear on both Alexander and her mother Amelia. He was a stocky man with thick salt and pepper hair. Farming left him with arthritic fingers and large joints that pained him as he worked. Amelia weighed no more than a hundred pounds and stood barely five feet yet she was the boss. When she spoke, everyone listened.

Shortly after Tom and his brother left to go to the war, her cousins Elijah and Grisham enlisted as well. With her cousins gone, the work on the farm fell mostly to Mary Ellen and her father Alexander. Elijah was sorely missed and his contribution to the farm became fully appreciated. Mary Ellen's Mother, Amelia, was sickly but she made a significant contribution despite her illness. Mary Ellen's three little sisters Nannie, Julia and Belle worked alongside the adults with each assigned specific responsibilities.

Alexander said Mary Ellen had become an excellent muleskinner. Plowing the cotton fields and keeping the furrows as straight as possible was exacting work. At the end of the day, you could look down the rows and see where the mule had strayed whereas Elijah's plowing would have been straight enough to line up a compass. Mary Ellen's plowing was good enough according to her father. He said that cotton did not know straight from crooked. She also chopped wood, cooked, pulled water from the well several times every day and through it all never complained. Her only thought had been of Tom and she lived for the day he would come home. Several suitors ventured to the farm looking to court her but none elicited the slightest interest in her.

Mary Ellen was responsible for teaching her three sisters how to care for the chickens, milk the cow, separate the cream from the milk and churn the cream into butter. Nannie fed the chickens and pumped fresh water for them every morning. Julia collected the eggs each morning in a special apron with two deep pockets, each of which would usually hold six eggs. Sometimes she was not careful, over loaded the pockets and ended up dropping several on the ground. The chickens liked fresh eggs as well as the people folk did and so the flock tended to follow her about waiting for the next calamity to happen.

Nannie, like most teenagers, resisted taking directions from her older sister saying, "You are only two years older than

81

me. So how do you know so much?" It was Nannie's job to take the milk and eggs to a cellar dug deep into the earth to keep them cool.

Belle, the youngest, idolized Mary Ellen and wanted to do everything just the same as her oldest sister. Whether it was bringing the milk cows into the barn or squeezing the teats trying to milk, she was content to be at Mary Ellen's side or underfoot sometimes too.

Before the war, Mary Ellen tried raising chickens. She bought a hundred young pullets for fifteen cents a pair and she knew she was destined to have a big egg business. When the hens were too old to lay they would go into the stew pot or become fried chicken dinners. The local rooming house also said they would buy live pullets for twenty cents each so it seemed like Mary Ellen was on to something.

Egg prices were high because of the war and once a week Mary Ellen would hitch a ride to town with her father. She would take five sometimes six dozen eggs to town and sell them for twenty cents a dozen. She always managed to buy a piece of candy, which cost a penny apiece from Hawkins General Store for each of the kids.

She built a hutch for her flock to roost but they were going to be free range during the day. As they got older, they began pecking all the feathers off each other's rear end. At Fate's suggestion Alexander shot some rabbits and Fate skinned them. Fate hung the rabbit hides up in the chicken hutch so they would peck them instead of each other. It seemed to work and everything went along pretty well, until someone left the hutch door open one night and the coyotes ate every last chicken.

Julia was the one who discovered the orgy by the coyotes. Nothing but bloody feathers and guts remained. She cried uncontrollably for over two hours. Mary Ellen suspected that Nannie was the guilty culprit but never said anything. After all, the chickens were dead and they were not coming back.

The sound of barking dogs interrupted Mary Ellen's chores. She looked in the direction of the commotion and saw two figures walking down the narrow dirt road that lead from Browns-boro, Texas, south to Poyner. One figure appeared to be a small boy and the other, a tall thin man who was leading a horse that appeared to be lame.

Strangers traveling the road had become more frequent than in years past so she did not think much about them. Seconds later, she heard her name shouted from the direction of the strangers. Startled, she looked more closely. The tall individual had a familiar gait and look about him. With a sudden lump in her throat, she recognized Tom but could not call his name. She dropped the hammer she held and ran screaming to Tom's open outstretched arms. She flung her arms around his neck sobbing with tears running down her cheeks. Tom collapsed flat on his back with her beside him on the dusty road. Neither Tom nor Mary Ellen could speak for several minutes.

Finally, Tom stammered, "I love you!"

Mary Ellen continued to sob and gasped, "Oh Tom! Oh Tom, I didn't know if I would ever see you again."

Orange sat on the ground and watched them saying, "I think she still likes you's Massa Tom."

Tom managed to gain some composure and pressed the most important thing on his mind. "Will you marry me?"

Mary Ellen looked into his eyes. His sun burned, dirt streaked face revealed lines around his eyes that had not been there the last time she had seen him. Despite the change, she sensed the same warmth and sincerity as before.

"Oh, yes! Yes! Yes! I have waited so long for you to come back to me and now you are here. Yes, I will marry you!"

☆ ☆ ☆ ☆ ☆

A small crowd of family members gathered round them. Alexander told Nannie to saddle a horse and go fetch Tom's family who lived a short distance away. Late in the afternoon, a horse drawn old farm wagon loaded with Tom's mother, Rachel and his father John and his seven brothers and sisters clattered into the Curry farmyard. Parents and other family members alike had a tearful, joyful reunion. Tom was disappointed to learn that there was no news from his brother. Meeting with his two younger brothers as if for the first time, John Dave now fifteen was only ten when the war started and wanted to be called by his initials J. D. Marion now seven years old had no memory of his older brothers. His five sisters smothered their baby brother with affection and he was as spoiled as rotten meat on a hot day. Martha Jane was five years older than Tom. She had two children and was a war widow. Irving her husband died in a prisoner of war camp in Illinois. Nancy was twenty, Mary was seventeen, Sally was twelve and Amanda was nine years old.

Seven year old Marion said, "Tom, how long we been brothers?"

Tom looked at the tow headed little boy, bent over and picked him up. Laughing loudly he said, "All your life Marion, all your life."

During the afternoon, Orange was simply a curiosity with little attention paid to him by Tom or Mary Ellen's family. He was happy just to be at the end of his and Tom's long journey. He was concerned however about what his role would be in the future now with Mary Ellen entering the picture. Previously she had only been a myth. She was a dream that Tom constantly had at the forethought of his every waking moment. Seeing her in the flesh brought the reality of the relationship between her and Tom as being paramount.

Chapter 10

Montague County

Upon arriving at the Pruit farm Orange felt displaced and confused as to where he fit in. First with Mary Ellen and now he observed the hearty hug Tom and Shad shared upon meeting and realized there was a strong bond between the two. Tom enthusiastically called, "Orange, come and meet my friend Shad! Shad this is Orange, he helped me to make it across the big Mississippi." The two Negroes shared a toothy smile and shook hands.

The fact that Tom was home from the war was not the only news. The telegraph office in Fincastle was receiving messages continually concerning the profound changes announced by the government in Washington and a huge crowd gathered every day in front of the office. The mood was somber. The local population was extremely nervous about the pending arrival of Union soldiers and the unfathomable impact on their lives.

When the first company of Union blue jackets marched into Fincastle, the detachment had both black and white troopers led by a white officer. They rang the church bells to call people to the little town square. A proclamation read by the officer in charge announced that all local government and officials were hereby suspended. Martial law and military government were now in effect and a provisional Governor appointed by the President would take charge of the State of Texas.

There was a group of colored men and women among a sizable group of civilians accompanying the soldiers. The crowd learned this group of blacks representing the Freedmen's Bureau and the white men, called carpetbaggers behind their back, were government bureaucrats charged with supporting changes in the local governments. A loyalty oath imposed by the Unionist Repub-

licans most Texans call the "The Damnesty Oath," required everyone to swear they had never borne arms against the Union or supported the Confederacy including voluntarily given aid, counsel or
encouragement to the Confederacy. Any person, who sold agricul-
tural products including grain or livestock to the Rebels, were denied the right to vote or hold office in any local, state or federal
government.

Tom and Mary Ellen's families were very upset by the dis-
enfranchisement orders. Tom's Father had never been political but
not being able to vote was very irritating to him and his friends.
They soon found most State and local governments run by former
slaves supported by Yankee Carpetbaggers. Unfortunately, these
people did not have the background or education to make the best
decisions in the eyes of the white population. This, in the opinion
of many Texans, was a government for black people only.

One week after the arrival of the Union troops, Jim walked
into the Pruit homestead. He had been a prisoner since the battle
in Franklin. His normally robust stocky frame reduced to that of a
scarecrow. However, after eating his Mother's cooking for a few
weeks Jim regained his strength. Tom was overjoyed to see Jim
and he felt as though his life was coming back together again.

The brothers took time to talk about the battle in Tennessee. Jim said, "Brother, we are both very fortunate to be alive.
Most of our company died in the battle or in a Yankee prison
camp. I took a bullet through my thigh. Fortunately, the bone and
artery were unscathed. A Yankee doctor forced kerosene and sugar
in the wound stopping the bleeding saving my life. Life in prison
camp was hell with little food or decent water to drink. Many soldiers died from malaria, starvation and filthy living conditions
where raw sewage ran down into the sole little creek providing our
drinking water."

Jim responded, "I know the conditions had to be terrible. I
am lucky to not have been captured."

Jim continued, "After Lee's surrender, the Yanks paroled
Confederate soldiers and started shipping us home. Hundreds of

us were crowded into open railroad freight cars with little fresh water or food and sent south to Memphis. There the Union Army arranged with a number of ferry companies operating on the Mississippi to provide transit down the river. Only thing is that the ferry companies didn't have enough boats and those they did have damned near sank with all the men they crowded on them. Once I was on the West bank of the Mississippi, I walked across Louisiana and a stretch of Texas to get home. We scrounged food along the way from loyal Southerners who wanted to help men they saw as patriots."

Tom listened and said, "We are the lucky ones. We left too many of our friends buried in shallow graves. I am resolved to distance myself from any involvement in political activity and never fight in somebody's war ever again. I just want to get married, and put a life together with Mary Ellen."

Jim said, "I have had a lot of time to think the last few months. I met some other prisoners from Montague County while in prison camp. Montague County is on the border of Indian Territory on the Red River and those boys told how the county there was full of maverick cattle. Why, you can roundup a large herd in a few weeks and make lots of money."

Tom laughed, "Yeah, the cows are wild and the country is infested with Indians. I expect you will earn every dollar you make."

"I think the rewards exceed the risks. There is going to be high demand for beef over the next few years."

Jim's proposition was attractive to Tom as he was not a farmer. It was too confining and being a cowman offered a better life in his mind. Tom's father, John, was happy to step behind a plow and stare down furrows while Tom was bored at the thought of his life only consisting of furrows.

Both Tom and Jim shared a love for fine horses and quality cattle. It took but a few days for the two brothers to decide to form a partnership. Tom said, "Before we go we need to help Poppa.

There are things that didn't get done while we were gone to the war and we need to give him a hand for awhile."

Mary Ellen and her Mother were busy planning the wedding, scheduled for September 9, 1865, so the brothers felt they had some time to make a trip west to at least explore the area and make sure the dream of ranching was feasible.

Before leaving, they took time to repair some fences and gather some stock and several bulls for their father John and Tom's future father-in-law Alexander. In ten days, with the help of Orange they were able to accomplish a lot.

Mid-day June 20, 1865, they were standing at the confluence of the Red River and Salt Creek. As they sat astraddle their horses taking in the view Jim said, "This is even more beautiful than I ever imagined."

Rolling hills covered in tall grass with clusters of post oaks and pecan trees lay before them. The country was more open than in East Texas. There the piney woods were so thick you could not see the horizon. This country was broken with rolling hills and it seemed every swale contained a creek.

They rode into a small tent settlement aptly named Forest Hill. Tents made up most of the living quarters. Among the tents sat a wagonload of lumber waiting for someone to build a new house. Several sod houses stood completed with several more under construction. North of the Red River was Indian Territory. There were few white settlers in the area as Comanche and Kiowa raids on the locals were common and savage. The Indian threat made both men nervous. They saw men of the community cutting trees to build a stockade, which would be used in the event of an attack.

While they were in Forest Hill one of the settlers introduced them to an old cowman by the name of O. W. Wheeler. Wheeler was a man whose entire life spent under the blazing Texas sun left him with a sunbaked appearance. He was so bowlegged from years sitting a horse that he had trouble walking. He had a bony frame with not an extra ounce of fat. His face creased with deep lines was the color of tanned leather.

Wheeler told them about Joseph "Cowboy" McCoy. McCoy was an Englishman who was building a stockyard in Abilene, Kansas, which was the railhead at the time. Wheeler was promising to take four dollars a head Texas steers up to Abilene and ship them east where the market was forty dollars a head. Wheeler was heading to south Texas to gather between two and three thousand head and trail them north to the railhead.

He told them, "Boys I will make you rich. Why don't you come with me and we can work together for two or three months to put a herd on the trail."

Jim eagerly accepted but Tom emphatically said, "I gotta date to keep back home to get married."

Jim argued, "Mary Ellen will wait to marry.

"Yeah, she might but I won't."

Tom was mad as a hornet. Jim pleadingly cajoled Tom the rest of the day. Tom finally consented for them to ride south with Wheeler for no more than ten days but only to familiarize themselves with the country. Putting a herd together would need to wait.

As they rode south, Wheeler kept up a constant barrage of information, which kept both Tom, and Jim fascinated. Wheeler's experience with Indians was an asset that would be of great benefit to the brothers. Wheeler advised that there would be no campfires at night. He said a cold jerky dinner was a hell of a lot better than a knife parting your hair. Tom and Jim had no experience with Indian fighting so they tried to absorb all the advice the crusty old man dispensed. He pointed out that the first thing you needed inside a stockade was a hand dug well.

"Never let the injun's make you die of thirst and camp as close to water as possible. When you are trailin a remuda, always have a couple of boys sleep among the picket line at night and tie a line off to one of the horses.

Jim interrupted, "What's a remuda?"

"You both need to learn a little Spanish. Remuda means your horse herd. Injuns like horses and they use it as their currency when they go to trading. Why, a Comanche brave can slip into camp while you're asleep and take your long johns off and not even wake you up."

Jim sarcastically responded, "Ain't nobody gonna get in my long johns without a fight."

Wheeler looked at him and said, "Boy, you need to believe everything I'm telling ya if ya want to live to be an old man. If you do meet up with a bunch of Comanche, don't dismount and try to stand them off. You are better off spurring your hoss and trying to out run em' and find some cover to get behind. Keep in mind that those Indian ponies don't have a shiny coat like a grain fed animal but they can outrun most any white man's horse. If you are smart you will sleep with your gun in hand and a rifle under your rig. I always carry two pistols and recommend it to anyone who wants to keep their hair. Have either of you fellas had any experience with buffalo?"

Tom and Jim allowed that they did not.

The crusty old man went on, "Well you're in buffalo country now and you don't want to bed down near their watering hole. You also need to post a lookout for a stampede. Everything north and west of this country is buffalo range."

Tom winked at Jim and said, "Stampeding buffalo or cattle?"

"Hellfire, you boys got a lot to learn. Why both, if you want to live through either one."

☆ ☆ ☆ ☆ ☆

On the second day, the three of them rode into a small community known as Tarrant County. There was stockade of tall poles buried into the ground for protection in the event of an Indian attack. Settler's log cabins and tents were scattered around it. The brothers and Wheeler set up a little camp on the outside of the stockade. Wheeler intended to stay for several days and make day trips out to see the settlers in the area to make contacts to buy cattle for his trail drive.

Tom and Jim wanting to look around the town left Wheeler at the only saloon in town saying they would meet him at three o'clock. The brothers walked down the main street poking into several stores until Jim met Lu Taylor a comely young blond girl of eighteen who willingly responded to his flirtations. She instantly turned Jim upside down in love. She had long golden hair that hung to her shoulders with blue eyes and a smile that smote Jim as though he suffered from a clubbing to the head. She suggested Jim come to a barn dance that night and he promised he would be there.

At three o'clock Jim and Tom met Wheeler at the saloon. They all ordered a double shot of rotgut whisky and sat there nursing it for a few minutes when all of a sudden an old bow-legged, red-faced, pot-bellied cowboy came into the bar, took his hat off, hit it against his pants leg to knock the trail dust off and created a cloudy haze of dirt. He stood at the door for a moment looking around the room until he saw Wheeler then let out a guffaw hollering, "Yeeehaww! Wheeler!"

The grizzled old cowboy pushed his way through the crowd to their table, pulled up a chair, pushed his hat back on his head and said, "Wheeler you old sumbitch what are ya doing in town?"

Wheeler with a smile exclaimed, "Boys, let me introduce you to Tucker Smith. He is one of the original wagon bosses on the trail from South Texas to Kansas. Tucker I heard you were dead. How does a story like that get started?"

Tucker reaching for the whiskey bottle said, "Give me a swig from your bottle and I'll tell ya."

Settling back in his chair Smith began, "Well, long story short, I was up in Dodge City and me and the boys had just finished selling our cows from a long drive outa South Texas for more money than I ever seen in my life. Being thirsty, we decided that we needed to celebrate by drinking some whiskey and loving some ladies. As the night was getting late and not being as young as I used to be, I decided it was time for this ol' geezer to get some rest. There was an ol' gal there that wanted to go to my hotel room with me. I didn't want to hurt her feelings none, so I said okay. When we got to the room, I lit a lamp to get a good look at her and she had a face on her that would have scared Stonewall Jackson. So, I just grabbed my chest, gurgled a couple of times and fell on the floor. She ran out the door an I ain't never seen her again. Guess she wanted no part of a dead man and the dead man wanted no part of her."

Once the story ended Tom, Jim and Wheeler all laughed until they had tears in their eyes.

The old cowboy said, "Let me buy you fellas a fresh drink."

Tom and Jim tried to say they had some business to take care of but Tucker was not about to be denied. They sat there for another hour listening to the two older men share story after story until Jim said, "Boys, I gotta go. It has been really interesting to listen to the two of you but there is a barn dance tonight and I aim to be there with bells on."

☆ ☆ ☆ ☆ ☆

When Jim arrived at the dance, Lu surrounded by leering lecherous eyes, did not lack for attention. She was dressed in white lace and wore a string of pearls around her slender neck. He thought how nice it would be to nuzzle such a neck. He walked over to her and said "Excuse me gentlemen, I would like to request the pleasure of the next dance with the young lady."

All of the men looked at him as if he had gone mad.

The biggest in the bunch with a stern look on his face commanded, "Stranger you need to wait your turn."

Ignoring the big fella Jim pointed at a skinny pimple faced boy gawking from to his left, Jim in his most formal voice said, "May I ask sir when you made your request for the next dance?"

"Well I am second after this guy but just a half hour ago."

93

"Well, begging the pardon of all you gentlemen, I made my request known to this young beauty earlier today. Isn't that correct my lady?"

She nodded. He held out his hand, Lu placed her hand in his and he briskly waltzed her away to the astonishment of the rest of her suitors. Jim held her appropriately apart with the dignity and greatest respect possible. Lu was as stately as a princess and all eyes followed her. Her feet scarcely touched the floor as Jim whirled her about the ballroom. The moment he placed his hand around her waist he felt a tingling throughout his body.

As they joined the dancers circling round the room, she broke into a big smile, "You were pretty bold just now."

"You make me bold dressed as you are, like an angel."

She blushed and giggled enjoying the gawking eyes of the crowd. At the end of the waltz, he purposely stopped on the far side of the room away from the other suitors. "It seems we are by the refreshment table; may I ask you to join me in a glass of punch?"

"You may."

When the next dance was beginning to start Jim could see the other men moving their way. He quickly took the cup from Lu's hand and swept her away around the dance floor once again. "I may not let you dance with anyone else tonight."

She coyly replied, "Well, I have to be fair so I may need to dance with some of the others at least once but I could let you escort me home if you would like?"

"How could I refuse such a request from a beautiful young lady!"

The other suitors managed to get a dance before the evening was over but Jim could tell that they were all running a far second as she only had eyes for him as they whirled her around the dance floor. As they walked home Jim asked, "May I see you tomorrow?"

"I need to work tomorrow morning but we could go on a picnic early in the evening down by the river."

"Wonderful, what can I bring?"

Smiling coyly she whispered, "Just yourself, my darling."

☆☆☆☆☆

Their stay in Tarrant County grew from a couple of days to five. Tom was growing antsy. He told Jim, "I got a wedding to go to and I will be leaving to go home in the morning."

Jim pleaded, "Stay with me for two or three more weeks. Let me get to know Lu a little better and then I will go with you."

Tom looked down at the ground and shook his head, "I am shut with this and I am leaving in the morning with or without you."

Jim decided to appeal to Tom's more sensible, monetary side and proposed, "Why don't we brand some mavericks and leave them with Lu's father?" It happened that Lu's father was a friend of Wheeler, and according to Wheeler, an honest man. "That way he can send them to market with Wheeler when he comes through next fall."

Tom and Jim had seen a fair number of unbranded cattle on the way south. Jim was finally talking sense to Tom. He needed to make some money even if the payday was out in the future. After listening to Jim's moaning, complaining and speculating on how much money they could make way into the night, Tom relented. He agreed to stay but only as long as the mavericks were plentiful.

Tom found a local blacksmith who was so old he could hardly swing a hammer. Tom wanted to make a one piece brand with his initials T and P. With the bottom of each letter connected as to a U. The old blacksmith nodded that it would be an easy request to fulfill. When Tom returned to get his iron the P had been turned into an F. The blacksmith told Tom that he had made an iron just as he wanted but the P was blotching when he tried it on a piece of wood.

Tom said, "Hell man, my calves are hair and flesh not wood."

The old man replied, "Son, using that iron the way you asked me to make it would have been a barbecue not a branding."

They had cattle waiting to be branded, so he took it as it was made. He decided later that an iron that said TUF might make a rustler think twice about the owner of a dogie carrying such a message.

Lu's father, Washington Taylor, known by his nickname of Wash, stood about five and a half feet tall. He covered his bald head with a big broad brimmed hat. Born in Georgia and migrating west he found his wife in Arkansas. Over time, they gradually drifted further west always in search greener grass.

The Taylor family lived in a sod cabin with the walls neatly chinked and then white washed. The roof's wood shingles mostly shed the rain. Originally built as a Texas dog run house it was long and divided into three sections. The center section left open without exterior walls served as the kitchen. Wash ultimately enclosed both sides at his wife's insistence due to the cold winters and the howling winds. A large fireplace dominated one wall and was large enough for two spits for roasting meat. A long metal rod ran along the right side and held cooking pots. The two side rooms, each with their own fireplace served as sleeping areas with one side reserved for Wash and his wife and the other for their five children.

Jim went to Lu's father and asked permission to marry his daughter before he proposed to Lu. Before the week was up a date was set for their wedding to be one month after Tom and Mary Ellen's date. Jim reasoned that he could be at Tom's celebration and return to Tarrant County in plenty of time for his own ceremony.

Wash gave his future son-in-law permission to use his set of corrals to do their branding if they would put his brand on two out of every five calves they brought in. He also would hold the calves and make sure they accompanied Wheeler to Kansas.

The brothers each purchased a pair of spurs. Jim especially liked the ones with large dull rowels that jangled with every step.

He also liked using a quirt, which was long enough to slap way-ward dogies back in place. Tom preferred keeping his hands free. Tom traded his McClellan army saddle at a local trading post for a double rigged saddle suitable for working cattle. It had a big skirt covered from withers to flank with long fenders, a stout deep seat and a two-inch cantle. They both purchased a pair of chaps to pro-tect their legs from thorns amid the thick brush.

Every morning they worked, as Jim liked to say, "From can see to can't see."

It was a hot dusty job. Tom swore up and down that every post oak and bush he rode by grabbed his clothes with a thorn that was at least three inches long. They grabbed his arm, back, or face and tore his clothes off his back. He was grateful for the leather chaps he wore to protect his legs. The cattle seemed to be attracted to the thick stands of oak. The only way to get them out was to ride in and push them into the clear where Jim waited. On the second day, Tom put his heavy oiled canvas slicker on while they were working. He was sweating so bad in it that he thought a thunder-storm might build up and wash him away but it did stop the thorns from gouging him.

Four dollar calves turning into forty dollar steers, was a big motivator to the brothers. Tom constantly thought of Mary Ellen and the life they would create together. He imagined the house he would build for his new bride and dreamed of living in it with her. Trading cattle attracted Tom because he didn't like being tied to a farm seven days a week. He wanted to be able to get on his horse and ride out to see the countryside.

Tom began to think that after the wedding he and Mary El-len would move to this more open country. The land was suited for raising cattle and farming too. Lu's little brother, Kenny, who was ten wanted to go out with Jim and Tom to help gather mavericks. He was a pleasant boy with sandy hair, a ruddy complexion and a mischievous smile. Kenny idolized the brothers and followed both of the men around like a little puppy.

"Please, please take me with you. I can ride a horse and I promise I won't be any trouble."

Jim said, "You have to get your father's permission."

After much persuasion, Wash agreed to let the boy accompany Jim and Tom.

Jim told the boy, "You need to stay close. We might run into some Indians and I don't want to have you get scalped."

☆ ☆ ☆ ☆ ☆

It was another long, hot day and they were making an ever-bigger circle away from town to find calves. By early afternoon, Tom noticed that Kenny's horse was lagging back, so he rode over to the boy. Once he was alongside Kenny, he told him to dismount. Tom loosened the cinch on the boy's saddle and found the horse had developed a saddle sore. The saddle blanket had worn out and the saddle was causing a set-fast on the little mare's back. Tom unsaddled the horse, turned the saddle blanket over and flipped it front to back then saddled the horse again.

Tom told Kenny, "This is gonna be hard but you need to put most of your weight on your stirrups. So stand up and get *your* butt out of the saddle."

Kenny stood as Tom instructed. Tom continued, "Now hold onto the horn and lean forward to take as much weight off the irritated area as you can."

They rode on for a couple of hours and Tom noticed Kenny was lagging behind and sitting down in the saddle. Tom rode over to the boy and ordered, "You need to keep up. I don't want you to get separated from us."

"But I'm tired. My legs are fairly give out from standing in my stirrups like you said."

Tom *said,* "I know it is tough, but you are going to rub a hole in your pony's haunch if you don't do as I tell you."

Jim kept about twenty calves bunched that Tom goaded from the brush and moving just behind Tom. Tom would ride into an area and then work his way back in small circles pushing the cattle towards Jim. It looked like a prosperous day of gathering mavericks. Jim thought that by day's end they might put together forty or fifty head.

The ride was long and the day hot and Kenny began to lag behind once again. Jim tried to keep an eye on him but the wild calves commanded most of his attention.

Suddenly a loud yell pierced the air. Kenny, who once again had lagged behind came barreling up screaming, "Injuns! Injuns!"

Jim looked at the area from where Kenny had bolted and sure enough, there were two Indian braves riding at a full gallop toward them. Jim drew his pistol and fired a shot at them, which caused the already skittish calves to bolt in ten different directions. The Indians then veered off and went over a little hill out of sight.

Tom came out of some thick oak brush almost colliding with Kenny shouting, "What the Hell!"

Jim pointed over his shoulder, "They went over that rise. Let's go get em'."

"Hold on. We don't know if they got company waiting for us out there. It might be a trap. We best try to gather up the calves we have and head back to town."

By this time, Kenny had calmed down and Jim knew Tom was right to be cautious. It took them almost an hour to put a group of eight of the scattered mavericks back together and then they headed into town. Kenny stuck with the two men like glue going home.

Over the next few days, they were able to put their brand on almost a hundred head of cattle. Tom and Jim did the math and concluded that they were going to be rich for sure. A week later old man Wheeler popped that conjecture with, "Boys you gotta remember, it's what you deliver that you get paid for, not what you start with. We got to deal with Indians, rustlers, tornadoes, hail, ice, floods, quicksand and drought. Just might lose half the herd between Texas and Kansas."

Jim looked at Tom and said, "Now he tells us."

Tom and Jim left for home August 1st, with Lu and her family standing outside their sod home waving goodbye. Kenny had begun to idolize Jim and wanted to go with them but Wash and his wife were having none of that saying, "I ain't having you go trapsin off. You would most likely attract an Indian attack on them boys."

The brothers followed an abandoned Butterfield Stage trail to Gainesville, Texas. As they rode into town, they passed a large tree with three men hanging from one of the limbs. They could tell by the smell and look of the bodies that it was a recent event. They stopped at the general store to buy some coffee, hard biscuits, jerky and bacon.

Curiosity got the best of them so Tom asked the storekeeper, "Sir, what did those men hanging from the big tree outside of town do to end up at the end of a rope?"

"You boys are not from around here are you?"

"No sir."

"Well sir, those fellas were white Commancheros who lived with the Indians in Indian Territory. They got what they deserved after burning homes and killing white folks just south of town two days ago. There's no law out here so the town folk gave them justice."

"Are you going to bury them?" Tom asked.

"No Sir. We want everyone to see what happens if you cross the line here in Gainesville. Why this ain't nothing. During the war, we hung nineteen Union sympathizers and then a few days later, we hung another seventeen."

Paying for their purchase, Tom and Jim mounted up and left for home. Tom said to Jim, "I suspect the fellas they hanged deserved what they got but I need to shake the dust of that place off of my boots. These folks are too happy to hang people and we don't need to take any of that with us."

"I agree. The sooner we've got this town on the horizon behind us the better off we will be."

Chapter 11

Home Again

When they arrived home, six weeks later it was to find everyone in a depressed mood. Black men had replaced all public officials, including the judges, the mayor and the sheriff. The military government made appointments without an election; not that it mattered, as many former leading citizens were no longer able to vote.

Tom and Jim decided to try their hand at gathering some of the stray cattle that lived in the piney woods of East Texas. They made a deal with their father to use one of his pastures to keep the cattle confined, offering to share the fruits of their labor in the same ratio as they did with Wash Taylor. They would quickly realize a profit, as the ferry boats in Jefferson were loading cattle to take to New Orleans.

Tom was pleased to find Orange fast friends with Shad. Shad was twenty-three years old. He married during the war and Mahalia was pregnant with their first baby. After emancipation, Shad agreed with Tom's father to work for a small house to live in and all the food he could eat. He received a small salary of twelve dollars a month. Once a year they would buy some clothes at the general store paid for by Mr. Pruit.

Orange lived in a lean-to next to Shad and Mahalia's little house during Tom's absence. There was a bunk with a mattress with ticking made of cotton grown on the Pruit farm. A small wood stove kept the place warm and provided a simple way to cook. A small table with a bench was the only other furniture. A window made of cloudy glass rippled the sunlight streaming into the room. In Orange's opinion, it was far better than sleeping outside as he and Tom had done for so many weeks. In fact, it was the best quarters he ever had in his whole life. Orange's friendly personality and keen sense of humor had won Tom's family over and he quickly assimilated into the routine of farm life.

Tom had plans for Orange. He wanted to show him how to be a cowboy. They cut a small mare out for him to ride and Tom adjusted the stirrups to his first saddle to fit the boy. He found a bridle but it needed new leather reins. He spent all of one morning working some leather, cutting it to length, punching holes for the bit ties and then sewing everything together with a heavy needle and waxed twine.

Orange learned the finer points of horsemanship: how to lift a hoof and check for rocks in the shoe, how to put the bit in the horse's mouth, how much grain to feed and what the signs of founder were. The boy rode the mare into a round corral and mastered how to turn and make the horse back up. Tom showed the boy how to put his tack away and then brush the horse down.

Shortly after daybreak one morning Tom, Jim and Orange headed out to begin gathering cattle. Tom showed the boy how to push the cattle out of brush and how to hold them by working them in a circle.

"Take it slow and easy. Don't rush them. You gotta learn to think like they do."

Jim was amused at Tom's helpful mentoring of the boy. He had come to like Orange too. He could see that Orange wanted to learn and he was not lazy. By late afternoon, they put seven head in the holding pasture.

Jim commented to Tom, "Not bad, but not as good as out West."

Tom said, "Yeah, but I didn't have to worry about getting scalped today."

Turning to Orange, Tom said, "I will pay you ten cents per head for every cow we take to market. But we gotta sell them first because I don't have any money right now."

The next morning Tom woke and went down to the barn to get his horse saddled. Orange was already there and trying to put the saddle on his mare. Tom smiled to himself and said, "Good morning. I see you are anxious to start working today".

"Yessa, I's sure is."

Just then, Jim showed up. Tom said, "You're late!"

Jim looked at the dark sky that was showing only a glimmer of sunrise and said, "Hell if I am. You are just anxious to make a few dollars so you can get married."

"Well, what about you? You better make a few dollars too friend, cause I seem to remember a little gal by the name of Lu that you promised your love to."

The friendly banter went on all day long. Tom was ecstatic to be with his family again. After enduring the death and destruction of the war, he gained an appreciation for the beauty and elegance of life and nature. He promised himself to never take anything for granted again and to always tell his family that he loved them every day.

When he was not chasing maverick cattle with Jim, Tom worked diligently on cleaning up a small one-room cabin located just behind his parent's house for himself and his soon to be wife. The family had not used it for years. He removed a rat's nest from the chimney of the fireplace and hung the door so it would open and close with little effort. There was a little pot belly stove they would use for heat in the winter that offered a flat place to set a coffee pot and if not in a hurry to cook simple things like bacon and eggs. There were two broken windows requiring a trip into town to get enough glass to make the repair.

The wedding for Tom and Mary Ellen was less than a week away, so their cattle gathering work was over until after the wedding. Tom, Jim and Orange took the cattle down to the holding pens in Athens. After a count, the cattle broker paid them off in gold coins for one hundred twenty head. It had worked to their advantage to gather and hold the cattle in a pasture of good grass for several weeks as they actually put on some weight and filled out quite nicely. The cattle broker liked what he saw. They were able to negotiate a price of seven dollars per head. Tom and Jim could hardly believe that they now had real gold coins in their pockets.

Tom told both Jim and Orange that they were going shopping. He led the way down the street in Athens to Virgil Hawkins's General Store. Hawkins was a genial middle-aged man with a big handlebar mustache that he kept waxed to perfection. He offered open account credit, which people paid generally once a year after the harvest. He always wore a canvas apron with two pockets on the front that held a pair of scissors and twine. He used those to tie packages or cut cloth from the bolts of fabric.

The first thing people saw walking in the front door of Hawkins store was a candy case. It was the most delicious sight Orange had ever seen. He stood mesmerized at the front of the candy case with his nose pressed to the glass while Tom and Jim were busy.

Tom picked out a new black suit with a vest for three dollars, a new white shirt for half a dollar and a felt hat with a silver hatband for three dollars. He also tried on several pairs of boots. The ones he was wearing had a hole worn in the outer sole and Tom had been placing a strip of cowhide on the inside allowing him to walk without getting thorns in his feet. He was attracted to a fancy pair with different colored stitching but selected a pair that would serve as work boots after the wedding. Jim likewise purchased an outfit that would also double for his own ceremony in just a little more than a month.

Before Tom paid his bill, he saw Orange staring at the candy with a drooling mouth. Tom said, "Mr. Hawkins, I want to pick out a new shirt and pair of pants for the boy too, and when we are done he gets to pick out a piece of candy.

Orange's face took on a look of complete surprise and a smile spread on his face from ear to ear.

When they finished at the store, they went over to see Mrs. Anderson the proprietress of a boarding house. It was a regal clapboard house with whitewashed walls and black shutters. A wide porch on three sides of the structure with chairs for guests to lounge in during the cooler part of the evenings offered a welcoming setting. The paint was beginning to peel in a few places due to a lack of attention; otherwise, it was a fine elegant building. Tom's family had known Mrs. Anderson since Tom was just a little thing. He knocked on the door and it was opened by a lady with salt and pepper hair done up in a bun. Once an attractive, matronly looking woman she possessed a welcoming personality.

When she saw Tom, a twinkle in her eye sparkled in recognition. She said, "Why, Tom! I haven't seen you since before the war."

"Yes that's right, Mrs. Anderson."

"Well what brings you to see me today?"

Tom explained his planned marriage to Mary Ellen Curry and he wanted to rent her parlor and bedroom on the second floor for his honeymoon.

"Well Tom, I have one condition for the rental of the parlor and bedroom."

"What is that, Mrs. Anderson?"

"An invitation to the wedding, of course."

"Mrs. Anderson our wedding wouldn't be complete without your graceful presence."

"I usually rent the room for $1.50 per night but in your case it will only be a dollar. I will also have breakfast each morning for you too."

"Thank you, Mrs. Anderson. I will need it for two nights and I will pay you in advance."

"I will make sure the accommodations are suitable for a honeymoon."

When Tom concluded his business with Mrs. Anderson, they headed to the closest saloon. As they walked through the swinging doors of the establishment, the familiar smell of tobacco smoke, beer, sweat and urine wafted into their nostrils. It was a dimly lit room with tables, chairs and crude benches made of hewn trees. The dirt floor covered in sawdust over time had soaked up copious volumes of whiskey and urine. A card game surrounded by gamblers was at the rear of the room. Older men played dominoes at a square table near the front door. A long bar made of wooden stave barrels with planks for a surface stood before the wall to the left of the swinging entrance doors.

They selected a table near the far side of the room away from most of the other patrons. Tom walked up to the bar and asked for a bottle of whiskey with two glasses and a glass of sarsaparilla so they could toast their hard work and good fortune. After the barkeep served their drinks, Tom lifted his glass to propose a toast.

Jim picked up his glass and said, "Orange, join us."

Tom spoke, "To brotherhood, family and friendships which surpass all others."

"Hear! Hear!" Jim said in a loud voice.

Tom counted out twelve silver dollars, which he stacked on the table in front of the boy saying, "We had a deal that when we sold our cattle that I would pay you for helping."

Breaking into a toothy smile Orange said, "Mr. Tom, I's ain't never had nobody pay me fer nuthin' in my whole life. I's rich now."

Laughing Tom said, "Well Orange, after we finish our drink, we can go back over to the general store and you can buy Shad and Mahalia a stick of sweet candy to thank them for helping you get your room set up."

Orange's smile got even broader and he said, "You's right Mr. Tom. That is what we gonna do."

The three of them luxuriated in their newly earned wealth until a couple of former Confederate soldiers swaggered up to their table and stood there looking disdainfully at them. The taller of the two crossed his arms, spread his feet and said, "Well, well, well, ain't this a cozy little group."

Jim heard the voice of the man and looked over his shoulder to see who stood behind him. The taller man had a pistol slung low on his hip. He also had a scowl on his face with an ugly scar running at an angle from his ear to his chin.

Snarling in a deep raspy voice the tall man said, "What the hell are you two doing sitting in here with a little nigger?"

Looking up, Tom pushed his hat back and studied the man's face for a moment before he answered "Mister, I don't know what your problem is but the boy's not hurting anybody and we didn't come in here looking for trouble."

Neither Tom nor Jim wore a weapon into town thinking there was no need. The tall man's partner, a short pudgy fella with a face lacking intelligence and not nearly as assertive hung back a couple of steps. He wore a Colt Army revolver slung low on his hip but his hands were trembling and his eyes flitted nervously between Tom and Jim

"Well, sometimes you don't have to be looking for trouble to find it. I don't cotton to white folks drinking with Niggers", the tall man said.

Suddenly, Jim tossed his liquor over his shoulder into the tall man's face. In the same movement, he grabbed the man's gun hand with his left hand and smashed his right fist into the man's big nose, forcing him back into his shorter partner. Springing like a cat on the shorter man, Tom hit him once on the jaw. The man dropped as if he'd been shot. Jim hit the tall man again in the face without turning loose of his gun hand and he too fell to the floor.

Running over with a Billy club in his hand the barkeep saw there was no need for further action. Looking down at the two men lying in filthy sawdust crawling with ants he said, "These two are trouble. They spend every dollar they got on whiskey and I don't know what they do to make their money."

Collecting the pistols carried by the two men Jim handed them to the barkeep saying, "Hide these guns until we can get our horses and hit the road for home."

Turning to Orange whose eyes were the size of one of the twelve silver dollars he had just been paid, Tom said, "Pick up your money Orange, we're going home."

Chapter 12

The Wedding

Tom went into town to fetch the preacher the morning of the wedding. When Tom got to town and knocked on the preacher's door, he learned the man was ill and that he would need to use a local judge. The preacher had arranged earlier for the judge to perform the wedding so it was only a matter of taking the buggy over to the judge's home to get him.

Guests started arriving that afternoon and small camps were set up all around the Curry farmhouse. Folks brought along their moonshine and the revelry was well underway by nightfall. Dancing and singing, some of it completely out of tune, filled the air.

The ceremony, outside under a large oak tree in the front yard of the Curry home was simple. The Judge asked Tom to stand a tall stump on end so he could use it as a podium. Tom and Jim along with their father and Mary Ellen's father arranged long logs for people to sit on resembling pews in a church. A center aisle for the bride and groom led to the makeshift altar.

Mary Ellen wore a long white dress with intricate lacework and several petticoats that both her mother and grandmother wore at their weddings. She looked beautiful. Tom and Jim both wore their new suits and when Mary Ellen saw them she laughingly said, "Jim, you look like you are getting some practice for your own wedding."

Jim smiled and kicked the dirt. "Yep, it's too bad that Lu isn't here to tie the knot with me today but since Mrs. Anderson only has one honeymoon suite its best that she isn't."

A fiddler started playing a screeching tune that was supposed to be a wedding march but it did not sound like anything familiar. Mary Ellen's sisters, Nannie, Julia and Belle attended her. Tom's little brother Marion was the ring bearer. The ring handed down through the generations originally belonged to Tom's great grandmother. When Rachel, Tom's mother, gave the ring to Tom, she said, "This ring was worn by my Grandmother. I give it to you to give to your wife as a promise to love her forever."

As Tom looked at the open palm holding, the ring his eyes filled with tears, "Oh Momma, I know how much it means to you and I know Mary Ellen will cherish it just as you have." Tom gave her a big hug and kissed her on her forehead.

When Tom stood next to the Judge immediately before the ceremony he smelled of liquor and seemed unable to keep a steady stance.

Tom said, "Judge, are you so drunk you are not going to be able to perform the ceremony? "

"Well son, this is only my second wedding ceremony so needed a little something to steady my nerves."

"Looks to me like you had more than enough to steady your nerves."

"Don't worry I wrote down the order of the ceremony so I wouldn't forget anything."

Everything went off without a hitch until the Judge said, "Tom, do you take this woman, Esther Marie as your...."

Tom immediately cut him off, "Now hold on Judge, you're about to ruin my whole life by marrying me off to the wrong woman."

The judge looked startled and said, "Well what is her name?"

"Mary Ellen, Judge! Mary Ellen! Do you think we can get on with it now?"

The crowd all laughed uproariously causing the poor judge to stutter and turn crimson. It took a few moments for the raucous crowd to settle down.

After the Judge pronounced them man and wife, Tom lifted the veil covering Mary Ellen's face. They stood for a moment looking into each other's eyes. As Tom leaned down to meet the lips of his petite bride, he thought he was experiencing a dream. She had been the single motivating factor in his surviving the war and here she was, face tilted up, eyes closed, eagerly awaiting his embrace.

As soon as Tom kissed Mary Ellen, people started shooting their guns up in the air and the celebration began in earnest. Following the wedding feast Jim tapped a spoon against a glass and all eyes turned to him. As the crowd quieted he said, "Ladies and Gentlemen, please stand and join me as I propose a toast to the Bride and Groom. Today, my brother and his chosen best friend are celebrating a life-changing event. To Mary Ellen, may the happiest day of your past be the saddest day of your future."

Many voices broke in saying, "Hear! Hear!"

"Tom, you need to learn that there are two theories as to arguing with a woman. Neither one works."

Laughter rolled through the crowd.

Jim continued, "May the road you travel together be filled with love and happiness forever." Jim lifted his glass and the cry of "Hear, Hear!" broke out again.

Tom and Mary Ellen honored their marriage by dancing the first dance. As Tom spun her round, his eyes looking deeply into hers he saw a radiance that filled not only her eyes but also her whole being.

★★★★★

Jim was feeling no pain and coerced his brother into taking several shots of a neighbor's homemade whiskey until Tom said, "I refuse to drink any more of this rotgut. My head is starting to spin and I would like to be awake and alert later."

Walking over to where his bride was squired around the dance floor by a lummox he had never seen before, Tom swooped his bride up in his arms carried her to the buggy that was hitched and waiting. The crowd gathered and cheered the couple. Climbing up beside her, he let out a rebel whoop slapped the reins and the horse and buggy bolted away from the wedding.

Tom drove the buggy over hills and along creeks while exchanging kisses with his bride. A deer bounding across the road startled their horse causing the buggy to swerve dangerously. The tilting of the buggy drew a gasp from Mary Ellen and she wrapped her arms around him ever tighter.

The bridal suite dimly lit in the upstairs window awaited them when they arrived. Tom eagerly tied the buggy to a hitching rail near the front steps and carried his new bride up the steps, across the threshold and up to the second floor. "Do you have the key, he asked?

She whispered, "Of course you silly boy, how could I forget something so important? Don't you remember, I put it in your coat pocket earlier?"

Tom fumbled with the key holding her with one arm, the other shoving the door open with such force that it thudded against the wall. Sounds of several stirring guests caused Mary Ellen to put her finger to her mouth shushing him. The room, lit by one lamp turned very low allowed shadows to play across the soft carpets on the floor.

He carried her into the little bedroom and laid her on the down comforters covering a most luxurious bed. She pulled him to her saying, "The moment I have dreamed of for so long."

They embraced, kissing, her breathing deepened into moans and panting. She was first to speak, "Wait, wait; let me get out of my gown."

Tom rose and stood facing a window uncertain as to what to do. Moon light streaming into the room fell across the bed casting a dim light. The newness flooded over him filling his virginity with total unfamiliarity. He beseechingly asked a higher power to be a good husband. He heard the subtle sounds of her undressing, recording it for posterity in the depths of his mind. He felt her beside him. She helped to remove his coat, then his shirt and pants. She took his hand in hers; it was dainty and warm. A hand, full of life made for just such a time. She led him to the bed reclining, pulling him to her. It was the most perfect time his life had known or would ever know.

Awhile the honeymooners were away a flurry of activity saw Alexander and John whitewashing the exterior with Orange and Shad splitting cedar shingles and repairing the roof. Jim rigged up a bell he purchased at Hawkins store and hung it beside the yard gate so visitors could announce themselves, teasingly saying, "Newlyweds need lots of privacy."

When Mary Ellen and Tom returned home, new curtains made by her mother and mother-in-law decorated their little cabin. A new cowhide rug covered the floor in the sitting area and flowers placed in a vase on the single table in the house welcomed them home. Tom and Mary Ellen thought it positively looked homey and were further surprised to find quilts and bedding donated by wedding guests.

Two days after Tom and Mary Ellen returned from their honeymoon Jim announced his plans to leave for Tarrant County. Tom regretted that he and Jim would again be separated, but Mary Ellen felt that she wasn't ready to leave her family just yet. After much discussion, Tom acquiesced to her desire to stay in Fincastle.

That night after supper Tom slipped out of the house saying, "I have something for you. It's a surprise so sit still until I call you."

In a few minutes, he called for Jim. When Jim came out the door, Tom was standing with Walker sporting a new saddle and blanket along with a new bridle on his head. "Jim, this is my wedding present to you. You are going to need a good horse to out run the Indians in north Texas." Jim tried to protest but Tom would have none of it. Handing the reins to Jim he said, "We got several horses here on the place that I can use. Besides, I ain't planning on taking any trips for a while and I want you to have a mount that will keep some Indian from getting your scalp. You can use your old mount as a pack animal. You're gonna need it to take all the wedding presents Mama has made for you and your new bride."

Tom paused for few seconds and said, "Look in the rifle scabbard."

Jim walked around the horse's rump to see the butt of a new Henry forty-four caliber repeating rifle protruding from a saddle scabbard. He took the gun out of the scabbard and whistled, "I heard of this gun when I was a prisoner. You can load this baby on Sunday and shoot all week long. I think those Indians better watch out if they aim to tangle with me. I heard it holds twelve rounds."

Tom said, "Fifteen."

All Jim could do was whistle again saying, "Thank you brother. Thank you."

"I wish Mary Ellen and I could be at your wedding but I promise, we will come and see you soon." Tom embraced his brother with tears in his eyes.

At sunup, the next morning Jim was ready to step in the stirrup. After he swung up into the saddle, he looked down at Tom and said, "I aim to marry and as soon as possible, move north to Montague County and settle. You remember that land just south of the Red when we first were on the top of the hill looking down on the river? That is where I intend to build my home. I will be looking over my shoulder every day to see if you are coming."

He spurred his new horse and waved goodbye as he rode away.

Chapter 13

A New Generation

Tom awakened to the sound of a baby cooing. Their daughter had been born almost exactly nine months after the wedding was now three months old. His little girl, Belle, lay cradled in his arm with her tiny arms and legs moving in motion as if dancing to the early morning serenade of birds chirping. He looked at his daughter's tiny hands and little feet. Realization of the perfection of this small being astonished him. The baby was truly a gift from God, a miracle. He loved Mary Ellen intensely but the love he felt for his child was different. With his wife, passion and carnal knowledge was strong. It was a beautiful magnificent thing. The child evoked intense emotion of the purest love that filled his whole consciousness.

The sun light beamed from the eastern sky. He marveled at how peaceful it was. The fragrance of fresh coffee wafted through the air of their small home. Suddenly the door opened. Mary Ellen entered the little one room house with a basket of fresh eggs.

"Well I see my lazy bones are awake now. The coffee will be ready shortly and I will get some breakfast started."

Tom marveled at her energy level. She continuously surprised him with her positive way of living life coupled with faith. She had a difficult time giving birth to Belle and now she was pregnant again.

Her eyes had flashed mischievously and a smile had come across her face saying, "I am not sure what I am going to do with you if you are going to keep me with child all the time."

Tom stood embracing her while kissing her gently on the lips saying, "I wouldn't have it any other way."

She picked the baby up letting her nurse while she expertly cracked several eggs with her free hand into a skillet. Tom quickly dressed. Outside at the well he pumped a pan full of fresh water. As he washed his face and hands, he heard his mother's voice calling his father to breakfast. Soon the sound of Shad chopping firewood and then softly talking to Mahalia drifted across the yard to Tom. She had been pregnant at the same time as Mary Ellen but she lost her baby. She started hemorrhaging and they thought she was going to bleed to death. She was pregnant again too. The sounds of the voices, the coolness of the morning and the peacefulness of a new day struck Tom. He thought what a perfect time of life. He finished with his chore, went inside and poured himself a full cup of coffee.

Mary Ellen sat at the table still nursing the baby. She smiled at him and said, "Come eat your breakfast."

Speaking admiringly he said, "It looks like that dainty little gal is still getting hers."

Tom sat and studied his young wife's face and saw that she seemed to be perfectly content. She became pregnant almost immediately after the wedding. While it had been Tom's intent to move out West to join his brother she asked him to let her have this first baby while she was close to her mother. Tom agreed, he knew how important it would be to have someone close to Mary Ellen during that time. The birth of their daughter was difficult and he was thankful for his mother-in-law's presence. He recognized that the women folk just naturally knew what needed to be done and how helpless he had felt during the birth.

Mary Ellen mused, "I think we need to have a preacher baptize Belle before she gets any older. I heard the new man at the church outside of Fincastle has done several baptisms at people's homes. We can arrange for the preacher to come out for Sunday dinner and do it right here at the farm. Would you ask him, please, the next time you get supplies?"

After breakfast, Tom joined his father, Shad and Orange splitting fence rails from pine trees. This was mind numbing work made more so by the heat and humidity. They would drive a wedge into the log and then another one a few inches away until the split ran the length of the lumber. They would then split that half into yet two more lengths. Their work yielded approximately four rails for each log. They were so proficient at this that they could produce consistently sixteen to twenty rails every hour. At midday, the sound of the dinner bell ringing across the pasture called everyone to eat lunch back at the main house.

After lunch, Tom needed to go to town to get supplies with Orange. He would also see the preacher and set a date for the Baptism. As Tom harnessed the horses to the wagon, he began thinking about the future where Orange fit in. Orange had gotten tall in the last year and a half growing by probably six inches. He was no longer a boy. Tom admired him for his willingness to work at whatever chore he was asked to do and to do it with a smile on his face. He was as much a part of Tom's family as his own brothers and sisters. In some respects, he had shared more with Orange than anyone except for his brother Jim. Obviously, the world had changed for young black men but at the time most of them were struggling more with life now than before the war. While he had not discussed this with Mary Ellen he decided to offer Orange the opportunity to go West with them.

The creaky old wagon rattled down the road to town, dust rising in a cloud behind them. Before the war Tom would have routinely strapped on his gun however since the war the Reconstruction government had made it illegal to carry a weapon. Since the run-in with the drunken Confederate Soldier, Tom felt vulnerable every time he left the farm. He was determined not to be surprised in the future.

Twice previously, Tom encountered the same Confederate soldiers. The first time, they stood in front of the saloon glaring at Tom as he went by. Pretending not to notice, Tom went about his business. The second time was at the cattle pens and several more of men were with them. It was apparent that the war was not over yet for this group of bitter individuals who persisted in wearing the Confederate uniform.

Today, Tom stopped the wagon on the street in front of Hawkins General Store. The proprietor Mr. Hawkins, greeted the familiar pair heartily. After the perfunctory exchange of pleasantries Tom handed Hawkins a list of supplies needed and said, "Mr. Hawkins, I will leave Orange here to get everything loaded while I go over to the bank if that is ok with you?"

Hawkins replied, "Why of course it's okay. Orange and I will be just fine. In fact, we just might find a piece of candy for Orange, isn't that right Orange?"

"Yessah, I's already got my eye on sumthin."

☆ ☆ ☆ ☆ ☆

Finished with his banking errand, Tom was accosted as he walked down the street by two men, "Mr. Pruit, my name is Albert Johnson and this is Dimmit Smith. We would like a moment of your time" the man began pleasantly. "We represent an organization that is putting a group made up of Veterans of the Confederacy whose aim is to counter the efforts of the carpetbaggers and the Yankee government. We want to restore our old system of government that protected our rights to own slaves. We know you served honorably and would like you to join us at our next meeting on Saturday at seven in the evening."

Tom stopped mid-step and looked at the two men. Both were well dressed and Johnson spoke as an educated man. He decided he needed to be careful in his response.

"Well gentlemen, sounds like your goals are just what we fought a war about and lost. What is the name of your organization?"

"We call ourselves the Klan, The Ku Klux Klan. It is a secret group. You would need to make a commitment and sign a secrecy oath in blood. "

"Where are you meeting?"

"We keep our meeting place secret. In fact, we change it every meeting. This week we will gather on the west side of the stockyards and then ride out to our meeting place."

"I appreciate your consideration gentlemen but I would like some time to think it over." Tom tipped his hat and said, "Now if you will excuse me I have some business to attend to."

As Tom walked down the street, he thought to himself that the invitation sounded like trouble. He fought a war, a war that was lost and he was ready to move on with life. Personally, he found slavery to be a repugnant practice that had no salvation.

As he walked down the boardwalk, he came upon a group of fancy carpetbaggers and Negroes with silk vests and plumed hats. The men, laughing and backslapping, enjoyed what Tom assumed to be a good joke. As he approached, one of the Negroes turned to him and said, "Boy, this is our side of the street. You best cross over to the other side."

Tom's focus snapped to attention. His first inclination was to continue to walk down the boardwalk. He had never been intimidated by anyone in his entire life. He grabbed his emotions and forced himself to stop and cross to the other side. As he did, raucous laughter erupted between the white and black men. Such an insult would never have happened before the war. A thought of finding the two men who invited him to a secret meeting of the Klan flooded into his mind. He had to think about his wife and daughter and what would happen to them if he were jailed for participating in such divisive activities.

Chapter 14

Rufus Snowden

As he passed The Emporium, a lady's boutique which often attracted his wife's eye on trips with him into town. She would longingly look at the window displaying fine women's attire standing outside on the boardwalk but always refusing to succumb to the urge to buy something. Today he was going to surprise her.

He went in and asked for help in picking something out. A matronly lady asked, "May I help you?"

"Yes Mame, I need to buy something for my wife."

"How tall is she?"

He held his hand out indicating, "Bout this tall."

"Is she thin or heavy?"

"Mame, she is just right."

She selected several items for his approval and he selected a blue skirt with flowers stitched along the bottom and a white blouse to go with it. It gave him great pleasure to be able to surprise her with store bought clothes. She wore mostly homemade clothes fashioned from inexpensive bolts of cloth or spun from flax grown on the farm. He also bought a pair of overalls and a pair of shoes for his little Belle.

While Tom was still in the boutique paying for his purchases, he heard loud voices coming from the area of the general store. He went outside and he could see a crowd of laughing men gathered in the street. Suddenly Orange literally flew out of the mass of men and landed hard on his back in the middle of the street. As Orange struggled to get up, Tom recognized one of the Confederate soldiers from their previous encounters. The man was laughing as he kicked the boy in the face. Raucous laughter from the crowd followed. Tom dropped his packages on the boardwalk of the boutique and dashed down the street.

As Tom passed the end of the wagon that was partially loaded with their supplies, he grabbed an axe handle. The Confederate did not see Tom come up behind him. Tom swung the axe handle with all his might hitting the Confederate in the small of the back. The man fell to one knee. He swung again catching the man full in the face. Several of the man's teeth flew out into the air. His next swing caught the man on the side of his face and he collapsed on the ground. Tom was on him like a wild man and starting to swing the axe handle again when several men grabbed him and restrained him. Tom was yelling for them to let him go but someone hit his head from behind. Tom went down and the next thing he knew he was lying on a bunk in the local jail.

When he could finally clear his mind he saw the face of a tall husky black man who looked to be about forty years old staring down at him. The black man had a badge on his vest and a frown on his face.

Tom said, "What happened?"

"Well sir, you just damn near killed a man today. You worked the fella over pretty good. I got him in the next cell and I got your boy Orange in the cell on the other side. I brought you both in here for safekeeping. Your man had a bunch of his friends with him and they were ready to lynch you."

Tom looked at the Confederate man who was still unconscious. His bloody face and head looked like he had sustained quite a beating. Tom returned his eyes to the black man with the badge.

"Are you the law?"

"Yeah, I was appointed Sheriff last month."

"Am I under arrest?"

"Nope, I just brought you in here to keep you from attending a necktie party as the guest of honor. Old man Hawkins told me what happened and I feel like you were justified in what you did."

"What happened?"

"Well it seems that your boy Orange was loading the wagon with your supplies and this guy picked a fight with him. Your boy tried to put up a good fight for a while but with a couple of others tripping him and shoving him, the sumbitchs got the best of him."

Tom looked at Orange's bruised face. One eye was swollen shut and he had blood spatters on his shirt and face.

"Are you okay, Orange?"

"Yessah. Orange is okay. I'se a little banged up but don' look like nothing broken."

Tom's head was ringing and the lump on the back of his head was hurting severely.

The sheriff handed Tom a pan filled with water and a cloth and said, "Here take this and put it on your head. You got some blood clotted and quite a lump on your head but I think you'll be fine."

Tom made a feeble attempt to clean the blood off the back of his head and neck and in a few minutes asked, "Are we free to go?"

"Yeah, you can go, but me and my deputy are going to give you an escort out of town. This guy has got a lot of no good friends and I suspect they are waiting to waylay you. I've got your wagon out front. Old man Hawkins finished loading your wagon and said you could settle up with him the next time you were in town."

As Tom and Orange climbed up on the wagon he remembered about his purchases at the boutique for Mary Ellen. I gotta go over to the ladies boutique to pick up some packages there too."

"I already got 'em for you. The lady proprietor brought them over to me. They are in the back of the wagon."

"I also need to stop at the bank."

"Probably best that I go with you there too."

"Much obliged Sheriff. By the way Sheriff, you got a name?"

"Yes Sir, I'm Rufus Snowden originally from South Carolina."

Tom went into the bank and withdrew every dime of his money. He felt that he needed the money in his possession should he need to leave the area. It came to seven hundred forty dollars, all from his cattle business. After the stop at the bank the Sheriff and one of his deputies accompanied them to Hawkins Store, so he could pay that bill and then outside of town for about two miles where they said goodbye.

After riding in silence for a few minutes Tom asked Orange, "What happened at the Hawkins store?"

"Well suh, I was totin' some sacks of flour out to the wagon and all of a sudden some men tripped me as I came out of the store and I fell down the steps of the store. When I got up that Confederate man hit me in the face and knocked me down again. After that, I don't exactly remember nothin'. I sorry, Massa Tom."

"Orange it wasn't your fault. That is the same man we had trouble with at the saloon when Jim was with us last year."

"Yessah, Orange remembers him."

As they arrived at the farm, Mary Ellen came running expectantly with a happy smile on her face that suddenly turned to a look of horror upon seeing Orange's face. She burst into tears crying, "Oh my God! What happened! Orange? Are you alright, Tom?"

Tom's father and mother, and all of his brothers and sisters along with Shad and Mahalia soon gathered in a circle around Tom and Orange. The questions came like a barrage. It was a half hour in the telling.

Tom hesitated telling Mary Ellen what his concerns were with the Confederate nor did he tell her or his father about his conversation with Johnson and Dimmit Smith. He did not want to give either any more to worry about.

After that incident, Tom tried to put the events in Fincastle out of his mind but they just would not go away. He knew that from now on every time he needed to go into town there would be a risk of something similar happening. He spoke with his father and expressed his concerns and they decided his father would be the one to make the supply runs in the future.

Tom and Orange took up gathering stray unbranded cattle, which suited them both just fine. There was a ready market for beef and the price was good. Since the end of the war, the folks back east had demanded more beef and the cowboys in Texas were ready to provide it.

About a month later, a letter arrived from Jim. A letter was an important family occasion and everyone gathered around the dinner table to have Mary Ellen read it aloud:

"Dear Family,

I hope this epistle finds you well. I am good and Lu and I are very happy. We have a little girl. Her name is Laura. We lost our first baby when he was just two days old. Lu is pregnant again and the baby should be born in the spring. We would like to move up close to the Red River but the Indians have held us close to Lu's family. Still hope to see you in Montague County soon. We are still staying with Wash just north of Azle, which is located on the west fork of the Trinity. He would enjoy seeing you and would be glad for you to stay there for however long you need to. The best place for you to cross the Trinity is at Trinidad. A man by the name of Earhart has a ferry there that will handle heavy wagon loads. I am holding your money from the cattle Wheeler sold for us. I have continued to gather cattle and will join Wheeler's next drive north taking them to market in Dodge City. I send my love to everyone. Jim

P.S. This is Lu writing

The letter brought both happy news and sad news but it was the first communication from Jim in over a year. Everyone was elated to hear from him and every one wished that it had been Jim in person to arrive, not just a letter. Tom was frustrated that Jim did not say how much money awaited him, but he was relieved that there was any money at all.

Chapter 15

The Negro Bureau

Several weeks later Tom, his father, John, along with his little brother John David were eating lunch with the family when suddenly the commotion of several men on horses and wagons clattered up to the front of the house. Tom's father got up from the dinner table and walked outside to see who was paying them a visit. There were three white men dressed in fancy duds astride some great horseflesh and five black men in two wagons. A short fat black man climbed down from the lead wagon and asked, "Are you Pruit?"

"I am. What can I do for you?"

"We are with the Freedmen's Bureau."

"So what's your business with me?"

"You got any Negroes working here."

"Yes, we have some. Why do you want to know?"

"We are here to check that you have a written contract with them."

Tom's father was a man just shy of sixty with a weathered face from years of working under the sun. He stood just over six feet tall with an impressive physique of broad shoulders and strong arms. He just stood silently for a short bit.

He said, "I don't have a written contract. We do business on a handshake. My word is good and so is theirs."

"Well Mr. Pruit, we are going to take you and your Negroes to town for a hearing before the Bureau to confirm what you are telling us. Where are they?"

Tom's Father who prided himself in a code of honor and truthfulness resentfully said, "They are down in our South pasture putting up a rail fence but let's get something straight. I ain't going

128

to town with you and neither are they. I am no liar and I resent you coming here and suggesting I am."

"Well old man, we are prepared to use force if necessary so I would advise you to cooperate."

A gunshot cracked the air. All of the carpetbagger's horses started pitching violently and one of the carpetbaggers flew off his mount into the dirt. Tom had left the house with his pistol through the backdoor and now stood to the rear of the Yankee carpetbaggers and the black men in the wagon.

Tom said, "You men best get off our property now!"

The short fat black man though visibly shaken, just stood there with his mouth open. Tom said, "My next shot may draw blood."

The little black man scrambled up into the wagon and announced, "You'll be sorry! We will be back with Union troopers."

As the group of Freedmen left the farm Tom's Father said, "I'll be damned if a bunch of Yankee's can come on my property and call me a liar."

Good to his threat the little black man came back three days later with twenty soldiers and the same three carpetbaggers. This time they surrounded the main house but Tom was not there. They threatened to burn the houses and barns down if Tom's father did not produce Tom and their Negro workers. Tom's little brother John David ran to the pasture to bring Tom, Orange and Shad back to the house.

When they presented themselves to the little fat black man, he told them they were being taken into Athens for a hearing. The carpetbaggers with them produced a set of irons and shackled Tom and his father's hands and legs. They then made them get up in a wagon with two Union soldiers to watch them. They put Orange and Shad in a separate wagon and all of them were taken to town. Mary Ellen and the rest of the family were screaming at the soldiers to let them go with little acknowledgment other than to be shoved aside.

Tom and his father were put in a stockade the Army had built for troublemakers on the outskirts of Athens. Orange and Shad were told to show up the next day at ten o'clock in the morning. Both of the young blacks were given twenty-five cents and told to find something to eat but no provisions were made for a place to sleep. Orange had no idea what to do. The only person he knew in the whole town was Mr. Hawkins at the general store. He and Shad walked to Hawkins Store to ask Mr. Hawkins what to do. Hawkins had come to know Orange from his visits to the store and grown to like the young black man.

"Orange! What brings you to my store today? Where is Tom?"

"Massa Hawkins, we gots a problem. Tom and his Papa, Massa Pruit, dey dun been arrested by the Negro Bureau and we needs to find a place to sleep and sumthin' to eat."

Hawkins frowned and said, "What were they charged with?"

"Don' rightly know fo' sure. Sumthin' bouts a written contract for us to work for dem."

"Well boys, come with me. I can let you sleep in my warehouse for a few days. In fact, if you are willing, I need to have some heavy lifting done and I will trade your time for some food and candy."

Orange looked at Shad. Shad nodded his agreement. "Thank you, suh. We's happy to do that."

Tom and his father occupied the same cell. A pile of straw for a bed, a water bucket with a ladle and a chamber pot were the only things in the cell. There were several dozen men in other cells. After the guards went outside the other prisoners wanted to know why they had been thrown into the stockade. When they told them it was a familiar story, as they too had experienced the same situation. Most had been fined and were unable to pay so they were forced to serve out whatever sentence they had been given. Several men confided that they had been members of the Klan and participated in burning Negro homes. There was a general mur-

muring of approval to create violence against Negroes including killing them. Tom disagreed as he realized that it wasn't the former slaves causing the problems but the Yankee Carpetbaggers who were white men.

That night several soldiers led a kitchen crew of black men and women into the cell area to serve the daily ration of weak potato soup and a piece of moldy bread. Each cell got a fresh bucket of water daily. The inmates emptied their honey buckets into a large barrel on a different small wagon.

After they had choked down the soup and bread Tom said, "Just remembered something I never got around to telling you about. A couple of men that approached me the last time I was in town to join a secret group they called the Klan. They say it is their intent to restore slavery and kick the Yankees out of Texas.

"Who were they?"

"Men I had never seen before; one by the name of Johnson, the other called himself Dimmit Smith."

"I don't know those men and I don't think you should go to their meeting."

"I am not planning on it."

Sleep that night was scarce for both Tom and his father. Tom had never been so happy to see the sun come up in his life. After daybreak a Negro Union Sergeant and two guards unlocked the cell door. He told them to get to their feet and follow him to an area that had a large horse trough. Given a bar of soap, the two men welcomed the opportunity to clean up. When they were finished, he led them back to their cell and told them that they would be appearing before a Union Colonel who would conduct the hearing at noon.

A Negro Sergeant accompanied by two soldiers arrived about a half hour early prior to the court proceedings to escort them. Shackled and shuffling with chains clattering, the two men entered the courtroom and were told to be seated at a table before the Judge. Tom recognized the room as the first place he cast a vote in an election many years before. It was different. The Republic of Texas flag that formerly hung on the wall had been replaced by the Stars and Stripes and was a reminder of how the world had changed.

The Colonel sat behind a long wooden table. Tom noticed most of the people in attendance were either carpetbaggers or Negroes. Tom scanned the crowd seeing only faces expressing curiosity but no friendliness. Finally, at the far end of the second row he saw his beloved wife. Her eyes filled with despair, blinking back tears, stared back at him. Her father sternly sat next to her, erect and stiff, as if ready for a fight. Tom wanted to yell out *"You bastards"* but knew that would only make matters worse. Controlling his emotions, he tried to console his wife with a loving look mouthing silently "I love you." She took a hankie and wiped the tears from her cheek smiling weakly at him.

The Yankee Colonel, whose face lined from years of sun exposure, was in full dress uniform and rapped a gavel on the table. He looked like a man who would not tolerate any disorder.

Calling the room to order in a voice of authority he said, "All stand and recite the Pledge of Allegiance."

Tom in his anger remained silent.

The Colonel took notice and said, "Mr. Pruit! If you don't say the Pledge of Allegiance, I will have you sentenced to thirty days in the stockade. How does that sound to you?"

"Not good at all, Colonel."

Well then, say it!"

Yes Sir, Colonel!"

Tom began in a low voice, almost mumbling.

The Colonel said, "Stop! Say it loud enough that they hear it down the street in the saloon."

The carpetbaggers and Negros laughed.

Tom swallowed hard, drew a deep breath and in his loudest voice recited the pledge and when it was over the Judge looked at him and smiled, "That's better. Both of you remain standing while I read the charges against you. I have here before me allegations that you refused a lawful request from the Freedman's Bureau to produce copies of your contracts with the Negroes employed by you. You are also alleged to have discharged a firearm at a Federal Officer, attempted murder and disorderly conduct. How do you plead?"

Tom's father quickly put his hand on Tom's arm indicating he should remain silent and said, "Colonel, we admit we don't have written contracts with our Negroes. We have a handshake agreement. Neither of these men can read nor write so a written agreement doesn't make much sense. Where is it written that the contracts need to be in writing anyway? Isn't your word of honor good enough anymore? As far as discharging a firearm, that is true, but we didn't attempt to murder anyone. If we had, you would have had several dead men to haul back to town rather than a couple of carpetbaggers with dusty clothes from falling off their horses. Disorderly conduct in my mind is questionable because when men come to your home and order you to go to town for what we consider to be unexplained reasons, we aren't going to comply."

"Well Mr. Pruit, what did you agree to in your handshake with your Negroes? Keep in mind I am going to call your Negroes as witnesses."

"Sir, we provide them with a house and food just like we eat. We also buy them clothes once a year and pay them twelve dollars a month."

The Colonel looked at Shad and Orange who were seated at a table on the right side of the room. The young Negroes, nervous and intimidated, looked as though they wanted to slip under the floor.

"Which one of you is known as Orange and which is Shad?"

Orange raised his hand stammered, "I's, I's, Orange and this here is Shad."

"Is what Mr. Pruit said here about your handshake agreement true?"

"Yes Suh."

"How long have you worked for the Pruits?"

"Mos' of two years, Suh. But Shad here has worked for Mr. Pruit mos' all his whole life."

The Colonel made some written notes and then said, "Thank you Mr. Pruit, you may sit down. I would like Tom Pruit to stand and give his answer to these charges."

Tom stood, rattling his shackles.

"So Mr. Pruit, I understand you are a veteran of our great Civil War. Is that correct?"

"Yes Sir, but I didn't find it to be none too civil with Yankee bullets whizzing all around."

The Colonel looked up at Tom and a slight smile softened his stern countenance.

"Did you get paroled from the war?"

"Yes Sir."

The Colonel looked at him and said, "Did you take a Loyalty Oath as part of getting your parole papers?"

"Yes Sir."

'Do you consider that you are abiding by your Loyalty Oath while shooting at Federal officers?"

Tom paused before answering; his mouth was dry but he managed to work up enough spittle to moisten his lips and said, "Colonel Sir, a man no matter who he is or what he is has to believe in something. I have come to realize I fought a war for the all the wrong reasons."

The crowd began to murmur. Someone said "Traitor!"

Mary Ellen uttered an audible gasp and began to cry.

The Colonel rapped his gavel sharply and said, "Order in the Court!"

Tom was silent for a moment, fixed his eyes on the Army officer then said, "Most Texans have a firm belief in honoring their word as a man. In my Fathers case, he firmly believes that if he were to lie he would answer to his maker. I also believe that we are answerable to a higher authority too and that is what made us resist the accusations of the Freedmen's Bureau challenging what we told them. They insulted us. When I swore the Loyalty Oath I did so with all sincerity."

Tom Paused again, looked briefly back at his wife. He had seldom spoken so many words to anyone before in his life continued, "Sir, I admit shooting my pistol up in the air. I didn't aim it at anyone and I had no intention of actually shooting anyone. I was just trying to protect my family and our property, not overthrow the government."

"Are you aware that I have the power to confiscate your property?"

"I have heard stories of confiscation going on since the end of the war but I honestly don't think that what we did justifies confiscation of our property."

The Colonel stared at Tom, his eyes fixed, the deep lines of his face unmoving, "What is justified here is what I determine is justified. Do you understand, Mr. Pruit?"

"Yes Sir."

"Have you ever owned any slaves?"

"No sir."

Shaking his head the Colonel said, "Yet you fought a war that was all about slavery. You may sit down now Mr. Pruit."

The Colonel announced, "This hearing is adjourned until tomorrow at nine o'clock in the morning. The prisoners are to be kept in the stockade until then."

As Tom and his Father were escorted back to their cell they found Mary Ellen waiting outside the courthouse for them with her Father, Alexander Curry. She had left the baby home with her mother. When she tried to talk to Tom, she was roughly pushed aside and told there could be no talking with the prisoners. Tom tried to say a few comforting words but was shoved along and told to be quiet.

Orange and Shad, not knowing what to do started to go back to Hawkins General Store. Mary Ellen called to them, "Are you boys ok?"

"Oh Yes Mame, we staying over at Hawkins store an he been feeding us too."

Mary Ellen relieved that the blacks were ok, continued to Mrs. Anderson's rooming house for the night.

The next morning the Colonel reconvened the hearing at exactly nine o'clock. Tom and his Father sat at the table for the accused and Orange and Shad sat with the Freedmen's Bureau representatives. Mary Ellen and her father were in the hearing room along with Mr. Hawkins and Mrs. Anderson. The others in attendance were a bunch of carpetbaggers most of whom had been there the day before. The rest of the onlookers were a mixture of the curious and Confederate sympathizers. The Colonel rapped his gavel on the table and called the hearing to order.

"I am prepared to announce my decision but before I do I want to say that I received a note from Hawkins, the owner of Hawkins General Store." He has requested to say a few words in support of the defendants. Mr. Hawkins, are you ready?"

Hawkins who had taken off his normal work apron and donned a suit coat, stood holding his hat in his hand, "Yes, Colonel I am."

"Please proceed then."

"Colonel, I have known the two defendants since 1855 when John Pruit purchased the farm where they live. I know them to be honest men of integrity who take their business responsibilities seriously. When Mr. Pruit and his son tell you that they have an agreement by shaking hands they mean it. I also know them to be reliable and credit worthy men. That's all Colonel."

"Is there anyone else that wants a say in these proceedings today?"

Mrs. Anderson stood saying, "Colonel, my name is Florence Anderson and I own a boarding house here in town. I too have known these gentlemen for many years and find them to be responsible members of our community."

"Thank you Mrs. Anderson. Anyone else?"

Mary Ellen stood saying, "Colonel, Sir, my father-in-law and my husband are good decent men. They have had an enduring relationship with both of the Negroes in this case. These men believe in fair dealings and have done so with these Negroes. They both work with our family because they know they are valued first as human beings and second as workers. Shad's wife, Mahalia, is pregnant with her second child after losing her firstborn. My father-in-law has continued to pay her the same wages she earned before all this happened during her troubled pregnancy."

"Is she here today?"

"No sir, she couldn't tolerate the wagon ride to town but I am sure Shad will verify what I have just told you."

The Colonel looked at Shad and said, "Is what this lady is saying true?"

Shad looked up and with large round eyes and a trembling lip said, "Yes suh."

The Colonel said, "I will give serious consideration to what I have heard here yesterday and today but I am going to recess until one o'clock today to give me an opportunity to digest what I have heard and to make a decision in regard to these defendants." With that, he rapped his gavel on the table, rose and walked out of the room.

Mary Ellen ran to Tom and her father-in-law and embraced them as she sobbed on Tom's chest. Tom did his best to comfort her before a guard forced her aside and he was led back to the stockade.

At one o'clock, the Colonel reconvened the hearing. "I have come to a decision concerning the case of Pruit versus the Freedman's Bureau. John Thomas Pruit please stand. I find that you are guilty of resisting an order by a Federal officer and I am levying a fine of ten dollars. In the matter of working Negroes without a written contract, I am assessing a fine of ten dollars. In the matter of the charge of disorderly conduct, I am assessing a fine of ten dollars and in the matter of discharging a fire arm, I find you not guilty. You may sit down."

"Samuel Thomas Pruit, please stand." Chains rattling Tom rose from his seat. "You sir, need to learn that there is a way to deal with a problem other than violence. I find you guilty of discharging a firearm at a Federal Officer. I also find you guilty of resisting a Federal Officer. On the disorderly conduct charge, I also find you guilty. I hereby fine you ten dollars for each charge. You will need to pay your fines before you will be released. I hereby sentence you to six months in jail with all suspended except for the time served. Further, you are both on probation for twelve months. This hearing is now over."

Both Tom and his father sighed in relief.

Mary Ellen openly sobbing managed to say, "Colonel! I am prepared to pay the fine for both my husband and my father-in-law now." She ran to Tom hugging him and her father.   "Very well Sergeant, as soon as Mrs. Pruit pays the fine to the clerk you may release both gentlemen from custody."

Out on the street, fines paid, once again free from the law, Tom noticed the now familiar figure of the Confederate troublemaker. He stood on the boardwalk across from the courthouse, arms crossed across his chest and a look of contempt on his face although missing some teeth. Ignoring his stare, Tom climbed in the wagon beside his wife and said, "Don't look across the street just now but the man who whipped Orange is watching us."

Tom snapped the reins and the horses trotted down the dusty street.

Mary Ellen said, "Is he the one who is leaning against the corner post?"

"Yes."

"He has a sinister look about him that scares me."

Chapter 16

The Decision

For the next few weeks Mary Ellen's father, Alexander fetched their supplies for them. Orange was happy to stay home and work saying, "I don' ever want to be roun' dem' fancy Niggers and Carpetbaggers no mo'."

It was hot, humid weather and work splitting logs into rails required water and rest breaks. Late one morning, Orange disappeared into a thicket of pines to relieve himself. Tom, his father, J. D. and Shad rested in the shade of a large oak tree. Suddenly Orange came crashing out of the thicket in a full tilt run hollering "Massa Tom, Massa Tom".

Tom jumped up in surprise and said, "What's wrong Orange?"

"Massa Tom, der's two white men back der and they tol me to give you's a message."

"What did they say?"

"Massa Tom, they told me to tell you's that Nigger lovers gonna be run outta Texas."

"What else?"

"That's all Massa Tom and then they rode off."

"Did you recognize them?"

"No Massa Tom, Orange ain't never laid eyes on them in my whole life."

"Which direction did they go?"

"They go that'a, way Massa Tom", said Orange and pointing over his shoulder.

"Damn it all! I didn't bring a gun or a horse down here this morning."

Tom's father, John Thomas said, "Best that you didn't because I think that may be exactly what they wanted to happen. You would have gotten yourself waylaid. Tomorrow though, we will both bring our guns and a saddled mount to be ready. Right now I think we need to go back to the house to make sure our families are alright."

Tom said, "You're right! I am going to run up there now."

When Tom, sweaty and breathless found Mary Ellen, she was hanging wash out to dry and his mother was picking corn in the garden with her daughters, Nannie and Belle. Matilda was boiling water for laundry.

Mary Ellen looked up in alarm. She said, "What's wrong?"

"Are you all alright?"

"Yes, of course. What's wrong?"

Tom briefly related what happened.

"Oh! Dear God! What are we to do?"

"Tom assured her, "Mary Ellen, I am sorry for all of this trouble. I promise that you and Belle will be safe."

For several days, Tom and his father slept with their guns close by and strapped their pistols on their waist first thing every morning. They kept their rifles within easy reach during the day as well. J. D. designated to provide security for the women and kids never let them out of his sight.

During one of their rest breaks Tom sat down next to his father and said, "Poppa, I need to talk with you. I want to move out West to be closer to Jim. The only reason we haven't already moved is because Mary Ellen wanted to stay here until after Belle was born. Now she is pregnant again. I know that if I bring up moving now she is going to be hard to convince under the circumstances." His father nodded his head in acknowledging these facts.

Tom went on to say, "It's not just the Klan that worries me. Between the carpetbaggers and the Freedmen I am made uncomfortable in my own home town. They lord it over us and seem to think we ought to ask their permission to cross the street. I want to move where they have less authority and a man can still move about freely. I would like everything to go back to the way it was before the war. I also know that won't happen. I don't want anything to do with the Klan. They advocate hanging people and burning their homes and fighting the war all over again and I just want no part of any of that. I also think you and Mama ought to leave and go with us."

His father was silent for a moment. "Neither you, nor anybody else should re-fight the war. It is over. Too many men died fighting for a cause that was immoral and they could not win it in the first place. Tom, I have been thinking about our circumstances here for a long time. Not only yours, but mine as well. Your mother and I still have young ones to rear. Your Ma has been a good pioneer but I do not think either one of us have enough years left to start over again. Your brother John Dave is eighteen and we still have Sarah who is fifteen and Amanda is twelve and little Marion is eight. This reconstruction thing makes me sick and I find it hard to swallow. We cannot vote and I am disgusted with how everything is so vastly different from the way it was before the war. I know that the South lost the war but I was never in favor of the damn war to begin with. I came west all those years ago to Texas because it offered us land and an opportunity. But the Republic of Texas doesn't exist anymore."

"So what are you thinking?"

"Well, first of all, I don't think your troubles with this Confederate soldier are over. In fact they may have just gotten worse with the beating you gave him." Tom thought a moment and nodded his agreement.

"Poppa, when Jim and I were out West looking for a place we heard that you could buy land for fifty cents per acre plus you can get a head right for a hundred sixty acres too and if you stay on the land for three years it doesn't cost you anything. If we work together and pool our money we should be able to put a pretty good outfit in place."

"Tom, I wish I could make this move but moving is a young man's way. When I first came to Texas, I was your age but the years have been piling up on me and I think your Momma and I must stay here."

Late that afternoon Tom hitched up the buggy and took Mary Ellen to see her folks. She was surprised he quit work early but did not question him as to why he wanted to visit her parents during the week. Sundays were usually reserved for family visits but an opportunity to spend time with her mother and younger sisters was not something she was going to refuse. When Tom and Mary Ellen arrived at her folk's home, the dust had not settled before her little sisters and mother gleefully appeared out of the house. Tom helped Mary Ellen and the baby down from the buggy and watched with happiness the reception his wife received from her family.

Tom asked no one in particular, "Where's Alexander?"

Mary Ellen's mother, Amelia, pointed to the log barn, which had a smoke house attached and said, "He is salting some hams. I am sure he would be glad for your company."

Alexander, a muscular man in his mid-forties, standing almost six feet tall was strong as a mule and sometimes just as stubborn. He worked hard to take care of his family and was intensely proud of his Tennessee heritage. He had been a good neighbor to Tom's family over the years, never refusing a request for help and generously sharing what he had; which frankly, was not much. Tom reasoned that since his father had also been born in the Cumberland Mountains of Tennessee, was initially the reason the two men were such good friends. As Tom entered the smoke house, Alexander looked up in surprise. "Tom! What are you doing here today?"

"I finished up early today and brought Mary Ellen and little Belle to see you."

"Well I had better finish up too then so I can go play with my granddaughter."

Alexander finished salting the hams, hung them up and threw some fresh wood on the fire. Tom watched the process for a moment and then he said, "Mr. Curry, I wanted to come over and tell you that I am thinking of moving west to Montague County along the Red River."

Alexander quickly turned from the hams he was working with and said, "I knew you were thinking of moving eventually but I hoped that day would never come. Also Tom, that's Comanche country. What makes you even consider taking your family where they could face the risk of being killed or worse by those savages?"

Tom recounted the visit from the men delivering the message to him concerning Nigger lovers earlier. Tom explained how the Confederate, the Klan, the Carpetbaggers and the Freedmen made powerful motivation to move west. Alexander sat on a small barrel listening to Tom. Quietly looking down at the ground for a short time, he tried to digest this news. He slowly shook his head side to side and finally let out a deep breath before he spoke. "Tom, I have found that most of the time, you can't out run the problems life throws at you. Have you thought about fighting fire with fire?"

"Well sir, I've had two run-ins with the Confederate. The first time was when Jim was with me and we whipped him and his friend. The last time was when he was beating the hell out of Orange in front of Hawkins General Store. I damn near killed him until his friends got me from behind. Now, I am fearful that they will waylay me or my father while we are working the farm."

Alexander looked at Tom and studied his son-in-law's face then stood and said, "Tom, I know you are a brave man. You have been a good husband to my daughter and a good father to little Belle. Naturally, I would like to have you be close to Amelia and myself but I understand the burden you are carrying. If you think this is what you need to do, you can do it with my blessing. I just do not know how Amelia is going to react. Let's go up to the house and break the news together."

The reaction from Mary Ellen's mother was worse than Tom had expected. She immediately broke down in a sobbing panic at the thought of having her daughter and grandchild moving away most likely never to be seen again. Mary Ellen also distraught at the thought of leaving her family tried to comfort her to no avail. It was a long buggy ride home for Tom and Mary Ellen.

144

The next day Tom rose early. He stirred the coals in the wood stove and added a couple of pieces of wood. He went out to the well and drew a fresh bucket of water to make coffee. While he waited for the coffee to brew, he walked back outside to watch the sun come up. It was going to be a beautiful calm clear day but Tom's mood did not improve with the weather. Absorbed in his thoughts of concern for his family he heard the door to his modest cabin open and shut. He looked up and saw his beautiful wife bringing him a cup of hot coffee.

As Mary Ellen walked to where he sat, she smiled and said, "I've got some bacon on the stove and I will fry you a couple of eggs. Do you want anything else?"

"Yes, give me a kiss."

"Well if we are going to do that let's do it right. Let me set this hot coffee down and then you better get ready."

Tom wrapped his arms around her small body, tilted her head back and kissed her gently on the lips.

"You can do better than that Mr. Pruit. I fully expect you to give me an enthusiastic kiss like you haven't seen me in a year."

As they embraced, Tom knew in his heart that the world revolved around his pregnant wife and little girl, Belle. He vowed to himself to keep them safe from the dangers confronting them. The sound of Shad and Mahalia stirring called them both back into reality.

Tom's enthusiasm for work on the farm was sorely lacking since he had made the decision to move west. His goal was to finish some uncompleted projects to make the place easier for his father to work through the next season. Shad and Orange painted the barn; he replaced some broken posts in the corral. Tom's father gathered their cattle and separated the ones he wanted to keep. Tom's little brother was whitewashing the house and a picket fence that enclosed the small front yard.

They would brand any new calves that evening before taking them to market. A little after noon, Mary Ellen's father, Alexander, rode up on a gray gelding and dismounted at the main house. Alexander said, "I have a request. My man Fate fell yesterday, he is laid up with a broken arm and is not much help. I was hoping I could borrow Orange for a few days to help get the rest of my corn crop harvested?"

Tom's father replied, "I think we can get along without Orange for a while. We have finished our harvest and fence building and only working on chores that we can do later if need be. Orange, get your gear and get ready to go with Alexander. I think you will like working with Alexander because Amelia is a great cook."

Tom and J. D. began work on an old Conestoga wagon their parents had used to make the trek from Tennessee to Arkansas and then to Texas. They used a forge to rebuild the iron rims on the wheels and replaced several of the wooden spokes. Tom found an old dried oak limb, fashioned a new tongue and replaced the boards in the bottom and sidewalls of the wagon. He caulked the boards with tar to keep water from leaking through to the inside. He also put several coats of a mixture of turpentine and linseed oil on all of the board surfaces inside and out.

Tom's mother and Mary Ellen took the old canvas top and began to patch tears and worn places with cotton and hemp cloth that Tom's mother had woven. When they were finished, Tom soaked the canvas in linseed oil and laid it out to dry for several days. Before stretching it over the wooden bows that would hold it in place, he covered it in a coat of white paint. He was hopeful it would keep most of any rain from leaking through.

A grease bucket was strapped to the side of the wagon and next to it was an old molasses wooden stave barrel for water. An extra wagon wheel was secured to the side along with a toolbox filled with extra bolts, chains and horseshoe nails hung on the other side. Tom built storage along the sidewalls and fashioned several wooden planks that could be laid cross ways to make a decent bed after a mattress of cotton ticking was placed upon it.

The harness had been in the barn for so long that the rats had chewed through parts of it. His father helped with working the leather to make all of the necessary repairs. Tom fashioned a new seat and a footrest from a piece of hickory hardwood that he found in the barn. The axles smeared of grease allowed the wheels to spin quietly. The doubletrees and singletrees were in good shape and did not require any maintenance.

Pulling the wagon would require at least four stout horses perhaps six. He knew he could not take a chance on going into town to find mounts so he decided to rely on his wife's father.

Alexander was a fine judge of horseflesh and Tom could trust him to select only the best animals. Tom knew that Mary Ellen would like a time to visit with her mother and she readily accepted his invitation to go for a short visit.

When they rolled into the barnyard in the farm wagon both Alexander and Orange were shucking corn and then stripping the kernels to be stored for the winter. Fate trying to help with his one good arm managed a wave of recognition. Orange dropped what he was doing and ran to greet Tom.

"Howdy Massa Tom, what brings you here today?"

"Howdy yourself Orange, are ya making a good hand for Alexander?"

Alexander chimed in and said, "You betcha he is. I do not know what I would have done without him. What is on your mind today?"

"Well sir, I have a favor to ask. I have great respect in your ability to judge horseflesh and I need you to find me some good strong draft horses to pull the schooner we are fixing up and I need a good strong mount to ride as a saddle horse, one that can run and have stamina. I remember you had a friend, a fella by the name of Coltharp, who trained horses before the war. Is he still in business?"

"I haven't seen or talked to him since the war ended. He had a place up in Van Zandt County about three miles north of Martin's Mills as I recall. He sold every animal he could get during the war to Lee's army. I suspect that business is not so robust right now. How soon do you want me to go?"

Tom thought a moment and said, "I need you to do this as soon as possible. I would go with you but with everything that has been happening I feel like I need to stay close to home."

Alexander nodded and said, "I can leave on Thursday if you will leave Orange to work with Fate until I get back. Depending on the weather, I should be able to get to Coltharp's place and back in eight maybe ten days.

Reaching under the wagon seat, Tom produced a leather sack and handed it to Alexander saying, "Good! I have two hundred in gold for you to take with you. If you can find the right draft animals, I think four yoke of oxen or maybe a couple of teams of mules. Sturdy animals will do me just fine; but I would like a fast saddle horse with endurance for myself. They do not have to be completely broke. I can finish them myself. That way they will get to know me and I will get to know them and we can probably pay a little less."

"I will do my best Tom."

Tom shook his father-in-law's hand with relish, gave a bear hug to Orange and said, "Mary Ellen and I will stay with your family while you are gone. Now, I think I had better gather up my family and head back home."

"Not before I get to play with my grandchild you ain't."

Chapter 17

The Hanging

Backbreaking work consumed the next five days for Tom and Shad. They dug a new well beside the main farmhouse and constructed a log building around it. An existing window of the main house converted to a doorway allowed access into the new well room. Tom and Shad finished the work on the roof by the light of lanterns. Tom's self-imposed deadline exhausted both men.

Tom's mother was thrilled she would no longer have to go outside in cold weather to fetch water. Despite the excitement of having water inside the house, everyone went to bed and slept soundly until a little after midnight. Suddenly there was a commotion of horses milling around and loud voices. Tom was instantly fully awake. Through the one little window he had made for Mary Ellen, he could see a flickering light that was not familiar to him. Mary Ellen continued to sleep with Belle snuggled at her side. Tom quickly pulled on his pants and boots, grabbed his pistol and went outside to investigate.

As soon as he opened the door he saw fifteen to twenty mounted men wearing white robes with round cone like hats that went up to a peak. A white hood covered their faces with a hole in the fabric cut for their eyes. Two men restraining Tom's father carried blazing torches. Tom ran to where his father was but before he could reach him, he felt a rope loop settle over his left shoulder and waist. Jerked to the ground the hooded men quickly stepped on his hand and took his pistol.

The shouting and commotion aroused everyone including Mary Ellen. She ran to Tom and his father but was quickly held back by one of the hooded men who said, "Hold on little Missy. You don't want to get in the middle of this."

Shad and Mahalia stood clinging to each other outside their little house wearing only nightclothes; their eyes reflected their fear and surprise. Mahalia was crying loudly. Tom's mother, Rachel, and his little brothers and sisters stood over to one side with two men watching them. They strained to hear what one of the masked intruders was saying to Tom and his father.

The man who seemed to be the leader pointed at Tom and said, "Bring him over here." The Leader edged his horse close to Tom and said "Where's the little Nigger you call Orange?"

Tom relieved that Orange was still working with Alexander said, "He's not with us anymore."

The leader slapped Tom in the face with a quirt he held and said, "I don't believe you, so if you want to protect your family you better get him out here."

Tom's father spoke up and said, "He is telling you the truth. The boy is not working here."

"Well now, pray tell where he went."

Tom interjected, "He's a freedman so he could leave any time he wanted."

"That's too bad. I had a surprise for him", said the man who appeared to be the leader. He then turned his horse to the left, waved to one of the other hooded men and said, "Bring the black bastard in."

They led a man tied on a horse with a black hood covering his head, was brought in to face Tom and his father. The leader said, "Take the hood off of our friend."

Tom was surprised to see a man barely recognizable as a human being, beaten so badly one of his eyes was actually hanging on his cheek. One of his ears flopped down partially detached from his head. The face Tom saw was swollen and behind severely cut lips some of his front teeth were missing.

The hooded leader said to Tom, "You know this man?"

Tom could not speak for a moment but finally said, "I think it is Sheriff Snowden."

"Well sir, he ain't going to be Sheriff no more. We are gonna make an example of him for interfering in our town. I don't think you are gonna take up with Niggers no more cause we are fixin' to hang this black bastard from one of your trees right here in your front yard."

Tom said, "He hasn't done anything to you. Your argument is with me so let him go. Turn me loose and we can settle this between just the two of us. I will fight you anyway you want; fists, guns or knives."

Guffawing loudly the man snarled, "Well I thought about that for a long time but I think that hanging this black sum-bitch here and now will have a bigger impact on you and the rest of the Yankee Carpet Bagging sumbitches than anything we can do. You need to take this as a warning. Don't cozy up to Niggers and Carpet Baggers."

Turning to one of the other hooded riders the leader said, "Pick a limb in that tree right there close to your left and throw a rope up there and make a hangin noose."

Suddenly, Tom rammed his shoulder into the chest of the man holding the rope around his torso. His movement knocked the man down. He slipped the rope from around his shoulders and tried to leap up at the leader but before he could another hooded rider hit him in the head with a gun butt. He crumpled unconscious to the ground.

The leader told one of his riders, "Get a bucket of water and wake his ass up."

Mary Ellen was screaming and trying to break free from the man restraining her to no avail.

Tom's Father said, "If you mean to hang my son take me instead."

The leader said, "I ain't gonna hang yur boy tonight. We're gonna hang the Nigger though as soon as we can wake your boy up. I want him to see how a black man jumps hanging from a rope. Maybe that will make him change his ways."

Tom awakened with water flooding his nose causing him to choke briefly. His head was ringing, pain surging through his skull. It was a moment before he could clearly get his thoughts defined. One of the hooded riders pulled him to his feet and tied his hands behind his back.

Another hooded man led the Sheriff's horse under a tree from which hung a hangman's noose. A man astride his horse alongside the Sheriff leaned out of his saddle, put the noose over the Sheriff's head and drew it tight.

Tom said, "Sheriff, I am sorry, so very sorry that your helping me has brought you to this."

The man lifted his head up off his chest and said, "Not your fault. Goes with the job, I knew the risks. Don't let the kids watch", he mumbled through his swollen bloody lips.

"Enough of this talking", said the hooded leader as he hit the flank of the Sheriff's horse with his quirt and it bolted into the darkness. The Sheriff jerked out of the saddle by the noose around his neck, his remaining eye bulging and his face contorted into a visage Tom would never forget. His legs kicked wildly for what seemed like an eternity, his body went limp and swung slowly, back and forth like a pendulum on a clock.

Tom had never seen a man die like this before. He was numb and speechless seeing a man alive one minute, and just a limp piece of flesh and bone the next. Mary Ellen was screaming. Tom's mother was trying to hold her skirt over the little children's eyes. The hooded leader rode up to Tom and struck him in the face with his quirt to make Tom focus on him. Tom looked at him and said, "You are nothing but a coward hiding behind your sheets and masks!"

The man looked down at him and said, "You best pay attention to what I am saying. Don't ever bring a Nigger into a saloon and drink with him again. If you do, I will be back and next time, not only will I hang your other Nigger, but I may string up your ol' man too or one of the kids may disappear while doing chores. Understand?"

Tom looked up and said, "I know who you are, you son-of-a-bitch!"

The man kicked Tom in the face, causing him to fall to the ground unconscious; then spurred his horse into the night.

Mary Ellen was bending over him with a tear stained face and a look of terror in her eyes when he regained consciousness. She helped him to his feet and called to Shad to come and untie Tom and his Father.

"Is my Papa okay?" Tom asked.

"Yes and your mother and the children are okay too."

At first light Tom, J. D. and Shad helped Tom's father cut the Sheriff down. They dug a grave in the woods about a hundred yards south of the main house in a small clearing. They erected a small cross at the head and the family gathered round it. John got his Bible and read several passages finally quoting Second Timothy 4: 6, 7, 8.

"For I am already being poured out like a drink offering, and the time has come for my departure. I have fought the good fight, I have finished my course, I have kept the faith. Now there is in store for me the crown of righteousness, which the Lord, the righteous Judge, will award to me on that day—and not only to me, but also to all who have longed for his appearing."

He prayed, "Dear Lord, this man tried to do what he felt was right. He died because of it. We ask that your blessing is bestowed upon his soul and that he live in the green pastures of heaven forever. Amen."

☆ ☆ ☆ ☆ ☆

For three days, Tom existed in a depressed state. None of the work necessary to prepare for their moving to Tarrant County was completed. Retribution and hate later pushed aside by fear for his family and an overwhelming helplessness so filled Tom's mind it prevented him from eating or sleeping. He slept on the ground a few feet from the Sheriff's grave. He became aware of his father asking, "Ok if I sit for a spell?"

Tom didn't look up but nodded. He heard his father saying, "Son, I went into town and reported the hanging to the military authorities. They got little interest in finding those responsible but at least I did what I thought needed to be done."

After a few moments of awkward silence John continued, "The Captain took a written report and said it would be looked into when they had time." Tom nodded again but said nothing.

John placed his arm around Tom's stooped shoulders saying, "Mary Ellen is very worried about you." After a brief pause he continued, "Having a hard time dealing with the killing of a decent man aren't you?"

Tom looked up and his father could see his red eyes were wet with tears. "Yes. Yes I am. In the war, I saw hundreds of men killed and I know I killed a few men but it was always in battle, never in a senseless, ruthless way like what we saw here. I am also asking myself why I haven't found those bastards and put a bullet in their heads yet. The only thing stopping me is concern for what might happen to my family."

John sat down next to his son and put his arm around his stooped shoulders. "I understand Tom, but vengeance in killing those men will only poison you with the same hate they are filled with. I have found that most times the good Lord has a way of punishing people like that. I have never spoken about this before but once when I was a young man some fellas stole a new pony I had worked long and hard to buy. I loved that young horse more than life itself. My father talked me out of going to find the men and settle the score. Some months later, I went into town and lo and behold, they just had a hanging. Apparently those fellas stole one horse too many and the law got them and performed the Lord's work."

Tom's father continued, "Justice delivered by the angels of God is much sweeter. You might kill them but what happens when their friends come to take vengeance on you or your family for their deaths? Don't misunderstand me. If they were to come back and threaten us again, I will stand beside you to defend our loved ones and our property. We have a bigger responsibility than vengeance and that is to take care of our families first. If you go kill the bastards it will make you a hunted man and the rest of your life will be one of always looking over your shoulder wondering if the rider coming over the hill is the law to take you in."

Tom yelled, "But those bastards need to pay for what they did!"

"Yes, I agree but you need to listen to what I am saying." John paused to let his words sink in and then continued, "Snowden was a brave man, he wasn't afraid to die and he never let weakness be shown. I suspect he prepared for death the day he accepted his appointment as a peace officer. I also believe he would not want you to take any vengeful retaliation. He would want you to live for your family. Tom, your wife and children need you alive and the bravest thing you can do is go to them and continue your life. I promise someday these men will get their retribution but not necessarily by your hand. Patience is a virtue that saves many a man. Let's go back and give our love to the people who matter most to us."

"I know you're right Papa but patience waiting for something to happen is hard, really hard. Just because Snowden was black doesn't mean nobody should care about what happened here."

"Oh, you care and I care. We will never forget but we can't let it ruin the rest of our lives. Come on let's go home."

John stood, held out his hand to Tom who took it and rose to stand beside his father for a moment before squaring his shoulders and walking to his loved ones.

Late that night Mary Ellen suffered a miscarriage. It was another little girl. They named her Francis. Tom lay on the bed beside his wife and held her in his arms weeping together for several hours. Both felt abandoned by God. The death of their little baby was crushing. Placed upon the events earlier it made a somber event even worse. Tom built a little coffin then dug a grave and erected a hand chiseled stone marker in the same clearing where they buried Sheriff Snowden.

Chapter 18

New Horses

A week later Mary Ellen's father Alexander arrived in his buckboard with two horses and six mules tethered in a line following along behind. He untied the animals and led them into the barn. When Tom and John first arrived at the barn, they were speechless. Alexander stood quietly and let the men look at some of the best horseflesh they had ever seen. Inside the stalls to the left was a sorrel stallion with a white blaze on his face standing over sixteen hands. The stallion was heavily muscled with intelligent eyes. He was not a long bodied horse but stout and strong. Next to the stud was a roan mare with four white stocking feet standing over fifteen hands with the same attributes.

The stallion was very spirited and seemed to be skittish as Tom opened the stall gate. Tom spoke in a low voice, "Easy boy, easy. I just want to look you over up close."

The stallion never took his eyes off Tom and sidestepped him at every approach. Tom slowly walked around the stall and the stallion kept backing away. "My, my, my but aren't you a fine animal. You don't know it yet but we are going to become best friends."

Tom next stepped into the stall with the mare. She was less skittish and had a regal look to her. He ran his hands down her neck, back, withers and haunch. He was able to lift her feet, checked her hooves then slipped a headstall on her and let her smell his breath. Alexander stood quietly letting Tom and John look over the two horses then said, "I don't know if I have ever seen a better example of Steel Dust breeding than these two animals. I don't know if you are familiar with the history of the breed?"

Since neither man answered he continued, "They are a mixture of the Spanish Barbs brought in from Spain by the early explorers. The Chickasaw Indians crossed the Spanish breed with English breeding stock stolen from settlements. They have strength, endurance and excellent speed over short distance. This stud horse is a grandson of Steel Dust who was foaled in Kentucky and brought to Texas in the forties. The mare has similar bloodlines. I thought you might want to do a little horse breeding out West. In fact the mare is freshly bred to the stallion in the last two weeks."

Tom asked, "Have either of them a name?"

Alexander said, "The stallion is Shining Star and the mare is Provocative Legs."

Tom nodded his head and said, "I can see why they got those monikers. The stallion will be a star no matter where he goes and just look at the long legs on the mare. I think I will shorten her name to just Legs."

"Tom, you and John might want to look in the pen on the north side of the barn too." Tom and his father did so and they found three matched pairs of the finest mules they had ever seen, three jacks and three jennies.

Alexander continued, "These are stout strong animals and hopefully will do a better job of pulling your schooner than the oxen I saw. They are already trained to harness and working as a team of six."

Tom asked, "How in the world did you buy these animals for two hundred in gold?"

Alexander said, "I admit, I didn't. I had to add some of my money to the deal but you are taking my precious daughter and my grandchild to a new home and I decided that Mary Ellen's momma and I needed to give her a present. The stallion and the mare are yours but the mule team belongs to Mary Ellen. You are going to need to put in some time with the stud horse as he is a spirited animal and it is important that you get acquainted but don't try to do it in a few days. Take some time and do it right. He's broke but you are new to him."

The first night after Alexander delivered the horses and mules, Tom was so excited that he could hardly sleep. The animals let his mind release the numbness of the killing of the sheriff and the loss of their baby girl. At first light, he went down to the barn and got a bucket of corn mixed with oats. Then he got a jug of molasses, poured some of the corn and oats mixture on a smooth piece of wood and began massaging the three ingredients together. He wanted a mixture that was not too wet with molasses but that had enough to bind the corn and oats into small balls. He rolled balls of the mixture into a diameter of about one inch and placed them on a flat piece of wood to dry. These little treats would reinforce the behavior and actions he wanted the horses to do.

Before breakfast, he took some hay into each of the horses and spoke to each in a low voice. The stallion seemed to be less spooky this time and did not move away as Tom put the hay in the feeder. The stallion only snorted once as he waited for Tom to leave the stall before approaching the feeder. The mare greeted him with a low whinny and eagerly began eating the hay. These horses were nothing like the raw broncs he broke at Boudreaux's. Most of those were outlaws and only in demand due to the scarcity of good horseflesh after the war.

After breakfast he asked Mary Ellen to pass the word that he was going to be working with the horses and tell everyone to stay away so as not to create any distractions. He eased into the mare's stall with a hackamore and a lead rope and slipped the headstall on her head without objection. He led her out into the alley leading to the corral. Once in the corral he simply led her around the perimeter. She accepted a lead rope and backed up on command. He gave her a ball of oats, corn and molasses after each requested maneuver. He also wanted to see if she would stand tied while he walked away. She did. He was able to pick up her feet and touch her without any objections. He accomplished all of this in about a half hour. Someone had done a masterful job of training this horse.

As he led her back into her stall the stallion nickered and pranced around his stall as if to say, "I missed you and I am ready for a little attention." Tom entered his stall and tried to slip the hackamore on him without success. Next, he got a lariat, shook a small loop out and slowly walked the stallion around his stall all the time speaking in a low voice, trying to be as calming as possible. He was able to slip a loop over the stallion's head without a reaction from the horse. Once the stallion knew he was caught the big animal became compliant. Tom opened the stall gate and led the big beautiful horse down the alley and into the corral.

In the corral, Tom slipped a bridle over his head and saddled him. As Tom worked with him, the stallion responded in a more spirited way than the mare but Tom expected that would be the case. The big horse responded to voice, knee and rein commands including stopping, backing up and turning quickly. He slowly touched this magnificent animal on the nose and forehead all the time talking in a low monotone of calmness. He stroked his hand down the stallion's withers and across his back to his rump. He gave him a treat and waited to see his reaction. The stallion instantly seemed to know which pocket in his vest the treat came from and nosed Tom for more. After pacing the horse through the same procedures as the mare, he was very pleased to see what a wonderful animal Alexander had bought for him. He took the stallion back into the barn and put him in his stall. The mare seemed to welcome them both. Tom stood leaning against the stall for a long interval just marveling at the beautiful horses and did not think again about the awful days of the hanging. Tom would let them rest now and would begin again after lunch.

The one working saddle he had was probably suitable for the mare but the stallion was a much larger animal. The only other saddle he had was a McClellan he came home from the war with but it had no horn and the cantle was too shallow to allow working cattle. It would have to do until he could make a trade for another.

Tom's spirit began to heal after spending the next several days working with his new horses. Becoming acquainted with his new mules and rebuilding his rigging for the Conestoga to a six animal driving harness was a tonic for his soul that gave him hope for the future. Mary Ellen saw the change wrought in her husband. His sullenness and refusal to share his grief with her began to wash away and she attributed it to the grace of God for which she was immensely grateful.

Chapter 19

Leaving Home 1871

The move to Tarrant County in the spring of 1871 began on a sad note. Tears flowed like water from Mary Ellen's family as well as from Shad and Mahalia. It was a gloomy day with storm clouds hanging low in the sky and a slight drizzle filled the air. The weather perfectly matched everyone's mood. They all accepted the fact that they most likely would never see each other again at least in this lifetime.

A last minute development was that Tom's younger brother J. D. who was twenty-one decided he too wanted to leave Henderson County for the excitement of what he saw as an adventure. This sudden turn of events took Tom's parents totally by surprise. After a soul-searching night, Tom's father and mother, John and Rachel begrudgingly gave their permission for J. D. to leave home. Tom, surprised by his little brother's decision, welcomed him wholeheartedly once the parents gave their blessing. J. D. was a hard worker and could handle horses. He also knew his way around cattle.

Mary Ellen's family came to see them begin their new adventure. Her mother, Amelia bravely tried not to cry but when little Belle cooed and wanted to crawl up in her lap she broke down. She knew that just as she had moved with her husband and left behind her family, Mary Ellen, Tom and grandbaby Belle would more than likely, never be seen again.

Amelia tried to be brave but under the surface, she was in a panic as was Tom's mother Rachel. Mary Ellen's little sister Nannie who was only thirteen was crying and saying to J. D. "I won't ever see you again."

He placated her by saying, "Yes you will. I will come back in two years and marry you; with God as my witness."

"No you won't! You will get yourself killed by some wild Indian or run off with some other girl," she said as she dabbed her eyes with the apron she wore.

J. D. gave her a peck on the cheek saying, "Yes I will. I am a Pruit and we always do what we say. Ain't that right Tom?"

"Don't worry Nannie. If he doesn't, he has to deal with me."

Tom's father asked everyone to gather round while he asked the good Lord for safe passage for all of the travelers saying, "Dear Father in heaven, thank you for the many blessings these members of our family have brought to us. We ask your protection on our family as they go west to start a new life. Provide your guidance not only for where they are to go, but for how they are to live their lives. Lord, as you led Moses out of Egypt to the Promised Land, so lead our loved ones in their journey. Amen."

Tom sat next to his wife and child on the wagon seat and held the reins tightly that controlled the mule team pulling his wagon. Orange, astride a filly, gifted to him by John was looking more like a cowboy than ever. He had a neckerchief around his neck and a large wide-brimmed hat, given to him by Alexander. J. D. was riding the stallion. All wore long slickers to stay dry. Legs, tied to the rear of the wagon along with Milk Cow and her calf each calmly followed.

Before they pulled out John said to J. D. "John David, you are our third born son and while your Ma and I have grave misgivings, we give you our blessing and pray you travel safely."

John David, for all is earlier bravado with a lump in his throat and tears bursting from his eyes could hardly muster a muted response of, "Thank you, Papa"

Tom planned to head west to Trinidad about fifteen miles from Athens. This was a different route than what he and Jim had traveled two years before when they had gone to Montague County, but it was a more direct route to Wheeler's place in Tarrant County. Tom estimated it would take two days to make it to Trinidad.

Early afternoon the rumble of thunder filled the air with constant lightning flashes and the steady drizzle soon became a downpour. Mary Ellen moved inside under the canopy with the baby to try to get some relief. The rutted trail they were on was beginning to get sloppy. Every little draw was flowing heavily with the run-off. About two hours before sundown, Tom pulled off the rutted trail into a small clearing. It would be a wet camp with no fire this night. Worse yet there would be four adults, and baby Belle trying to find space to sleep under the tarpaulin.

They hobbled the mules and the horses. They strung a picket line between two large pine trees that they would tie the horses and mules to later in the evening. After securing the livestock, J. D. and Orange decided that they would throw a tarpaulin under the wagon and sleep there. Fortunately, Tom had stopped on a small rise, which was well drained. J. D. and Orange tied off a tarp along one side of the wagon and another across the back letting both drape down and underneath the wagon. They hoped this would provide protection from the freezing rain blown in under the wagon and give them a dry surface for their sleeping blankets.

The storm continued to rumble and the intensity ebbed and flowed for most of the night. Shortly before daylight, the freezing rain stopped, exposing a sunrise behind mottled clouds. Tom climbed out and sat on the wagon seat to put his boots on. The boys were still asleep under the wagon so Tom decided he would start a fire using some of the kindling he had stored in a box on the side of the wagon. Several down and dead branches in the area were full of pitch and he could use them to get a fire going to take the chill off the morning air. He knew everyone would want a hot pot of coffee too.

☆☆☆☆☆☆

The sunrise was a welcome respite for Mary Ellen. It was springtime in 1871 and Texas was still a wild frontier where the law was on the side of the fastest six-gun. She was hesitant to leave family and everything that was familiar but felt they had no option due to Tom's difficulties with the Klan. She was not sure what life was going to be like in Tarrant County; but prayed this move would be a good decision. If the carpetbaggers and Yankee government people would be few and far between, then it was all right by her. She put her complete trust in her husband's ability to take them to this unknown place safely.

Her dreams for several nights were fraught with wild Indians, bandits and renegades and she woke this morning in a terrible mood. Last night's cold and frost still covered everything including the canvas atop the wagon. The icy frost stung her hand as she prepared to climb down from the wagon tailgate. She needed to prepare breakfast for Tom and the boys and was grateful for the fire Tom made earlier which warmed her while she worked.

A pot of coffee perked on the fire and the smell permeated the air. Mary Ellen skillfully milked the cow getting enough milk for biscuits and for Belle to drink. She mixed lard, flour, a pinch of salt, a pinch of sugar and fresh milk in a bowl to make dough for biscuits. A blackened, well-used Dutch oven, her mother and grandmother used before her, was already warming. A large sooty frying pan lay waiting at the edge of the fire to cook the bacon. The chickens with them provided no eggs today, probably because the chickens were not used to all the rocking and shaking of the wagon.

The food supply was stored in the chuck box in large crocks with tight lids to keep the dust and bugs out. She quickly got the bacon out and cut several pieces, which she threw into the skillet. The activity of the morning routine helped clear away the distress she felt upon awakening. As soon as some of the bacon fat began melting, she stuck a long fork in it and rubbed it around the inside of the Dutch oven. Forming small round gobs of dough, she placed them in the Dutch oven; then placed some of the coals from the fire on the top of the oven. The biscuits would be ready by the time the bacon was done.

Tom harnessed the mules and hitched them to the wagon. The saddle rigging lay on the tailgate of the wagon waiting to be thrown on the back of his newly acquired stallion, Star.

Tom gruffly yelled, "Rise and shine girls. It's time to roll out and go to work."

"We ain't no girls", J. D. yelled from underneath the wagon.

"You must be. Ya'all got enough beauty sleep to turn an ugly gal into a princess."

Mary Ellen enjoyed the good-natured teasing of the boys by Tom. It helped to relieve her anxieties about leaving her family. She tried daily to have a positive outlook but it was only camouflage for her deep-seated longings for her familiar family lay just below the surface.

Tom picked up the jesting again saying, "J. D., today I want you to be the mule skinner and I am going to ride Star. You need experience driving a six mule team, but be careful; you got precious cargo with my wife and babies aboard."

Mary Ellen chimed in, "You better be careful or I will bang your head with my big skillet."

Chapter 20

La Santisima De Trinidad

It was about three in the afternoon when they pulled into Trinidad. It was not much of a town. Tom estimated about thirty people lived there. There were only a few log structures with one of them serving as a little church, another as a small general store and livery stable and a saloon. Tom told the boys to stay with Mary Ellen and the wagon while he inquired in the store about the ferry. He tied Star to the lone hitching post in front of the store and climbed a couple of rotten stairs that were ready to collapse up to the porch. An old-timer sat sound asleep in a cane back chair on the porch to the right of the door. An upside down flour barrel with a checkerboard on it sat next to the sleeper who never stirred as Tom walked by with spurs jingling.

Several lanterns inside the store cast very little light. The front of the building housed the store inventory, which included dry goods and some cans of medicinal products. To the rear, simple planks lay on barrels to form a bar. A few tables and benches sat to one side. There were four older men playing dominos and smoking their pipes. They looked up from their game at Tom inquisitively but soon continued playing.

Two women talked to a man who looked to be the proprietor. He was a tall skinny man with gray hair. The man acknowledged Tom with a wave saying, "Be with you in a minute sir." The shopkeeper finished his conversation with the women and then came out from behind his counter saying, "What can I do for you stranger?"

Tom said, "Looking for Earhart who runs the ferry."

"Well sir you have found him; but if you are looking to cross the river today I can't oblige you as the water is high and fast.

Maybe we can make it across in a few days. We have had a lot of rain upstream and my loading dock is under water. You got folks with you?"

"Yes sir and stock that needs feed."

"You're welcome to put your animals in the corral at the back of the store. Course boarding the animals will cost you ten cents for a bucket of oats and ten cents for each animal for hay and I can rent you a room for the night too."

"Thanks but I will only need to feed the stock. Me and my party will camp next to the corral if that is okay."

"Why yessiree, that's not a problem. We got good clean well water too. You can gather some river trash wood that is scattered along the bank for firewood. Just take yourself around back and help yourself. We can settle up later. By the way, there are several wagons headed west camped just downstream that you might want to join up with, more protection for you from bad men that prey upon travelers."

Tom touched his hand to his hat thanked the man and went out to get everyone settled in for the night.

☆ ☆ ☆ ☆ ☆

The next morning Tom, J. D., and Orange rode along the bank of the Trinity both North and South. The river was a turbid, opaque body of water that rushed rapidly along causing whirlpools in places. It looked most inhospitable and dangerous.

Waiting for the Trinity's flow to come down, Tom found an opportunity to visit with Earhart. The old man explained that the first Spanish explorers named the river La Santisima Trinidad which meant The Most Holy Trinity. He said settlers new to Texas spoke little Spanish and changed the name to the English version of Trinity. Tom appreciated the old timer's knowledge of the history of the river and the fact that he was familiar with its seasonal flows.

On the second day of their wait for the river to come down two men rode up to their camp behind Earhart's store. "Howdy. Me name is Ransom, Ransom Meador. Mind if me and me brother get down and visit a spell?"

Tom feeding the horses said, "You bet friend". He walked over to Meador and held out his hand in greeting.

"We got a pot of hot coffee. How bout a cup?"

"Aye laddie, that sounds good."

Both men dismounted and tied their horses to the rear wagon wheel. As Tom poured coffee, the second man introduced himself, "Jubal Meador."

Tom looked up at him and said, "Jubal, glad to meet you!"

"This is my wife Mary Ellen and my little brother J. D. That fella there is Orange; he works with us."

J. D. excused himself saying, "Sorry, gents, but I gotta milk the cow. Little Belle needs her dinner," motioning towards the toddler.

Tom studied both of the men and determined they were about his age. Ransom appeared to be the older and walked with a slight limp. Jubal was taller than his brother, standing a little over six feet. Tom thought both appeared to be stout sturdy men with a friendly manner about them. One of their horses had a bridle with the letters CSA on the headstall. Ransom and his brother spoke with an unfamiliar accent totally unlike the Texas drawl that Tom was used to hearing.

As Tom handed the men their hot coffee he asked, "So what are the Meador brothers doing in Trinidad?"

Ransom sat his coffee cup on a rock while he rolled a smoke and responded, "Headed to Fort Worth. We have two wagons with me wife and two children, Justin and Julie Ann. The other belongs to Jubal and his wife Sally. Jubal here is a newlywed. He and Sally don't have any pups yet. We would most welcome yee' joining us in the trek. That way we have the ability to help each other in the event of trouble. We have been waiting here for the rains to end and give the trail time to dry up nigh onto ten days."

Rather than accepting the offer immediately Tom decided it would be prudent to learn more about his prospective companions. "Looks like at least one of you fought for the Johnny Rebs in the war."

Ransom said, "Aye laddie, me and me brother both did. Him and me are from Virginia and served with Stonewall Jackson's brigade. Me and me brother were with him at Chancellorsville when a Yankee musket ball killed him. Stone served with General Jubal Early. He admired the man so much that he changed his name to honor the great man."

Tom looked at Jubal appreciatively and said "What a gesture of respect." Jubal looked up from where he was squatted by the fire and said, "Well it wasn't totally from the goodness of me heart as I hated me given name and decided I'd take the General's. I respected the man a lot. Me mother was disappointed though."

"What was your given name?"

"Francis shortened to Frany. Saw yee saddle as we rode up and figured yee must have been a Johnny Reb too."

"Yeah the war isn't something I like to remember though. I was wounded at the battle of Franklin in Tennessee when we lost thousands of our good men trying to overrun the Yanks and their repeating rifles. Lucky I made it out of there. So, how long have you been on the trail?"

Ransom spoke up, "Me and him went home after the war but it was tough with the carpetbaggers and all the politics so we sold everything to some Yankees and been on the trail ever since. We tried to bring our parents with us but they are older now and didn't want to leave Virginia where me Mother had lots of family. They are especially close and all came over together from Ireland."

Tom interjected "Ireland! That's' the brogue that I hear."

"Aye, that's the Irish brogue talking to you. Anyway, me and me brother planned to settle somewhere out West, preferably Texas. We been harassed all along the trail by black fellers in fancy suits accompanied by carpetbaggers. We still are not where we want to be. Too much Yankee influence now even in Texas. Where are yee headed?"

"I plan on meeting up with my brother somewhere northwest of Fort Worth in the Cross Timbers where Ash Creek joins the Trinity River. Eventually we both plan to move to northwest Texas in Montague County. Good country for either farming or cattle but it is so sparsely settled that the Indians are still a problem."

Jubal rose to his feet and said, "Looks like the Missus has just about got dinner ready so best we mosey on. When are yee heading out?"

"Just as soon as Earhart feels it is safe."

Ransom added, "We are camped just about a half mile south of the ferry crossing, so stop by and we can get the ladies acquainted in the morning and if yee are agreeable we can go down the trail together."

Tom looked at Mary Ellen. She turned to face Ransom and Jubal and said, "It would be nice to have the company of other ladies for me, and the children for Belle. We look forward to meeting your families tomorrow."

The next day shortly after sunup Earhart came out the back door of his living quarters at the rear of the store and announced that the crossing would take place the next morning. This was surprising but welcome news to Tom who was anxious to hit the trail. Tom had been watching the river too but had not noticed a significant reduction in the flow of the current. If Earhart thought it was time, he had to depend on the judgment of the older man as he had the years of experience on the river.

After breakfast Tom and Mary Ellen took Belle to meet the Meador family. When they arrived at the Meador camp, Ransom introduced his wife Vivian and Jubal's wife Sally. Both women immediately began oohing and ahhhhing over Belle.

The next morning brought a flurry of activity. All the stock needed to be fed, the cow milked, and the mule team hitched to the wagon. Earhart told Tom to saddle the stallion and Legs to be ready to help get the wagon off the ferry and up a muddy slope on the far side of the river. As a safety precaution, all the women and children would wait until the wagons and teams were on the far side of the river. Earhart suggested that Tom, Ransom and Jubal draw straws to see which family's wagon crossed first. Ransom walked over to Earhart's barn and came back with a long straw of hay, which he cut, into three pieces.

Turning to Tom he said, "Okay boys, long straw goes first, short straw goes last."

Tom drew the short straw making him last to load.

Earhart's ferry was made of logs lashed together with wooden planks nailed on the top surface. A long line of thick rope was stretched across the river and secured to a large oak tree. A triangular pulley system rode the big rope and attached to the ferry at both ends of the upstream side of it to keep the ferry from floating downstream. Another long rope line stretched from each end of the ferry across the river and attached to a team of horses that would pull the ferry across. Tom last crossed a river on a ferry in the war but he had not been in charge. The Army always had a surplus of men available, which was a huge advantage whereas Earhart depended on his customers participation in helping to load the wagons and stock.

Earhart directed Jubal to take his rig down a slope leading to the ferry with a cautionary word of "Not too fast. Use your brake to hold it. Keep a tight grip on the reins and don't let the team get its head."

At the bottom of the dirt ramp, Jubal's team spooked by the rushing water boiling around them and the lead horses reared up until he tightened all the slack out of the reins. The ferry rocked up and down each time they shifted their weight and the horse's eyes were wide with fright. Jubal did his best to calm them until Earhart brought some old flour sacks and yelled to Ransom and Tom, "Wrap the sacks over the horse's eyes so they can't see."

Ropes were tied from the raft's floor to the wagon on both sides and front to back to stabilize it.

Earhart cast off and his men on the far side of the river began to draw the ferry across. About a third of the way across the river current was washing up and over the ferry floor. Earhart and Jubal were the only men aboard. Earhart was busy trying to keep the lines straight and not tangled. Jubal set the wagon brake and stood between the lead horses with a grip on their headstalls. Suddenly one of the bowlines leading to the pulley system popped. The ferry immediately swung around and the wagon tilted to one side where it hung precariously for a few seconds and then crashed on its side into the rapidly flowing current, dragging the team of horses with it. Jubal thrown into the river tried to catch one of the trailing lines from the ferry. Flaying in the swift current he tried in vain to keep his head above water but the raging current swept him rapidly downstream.

Earhart managed to stay aboard the ferry. Without the weight of the wagon and horses, it regained buoyancy. Seeing Jubal in the river Tom mounted the stallion. He spurred his horse and raced downstream. Ransom likewise scrambled for his horse following Tom. Tom quickly took his lariat, shook out a loop and made a throw at the first clearing but it was short. Tom again drew the rope back and formed another loop. Crashing down the riverbank through underbrush and large trees made it impossible to get close enough. He spurred the stallion urging him to a faster gait to get ahead of the current.

Tom yelled "Jubal! Swim to me!"

His next throw was closer but the current continued to sweep the man downstream. A quarter mile later Tom was able to find an opening in the brush. Urging his horse into some chest deep water allowed Jubal to grab the loop and tighten it on his arm. Tom towed him toward the bank. Jubal was in waist deep water when Ransom ran to help his brother to his feet. Jubal choking and coughing up river water was trying to catch his breath. Sally hysterically ran to him and helped Ransom carry him to the shore.

Earhart's men on the far bank ran downstream and helped the floundering team of horses out of the river. The wagon splintered after it hit a rock outcropping, scattering the contents throughout the water.

Earhart had the ferry ropes repaired late the next morning and they were able to bring the Ferry back to the east side of the river. Earhart profusely apologized, accepted full responsibility then promptly took Jubal to his store and gave him two sets of dry clothes. Earhart's wife helped Sally with some clothes since everything they owned washed away in the river. Earhart also provided some supplies, blankets and kitchen utensils. He apologized about underestimating the flow of the river and sincerely attempted to make things right for his blunder. He made an old freight wagon available to Jubal and Sally. The tongue was broken but Earhart salvaged the tongue from Jubal's wagon. By midafternoon, the replacement wagon was road worthy. It was heavier and more solidly built than Jubal's old wagon, so there was some small benefit to having a wreck on the river.

The next morning, to avoid overloading the ferry again, Earhart decided to take the wagon teams across separately then transport the wagons individually and finally the families. This would take longer but nobody wanted to chance another disaster. Once again Jubal was first to venture out on the river.

The next trip they brought over Ransom's team of stout draft horses. Ransom returned with Earhart and loaded his wagon. Once it was across J. D. and Orange took the Pruit mule team across and remained on the west bank. They would be ready to hitch the mules to the wagon as it arrived.

By midafternoon, everything and everyone were on the west bank of the Trinity. Earhart previously agreed to a price of five dollars for each crossing but the old Gentleman ended up charging only two dollars. He said it was an honor to take such a lovely families across the river.

The women dictated that they should camp immediately and share a meal of thanks for their safe passage over the Trinity

River. After supper, Ransom disappeared to the far side of his wagon returning with a bottle of white lightning and five or six tin cups, saying, "Boys, Ol'man Earhart gave me this bottle and now seems like a good time to drink it."

He handed a cup to each man including J. D. and Orange, uncorked the bottle with his teeth, and poured each a cup full. Orange who had never taken a drink stronger than sasparilla before sniffed the liquor, "WhooWhee! That thar is some strong stuff."

Two drinks later Orange tried to stand up, "Whoa, ever thin is movin and I don' feel so good."

J. D. scrambled to his feet and fell flat in the dirt. Tom and Ransom grabbed each of the boys slipping an arm under theirs and helped them stagger to their beds. Ransom produced a banjo and began playing old familiar tunes. Everybody was happy for the lighthearted moments and relieved that the treacherous river crossing was behind them. Joyous singing continued long into the night.

The next morning the sun burst across the horizon. It was a beautiful spring day in Texas and everyone prepared to get under way except for J. D. and Orange. Both of the boys rose twice in the night and retched outside the wagon. The smell of vomit ruined everyone's appetite for breakfast. Tom walked over to the boys extolling the virtues of sobriety and moderation bantered loud enough for everyone to hear, "Rise and shine men. I use that term loosely since I don't think girls would have gotten drunk but I need the teams hitched to the wagons. I would invite you to breakfast but you might be better off without it."

The mud was drying up along the trail and the weather was sunny and bright. They passed groves of pecan trees standing in lush green grass as high as a horse's belly. Texas Bluebonnets were blooming and every creek was running with water leading to several small lakes. In three days, they were in Fort Worth and the Meador's said farewell as they were going to push on to San Antonio. It was an emotional parting. Everyone realized they might not have survived the river crossing without the help of the others.

179

Chapter 21

The Homecoming

The Pruit family continued to push north and west along the West Fork of the Trinity River. Arriving in Tarrant County, they learned Wash had moved his family to Forestburg in Montague County. It took another three days to traverse the trail to the Taylor homestead only to find Jim gone on a trail drive to Kansas. Both Lu and Wash were excited and surprised to see them.

Tom asked, "Wash, it's good to see you but when will Jim be back?"

"Well, l got to count up the days. That herd started on the trail back in June I think. I reckon he will be home in four maybe five weeks."

Wash seeing Tom's disappointment said, "We got lots of room here so why don't you plan on staying with us till then. You'll have time to rest after your trip and familiarize yourself with the country."

Mary Ellen appreciated the opportunity to sleep under a roof again. She and Belle quickly adapted to the Taylor household. Belle being the only child in the house quickly stole everyone's heart and waddled around chatting up a storm in unintelligible baby talk. The work of cooking, laundry and childcare while on the trail was lessened and the company of other women made the lost association of her mother and sisters more bearable.

The second evening, after supper, Lu sat down at the dinner table and handed Tom a small cloth sack. He looked at her quizzically and said, "What's this?"

"Open it. This is your share of the sale money from last year's cattle. The ones you and Jim branded before you went back to Henderson County."

Tom looked at Mary Ellen. She was smiling expectantly. He slowly loosened the drawstring spilling its contents of tightly rolled bills on the table. With Mary Ellen's help, he began counting. When he finished, he looked at Mary Ellen saying, "This can buy us a section of land with enough left over to build a house."

In the following weeks, waiting for Jim to return, Tom started looking for a place to live close to the Taylor spread. During this time, Mary Ellen and Lu twice killed rattlesnakes in the house. Once, little Belle was crawling along the floor when a big snake came slithering across not more than three feet away. Fortunately, Mary Ellen was able to grab the baby while Lu used a long handled broom to push the viper out of the house. Lu grabbed a double barrel shotgun that hung above the door and discharged both barrels killing the snake. That provided more excitement than Mary Ellen could tolerate.

Mary Ellen told Tom "Living in a soddy house with dirt floors and no threshold is not going to be an option. Snakes, centipedes and spiders live in the walls and rain leaks through the roof. Besides we are going to have another baby."

Startled out of his thoughts Tom quickly turned to look at his wife.

She plaintively asked, "How do you expect me to keep our children clean when they are crawling on dirt all day long?"

Tom stood, took two steps across the room to where she sat and pulled her up wrapping her in his arms. "When were you going to tell me?"

"When I was sure."

"Well are you?"

She gazed up into his eyes and answered with a mischievous smile on her face "Yes Darling. I am sure."

"I promise, we'll find a place for you to raise our babies."

Shortly thereafter Wash suggested, "There is a sad case of a lady who recently died leaving a husband and two children. The man is returning to Tennessee to take his children to be raised by his sister and their place is only a mile up and across the creek."

Tom hitched up a team to Wash's buggy and took Mary Ellen to see the prospective home. It was a small poorly built two-room frame affair. The exterior lumber, raw from exposure to the elements, needed a coat of paint and the roof shingles were curling. The buildings sole appeal was a single glass pane window in each room. After looking at the house, Tom couldn't find anything to like about it. It did have one saving grace about it. It was up off the ground. Mary Ellen on the other hand saw possibilities. She told Tom, "I want you to build a fire in the fireplace."

"Honey, it is hotter than the hinges of hell today."

"I know that Tom, Sweetheart, but I want to know if the chimney will draw smoke."

Shaking his head, Tom gathered some dry wood and lit a fire. Mary Ellen continued to walk in and out of the little house. Once the fire was going and it was apparent that the flu would draw she spoke again, "It will require an addition for our private sleeping room. It is elevated up from the ground and has a nice tight door and threshold, which is one thing I insist upon. I want the new room attached to the house to form an "L" so we can have a sheltered place for the babies to play out of the wind. I want a shade arbor to the side of the new porch built right here for a cool place in the summer. If you tuck it against the side of the house, it will almost be like an extra room. I also want you to build me a separate kitchen on the south side near the well and I want a wood stove in our new bedroom."

Pausing for a moment almost as if an afterthought she added, "Of course you will paint the house white with black trim on the windows and doors."

Tom looked at her open mouthed with the list of desired additions floating through his mind as he calculated the cost and time to accomplish them. Her requests were a surprise, as she had never made demands of him before in their marriage. He felt obliged to accommodate her requests as she had, after all, uprooted her entire life to accommodate him. Besides he could tell from the way her face was set in a determined little frown that her mind was made up and he better agree.

"Well, I can do it, but I can't imagine why you want a stove in our bedroom?"

She coquettishly looked at him, her face changing into a sly smile, "Why my dear, to be better able to conceive more babies with you, silly boy."

Tom made an offer of one hundred dollars to the widower and they owned a new home that afternoon. The seller also sold them a quarter section of land that joined Wash's property for fifty cents per acre. Tom felt quite smug. He spent less than half of his original savings and he still had the thousand dollars from Jim's cattle sales.

A sawmill located several miles away on the North Fork of the Trinity River sold rough sawn lumber. Tom took J. D. and Orange and made several trips there to buy the necessary additional material. He hired a crew of men that hung around the lumberyard to help and in a little more than four weeks the house was finished to Mary Ellen's satisfaction They also built a bunkhouse and began work on a small barn and a set of corrals.

Orange was on the barn roof nailing down some shake shingles when he suddenly called out, "Massa Tom, looka there. Yur' brother Jim is here."

The celebration of Jim's homecoming lasted well into the night. He spun yarn after yarn of the places he had been and the people he had met. Orange and J. D. both declared that they were going on the next cattle drive north declaring their desire to become rich despite the Indians and rustlers. Tom listened in awe too, but knew his responsibilities to his family were going to take precedence. Jim and Lu had a child, but they lived with her mother and father so she had supportive family close by while Jim was gone.

Once the excitement died down over the next few days, the brothers began to make a plan for the coming year. With the influx of new settlers coming into the area, the opportunity of branding

183

yearling heifers and bull calves was decreasing. Jim suggested that they form a partnership and take the money they had accumulated thus far and begin buying cattle from other ranchers. They would make proposals to purchase cattle paying half cash up front and the balance after the cattle were sold in Kansas. Any profit above the contracted price would belong to Jim and Tom. Jim would accompany the herd and be their association's representative to monitor the trip and final sale. Obviously, there was some risk in that they were guaranteeing the price to the participating ranchers without knowing the final market price. Jim was an astute trader and felt he knew enough about the future cattle market to make the gamble.

The three brothers and Orange worked long days buying, branding and castrating bull calves. They were extremely lucky that the weather cooperated. Heavy rains and warm temperatures helped grass to sprout making excellent forage all over their range. Orange and J. D. enthusiastically took to the life of a cowboy becoming almost as good at riding and roping as Tom.

☆ ☆ ☆ ☆ ☆

Some of the cattle they bought from other ranchers had no fear of a man horseback. A big bull, with extra-long horns even for a Texas Long Horn got up in the middle of a bunch of post oaks and refused to budge. Tom was riding a gelding he had broken and trained for several months and he decided that he would try to get a rope on the old moss back.

He worked his way into the heavily wooded thicket and quirted the bull on his right flank. The bull bellered, took a couple of steps forward, as Tom, quirted the bull a second time. The bull bellered again, jumped out of the brush, and turned as Tom came into the clearing. The snorting bull facing him, Tom tried to make a clean break away but the gelding was not fast enough. The bull ducked his head down and slammed a long horn up into the soft underbelly flipping the gelding and rider upside down. The horn penetrated the flesh as though it were hot butter.

As the gelding fell on its right side, Tom baled off and ran back into the oak thicket lucky not to be trampled or gored himself. The bull backed off and rammed his horn into the horse's belly again. The squealing horse desperately tried to flee but could not rise to its feet. As the bull prepared to charge again, the crack of a rifle shot echoed through the air. Jim fired three times before the bull went down for good.

The horse, mortally wounded, kept trying to get up but only managed to flail his legs uselessly scraping up a cloud of dust. Tom eased over and tried to see how badly hurt the horse was. The loss of blood was immense as one of the horn thrusts severed a main artery. Tom drew his pistol and shot the horse in the head.

Retrieving the saddle and rigging from the horse took several minutes. Collapsing on the ground Tom said, "I gotta sit down and let my heart catch up with the rest of me for a few minutes."

He muttered to anyone who would listen, "Not a profitable day. Dead bull. Dead cow pony. Damn near dead cow puncher."

Later that afternoon, Orange and J. D. teamed up to rope calves so they could be branded. Orange threw a tight loop to head and J. D. was heeling. An unusually large steer, one that they missed the year before, was extremely hard to catch. The chase was on and Orange urged his pony into a full gallop to catch the steer. He stood on his stirrups giving his horse his head all the while winding a loop over his head. Tom and Jim were waiting for them to catch this maverick and lead him to the branding fire.

Tom admired the style Orange used. It was exactly as he had taught the boy. He threw his loop drifting in a perfect arc, falling over the steer's horns settling around the animal's neck. Orange drew his horse's head back putting the brakes on. Orange was taking a dally around his saddle horn when the steer hit the end of the slack snapping the rope taunt. Orange suddenly screamed in pain. The rope spun around the horn and took Orange's thumb off as cleanly as if a surgeon's knife had been used.

Tom rushed to the boy yelling, "Jim get a hot iron. J. D., hold him still."

They pulled Orange to the ground. Blood squirted everywhere and the ligaments hung limply at the end of what was left of his thumb. Orange held his hand, looking in disbelief at his hand. Jim ran up with a hot red glowing iron.

J. D. held Orange's right arm and Tom his bleeding left. Jim took the iron and pressed it to the end of the thumb. His flesh sizzled, smoking as it cauterized. Orange writhed, screaming on the dirt.

Fifteen minutes later Orange still whimpering in pain asked, "Is I'se gonna be able to use my hand?"

Tom said, "Orange, I think you were lucky. You only lost the part south of the first knuckle on your thumb so you should be able to still grip something with effort and some practice."

Jim chimed in, "This advice comes after the barn door was left open but next time I don't think you will forget to tie the end of the rope to your saddle horn!"

☆ ☆ ☆ ☆ ☆

Late one afternoon in early fall of 1872 three Texas Rangers traveling to Fort Richardson in Jack County from Spanish Fort on the Red River stopped at Wash's home. They reported a series of Comanche attacks that occurred in Clay County, which bordered Indian Territory along the Red River down south and west to Palo Pinto and Stephens Counties. The Rangers were recruiting young men to help fight the Indians. They reported many abductions, rapes, mutilations and killings of men, women and children.

The Rangers offered grand adventure and a salary of twenty dollars a month in exchange for an enlistment of sixty to ninety days. Food and ammunition would be provided to the recruits and feed for their mounts. They, in turn, were required to bring their own horse, saddle, side arms and rifles. J. D. and Orange announced at dinner that night they were joining the Rangers. They reasoned that the work of accumulating a herd for the drive to Kansas was over and done.

Both Tom and Mary Ellen tried to talk them out of enlisting but could not change their mind. J. D. told them, "I am twenty-one now and Orange is twenty. We are plenty old enough to make the decision."

Before they left the ranch, the Ranger Captain wanted to swear them in as official Rangers. Everything was fine until he asked Orange his name. Orange replied, "Orange."

"Yes, I know Orange, but what is your other name, you know, your surname.

Orange stuttered and had no answer until Tom spoke up, "His last name is Pruit, just like the rest of us."

Later Tom told his wife and brother, "He earned our name and I am proud to give it to him."

Orange and J. D. packed their gear. Each carried two pistols and a Henry forty-four caliber repeating rifle. Tom loaned them his old fifty caliber Sharps for long distance shots. They departed with the promise of being home before the first frost. Mary Ellen, unable to dissuade them, tearfully offered up a prayer for their safe return.

As they disappeared over the horizon, Tom recollected J. D., a few years earlier declaring his maturity to his Papa, John upon leaving home with a face still covered in freckles and pimples. He also remembered how he felt the day he left to go to the war. His youthful, naive enthusiasm had kept him from listening to the words of caution from his loved ones then too.

While the boys were gone, a detachment of soldiers from Fort Richardson bought twenty head of steers from Tom. The six troopers left in late afternoon to return to the fort with the cattle. Tom advised, "Sergeant, wait and leave early tomorrow morning. You can camp here and have supper with us. You will need to make camp tonight anyway and we have water and shelter for you and your men."

"Thank you, Pruit, but my commanding officer is expecting us to return by mid-afternoon tomorrow. He wants to kill one of the beeves and put on a feed for the men at the post the next day."

The detachment had been gone for about two hours when Tom recounted the government script and realized the Sergeant mistakenly overpaid him. It was still twilight and Tom thought he could catch the soldiers before nightfall and have the Sergeant correct the requisition.

The soldiers must have pushed the cattle hard because when their campfire came into view it was full dark. A soldier sat against a wheel of a supply wagon. A second appeared to be asleep next to the fire. As he approached the ring of light cast by the fire, he was surprised that neither man acknowledged his presence. Tom was preparing to dismount when he saw an arrow protruding from the back of the trooper who lay on the ground. The sitting man had an arrow so deep in his chest only the feathers protruded.

Tom could feel the hair all over his body stand on end. The only other time he had felt such a sensation was in a lightning storm. Suddenly an arrow embedded itself in the wagon beside his head and the whooping cries of Indians hit his ears. He never finished taking his boot out of the stirrup, instead spurring his horse through the camp riding low on the horse's neck.

He did not need to look back to know he was being pursued by Comanches. He saw no other soldiers, dead or alive, nor any cattle. The landscape offered little cover other than a few copses of oak trees. Star was fast and had great stamina but the Indian mustangs stayed close. A small rise came into view. He recognized the terrain and knew that immediately after the rise, a depression deep enough to hide in existed. Swinging out of the saddle, he lifted his carbine from the scabbard and took cover behind some rocks. A full moon silhouetted the two Indians. They were coming fast. Tom levered a shell into the chamber, took careful aim and fired at the leading brave. The bullet hit the lead horse passing through the neck. The horse somersaulted, throwing the rider forward and rolling over him. Upon seeing his fellow Comanche fall, the second turned and raced back in the opposite direction. Tom did not take time to confirm if the first Comanche was dead. Swinging up on Star he returned home as fast as his mount could run. Fortunately, his family was safe.

After daylight, the next morning Tom and his neighbors buried the two dead troopers he had seen the night before. They scouted the area finding three more dead soldiers and buried them too. Tom rode down to Fort Richardson the next day and told the post Commander what happened. Tom offered to make the adjustment but the Captain said, "Pruit, I appreciate your coming down here more than I can say but go ahead and collect your script. It in small measure expresses my appreciation to you for your report."

Chapter 22

The Trail Drive of 1872

Jim became aware of someone or something kicking his foot and heard a voice telling him to wake up. He groggily blinked his eyes, rolled from a fetal position on his side to his back and mumbled, "What time is it?"

"It's two in the morning and you're on night herd from two to four."

His close friend, Cush, stood over him holding a cup of steaming coffee. The smell wafted down to his nose. He had been asleep for two hours. Cush's real name was Chandler Cushing. Cushing, a top-notch cowpuncher and Jim were on a drive together for the second time. Cush had saved Jim from being trampled the year before. A fierce thunderstorm had caused a stampede and in the resulting melee Jim's horse stepped in a prairie dog hole breaking his leg. Fortunately, for Jim a lightning flash allowed Cush to see where he was. Cush maneuvered his own horse through the rushing cattle, held out his hand and helped Jim swing up behind him.

Jim sat up and reached for his boots then realized he never took them off before falling into a deep sleep. It was a short night as he had only gone to bed after his shift ended at midnight. The herd stampeded the night before and it took the entire crew all the previous day and night to gather the scattered herd. Every man spent over twenty-four hours straight in the saddle, dismounting only long enough to take a leak.

Jim gingerly took the hot metal cup. He took a small sip of the black coffee as it was still boiling. He smelled bacon cooking and his stomach twinged, as he had not eaten for two days.

Cush said, "I already saddled one of your night horses and he's tied at the rear of the chuck wagon."

"Thanks pard, much obliged."

Jim walked over to the wagon where Cookie held out a slab of bacon resting between two pieces of buttered biscuit. The bacon and biscuit went down in two bites. The cook, usually known as "Cookie," was not only a purveyor of nutrition but mother confessor to the men. He consoled them in loneliness and matters of the heart when they pined for a distant or lost love. He was always ready with hot coffee and a generous helping of the days fare. His was the first voice they heard every morning while simultaneously ringing a triangular bell and yelling "CHUCK" announcing breakfast.

Jim mounted and rode out to the herd. He tried to sing a tune he heard once in a saloon but could not remember all the words so he hummed it as he rode slowly around the herd. It was a full moon night with a cloudless sky. He could clearly see most of the cows bedded down resting as it had been a strenuous time for them too. A few grazed in stands of grass not totally obliterated by the sharp hooves of almost three thousand cattle.

A small stream trickled along the West side of the herd. When Jim reached it, he dismounted knelt down and washed dust from his face and eyes. The water was cold and sweet and helped to stimulate his mind. He needed to be awake and aware. Some drovers could sleep in the saddle as their horse made their way around the herd but Jim knew his very life might depend on quickly reacting to anything that might disturb the herd or his horse.

This was Jim's fourth trail drive with O. W. Wheeler. He appreciated Wheeler's experience in not only the cattle business but in how to find and keep the trail, locating water and the signs shown by wildlife to lead the way. Doves were plentiful on the plains. The birds usually roosted close to water, as they required it daily to survive. You needed to watch which direction they were flying in the evening, as they would lead you to water. Wild mustangs also gave clues as to the whereabouts of water. If they were head down grazing, they most likely were coming from water. If they were walking and not grazing, they were going to water.

191

After Tom and Mary Ellen's wedding, Jim spent the better part of 6 months branding abandoned dogies and unbranded mavericks. He ultimately assembled a small herd of about two hundred head. The first group of ninety head he and Tom branded had been picked up by Wheeler on his way to market in Abilene, Kansas. Wheeler's offer was to pay the brothers after delivery, less his expense for the drive. Jim paid his-father-in-law for the use of his pens and pasture netting a little over two thousand dollars, half of which he set aside for Tom.

Jim thought it was to his advantage to join the drive throwing their cattle in with Wheeler's herd, and working on straight shares of income and expenses and sharing the work of trail driving the herd to Kansas. It was not a matter of trusting Wheeler, but better to see firsthand what the business required to be successful.

Last year they trailed a mixed herd of cows and calves along with steers. If there was a pregnant cow that dropped a calf Wheeler instructed they be killed because they would not be able to keep pace with the herd. The sound of gunfire created a depressing time for Jim and when it was his turn to cull the new calves, he really hated it. Killing the calves distressed the momma and they became hard to keep with the rest of the cattle, wanting to return to the last place their baby had been alive. Wheeler explained that they wouldn't get paid for the calves even if they were lucky enough to live through the trail drive. To Jim it was not the money. It was killing one of God's little creatures and he always detested it.

The crew consisted of McCoy, the drive boss, two point men who were usually the most experienced men, two flankers, a cook and some helpers who usually rode drag. Drag was a hellhole of boiling dust that choked lungs and irritated eyes. After a day on drag caked in dirt, a man was unrecognizable and some would quit if the drive boss did not rotate them around. When drovers got sick or injured, the cook did the best he could for the cowboy or they would take him to the nearest town if they could make it. If the drover could not make it in time, they buried the poor devil.

The trail boss tried to coordinate the day's drive so the cook could have time to move, fix lunch, move again and then prepare dinner. The men always thought that Cookie's biscuits and gravy and apple pie were every bit as good as their mothers but their favorite meal was the son-of-a-gun stew he prepared on most days when they killed a cow.

The Son-of-a-gun recipe called for tripe, tongue, heart, kidney, liver, brains, and sweetbreads with onions, potatoes, salt pork, salt, pepper and thyme added to the pot and cooked for several hours in a big kettle hung over the fire. The mixture thickened with flour and some cornmeal made a delicious meal. Several pans of crusty cornbread swimming in butter topped the meal off.

The weather was so changeable that you could be scorching one day, go to bed that night and wake up in the morning to five or six inches of snow on your bedroll. Late in the season, a blue norther bearing snow, wind and ice could blast the land, sweep down into North Texas without warning, scattering the cattle before it for a hundred or more miles and causing many to freeze to death.

Crossing the turbulent Red River into Indian Territory the drive lost Buster, a pimple faced skinny youth who had not had his first shave. When his horse panicked in the fast rushing water so did he. Jim was not more than fifty feet ahead of the boy when it happened. Buster screamed for help and before Jim could turn his horse to help; the boy washed away in the current. They recovered the horse but not Buster. The water was a muddy murky brown and Jim and the other drovers searched for two days before they found him in the roots of a cottonwood tree down river about a mile. They buried Buster above the high water mark in a grove of cottonwood trees.

Jim and Cush took the ax from the chuck wagon and fashioned a cross to mark the grave. Cush was handy with a knife and carved Buster's name and the date on the timber. The whole crew gathered rocks from the river to put on the grave-site. They laid a tarp out and stacked rocks on it and then tied a lariat from two horses to two corners of the tarp and pulled it to the grave where they covered it in a double layer of rocks. They hoped it would be enough to deter the wolves.

Wheeler held the herd on the North bank of the Red during this time. After the grave was ready, Wheeler gathered the crew around Buster's grave, doffed his big flat brim hat and said a few words, "Men this boy never got a chance to grow up to manhood. He was a good boy and I know that the Pearly Gates were flung open to accept his soul. May he rest in peace."

With that, he pushed his hat down on his head, gathered the reins of his horse in hand, mounted and rode back to the herd saying, "We wasted enough time. Let's push beef." The somber group of men slowly followed.

☆ ☆ ☆ ☆ ☆

All through Indian Territory when they encountered Indians, usually there was no problem. Other times the Indians wanted to cut out a calf for trespassing on their lands. Wheeler thought it wise to accommodate this practice as long as it was not onerous. Sometimes the Indian demands required several hours to negotiate. A demand for liquor was always refused. Sometimes it turned ugly with the cowboys drawing their pistols and rifles to refute a ridiculous demand. Had they been further west following the Chisholm Trail it might have been another matter. The Comanche and the Kiowa Indians ruled the land there and a gunfight would most certainly have occurred with a loss of life on both sides.

Just South of Eldorado, a band of Cherokee braves followed behind them for several days always staying back a half-mile or so during the day. Wheeler knew they would try to steal cattle at night and decided it was best to ride out and parley with the braves. Their leader was an old toothless man but the young bucks looked like they could and would be glad to have a confrontation. The old chief who spoke only a little broken English wanted twenty head. Wheeler almost drew his pistol and shot him dead but knew he would himself, be killed by the young bucks. After much haggling Wheeler told Jim to cut out five of the worst looking cows and bring them to him.

After more bargaining, Wheeler again sent Jim to cut out five more cows. This satisfied the old chief. The Indians took their new bounty east off the main trail. They were hardly out of site when two gunshots were heard. Wheeler sent Jim and Cush to see what was going on. The two men thought it best to be cautious. Cush pointed out a small rock outcropping from which he thought might provide them with a valley view. They stopped just below the summit and in a low voice, Cush suggested a plan to Jim, "I have a small spyglass in my saddle bags. Why don't I climb up the rocks where I can see what's going on?"

Jim nodded agreement. Cush dismounted leaving Jim with the horses. He quietly crept up to the top of the rocks, took his hat off and laid it aside before peeking over. He opened the glass and peered down at the valley. Momentarily, he was back. He mounted his horse not saying anything until they were a short distance away.

Shaking his head in disbelief he said, "Those savages were already butchering one of the smaller cows and eating the damn thing raw."

Two nights later, black low lying clouds with rumbling thunder and lightning flashing almost constantly overhead, rolled upon them. The nightriders did not need to ask for help as all hands were in the saddle trying to keep the herd calm. Lightning struck in the middle of the herd killing several head immediately.

The cattle bolted while Jim and Cush were on the right flank. Cush tried to yell something to Jim. The wind, pelting rain and thunder, as well as the sound of more than four thousand hooves pounding the ground, made it impossible to hear. In the confusion and madness of the stampede, Jim could only hold on to the pommel; let his horse have the reins and pray. In the flashes of lightning, he was able to make out the form of a rider ahead of him for a few minutes.

When he saw a rider again, it was impossible to know if it was Cush. The herd began to mill. The leaders, winded now, would be easier for a man horseback to keep turning them. The ferocity of the storm moved away from the herd. Finally, the rain came less intensely turning into a slow drizzle. The clouds cleared and he was able to see across the narrow valley in the bright moonlight where several cowpunchers were singing a familiar tune trying to calm the cattle. Jim began to sing too. Slowly the herd began to graze and Jim realized that the danger was for the moment over. He was drenched and his hat was missing but he was alive.

After daybreak, they found one of the cowboys was missing. It was a young fella from Jack County on his first time away from home and his momma. Jim thought about the slightly built young boy who wanted so badly to be a man. The kid's name was Joe Bob and he had the clearest blue eyes Jim had ever seen. Jim prayed they would find him alive. The boys had hurrahed him a good bit of the time on the trail but the kid seemed to take it all in stride. The boy was innocent, naive and a virgin not only in a physical sense but also in every distasteful thing in life.

Jim recalled one afternoon a few weeks back, the herd passed a lone farmhouse that appeared abandoned. That evening, Slick Powell, the camp jokester so named because he used axle grease on occasion to comb his hair, started in on Joe Bob.

Slick, who was not much older than Joe Bob but a whole lot more worldly, got to hazing Joe Bob about his lack of experience with a woman.

"When we came by that old house this afternoon there was a little blond gal waving a blue scarf at me as I rode by. She was pretty as she could be and I just had to stop and tip my hat to her. She smiled real purty saying she was real lonesome and asked me to get down and come in for a spell but I done told her that I had my duty to do for the herd."

Joe Bob bit instantly, "So why don't you ride back down there this evening before you got to night herd?"

"Well, ya know I ain't no stranger to the ways of women and I am particular towards women with dark hair."

One of the other men piped up and said, "Yeah, but they all smell like the back end of a dogie."

Slick responded, "Friend you ain't never seen me when I was romancing no gal. This filly was sure nuff pretty but I think she is more like what Joe Bob would like. Ya know, young and innocent, not a soiled dove that the likes of this bunch run with in saloons."

Slick had Joe Bob swallowing not just the bait but the hook, line and sinker too. Slick says, "Joe Bob, why don't you let me escort you down there this evening for a rendezvous with this luscious young thing?"

"Well I don't know if I should or not Slick. I'm mighty nervous just thinking 'bout it."

That brought a cacophony of catcalls from the rest of the boys.

Slick says, "Now how in hell do ya think yur ever gonna learn 'bout women if ya don't get started? Now's the perfect time!"

That brought more cacophony from the bunch around camp.

"Now's yur chance boy. Let's go do it."

Not wanting to appear fearful, Joe Bob relented. Unbeknownst to him the rest of the boys were in on the joke and one had been dispatched a short while before to hide inside the house. When Joe Bob and Slick rode up to the old house, there was no lantern light or smoke coming from the chimney.

Joe Bob looked nervously at the house and said, "Don't look like anybody lives here Slick. Best we go back to the herd."

"Now don't be so quick to quit here Joe Bob. A young gal like this one is probably doing her chores for the family."

Slick says to Joe Bob, "Step down and go knock on the door. I'm gonna ride on back to the herd so as not to be late for my shift. Besides three is gon'na be a crowd."

With wide eyes filled with anticipation and as much trepidation, Joe Bob climbed down, threw the reins across a portion of the fence and walked through a gate that was half off its hinges, climbed some rickety old steps and knocked on the door. By now, Slick was loping up the trail a half mile away.

Suddenly, Joe Bob hears a man's voice, "So you're the no good sorry ass who has been seeing my wife." Two gunshots rang out. Joe Bob was off the porch, jumping the gate and flying into the saddle as he urged his horse into a gallop.

When he arrived wide-eyed and breathless in a cloud of dust at camp the entire bunch were rolling on the ground laughing. As he saw the raucous laughter he wised up, then he got mad, "Where is that damn Slick? I'm gonna shoot his ass off. Ya sonsabitches."

Slick doubled over in mirth was hiding behind the chuck wagon.

Wheeler said, "Pull in yur horns, Joe Bob! They just having a little fun at your expense."

"Well maybe so, but I still don't like it."

Slick chimed in, "Next drive you get to be the fella in the house."

☆ ☆ ☆ ☆ ☆

Jim, Cush and Slick Powell filled with anxiety as they rode back down the stampede ground looking for any sign of Joe Bob. The rest of the boys started a count of the remaining herd and others began trying to gather cattle that were scattered in the brush. It was highly unusual for a wrangler's horse not to find the way back to the herd but Joe Bob's mount was not to be seen.

Jim remembered how the young man, a boy really, just barely sixteen, had begun to fit in with the entire crew. He was not a shirker and willingly accepted whatever chore he was given. Jim being almost thirty had taken an interest in Joe Bob who reminded him of himself and the boy looked up to Jim as if he were his older brother. As a veteran of the war, Jim had experienced the toughness of life yet he maintained a sympathetic outlook for the youngsters.

They found several steers still alive with broken legs that they shot. All told, probably ten or twelve had to put out of their misery. Cush within earshot of Jim yelled, "Joe Bob's horse is over here."

Both Jim and Slick galloped over to see the trampled remains of Joe Bob's mount. Jim scanned the area then screamed, "He can't be far. Spread out and look at every depression, any place a man might lay."

A quarter mile further down the trail Jim squinted into the sun and saw what looked like a man standing in a tree. He quickly spurred his horse and just as he rode up he recognized Joe Bob. Jim reached for the boys limp arm to see if there was a pulse. The boy was still alive, impaled on a low dead branch of a large oak tree. Apparently, he was riding hard during the stampede and in the pitch black didn't see the tree until it was too late. Jim had to force down a gag reflex at seeing the young boy run clean through as if he had just lost a jousting match.

Jim urgently blurted, "Joe Bob, can ya hear me?"

The boy's eyes fluttered and opened slightly. He weakly gasped, "Water."

Jim grabbed his canvas water bag from the horn of his saddle and poured water on the boy's lips and partially open mouth.

Jim fired two quick shots followed by two more to bring in the others to help him get Joe Bob off the limb. They tried to extricate him from the jagged branch piercing his chest just below the sternum.

When they moved the boy, he screamed in pain saying, "No! Don't move me! Leave me be. I'm done for anyway. Jim, ya been like a Pa to me. I need ya to take my things to my Momma back in Jack County."

Jim countered, "Joe Bob, we got no chance of saving you if we don't get ya outta this tree."

Jim was not sure the boy heard what he said as his head immediately dropped with his chin resting on his chest. The realization that Joe Bob was dead brought a wail from the depths of Jim's being. Jim slumped to the ground and began sobbing.

Cush and Slick knelt beside Jim and put their arms around his shoulders. Slowly Jim was able to recover. He finally said, "I'm all right, let me get up now."

After they got the limb out of Joe Bob's torso, Jim climbed up in his saddle and told the boys to lift the dead boy up to him. Jim carried the youngster like a baby in his arms back to camp. From where he was found, Jim estimated that Joe Bob had been hurt soon after the stampede began. It was an emotional blow to every man in the crew. Joe Bob was every man's little brother. It just did not seem right that someone so young and innocent could suddenly have his life taken away in such a godforsaken place. Jim picked a spot for a grave on a little knoll just down from a rock bluff that would be easily recognizable.

When they finished digging the grave, Wheeler said words over Joe Bob, "God, I don't profess to know much of your ways but I shore do think you killed the one amongst us who deserved it the least. Anyone of the rest of this bunch was a better choice for you to make. Since you took Joe Bob, I hope you give him a seat on the side of your throne so you can comfort him forever. Amen boys."

Men and cattle were both exhausted. Wheeler put a couple of men out to watch the herd while everyone else slept for a couple of hours. Wheeler thought they were lucky to only loose twenty-seven head out of twenty five hundred. Jim was savoring some coffee as Wheeler rode up to the chuck wagon and climbed down off his horse.

Wheeler looked at Jim and with a serious note to his voice said, "Well Jim, I shore do feel lucky that all those cows we lost carried your brand."

Jim snorted, "The hell you say! Better go look um over again. I know I shot at least a dozen of your cripples this morning."

All of the hands gave a loud chuckle hearing that.

Three weeks later the herd was bedded down just south of Abilene. Wheeler wanted to hold them there because there was good grass and water until he could finalize the sale with his buyers. They would take the herd up to Joseph McCoy's stockyards north of Abilene as soon as McCoy said they were ready for them.

Wheeler called the boys together for a short meeting, "Boys I'm gonna let ya take turns going into town. We will draw straws, half will go in tomorrow morning for twenty-four hours and the other half will go for twenty-four hours the next day. I am advancing twenty dollars today to each of ya. I will be paying every drover off as soon as I get paid for the herd. Any man not back to start his work shift, will be fired and docked a month's wages. I know all of ya need a bath, a shave, new clothes and a drink!" The cowboys whooped and hollered throwing their hats in the air.

"Just remember, don't be shooting up the town or the Sheriff, Bear River Smith, will throw your asses in jail. He's a tough hombre, the kind of man who won't take shit off nobody. He got his name from killing a grizzly with a knife while being swept down a river. So watch yourself and look out for your pard while in town. There are a lot of bunko artists and card sharks in the saloons and they will cheat you out of everything ya got. So be smart. Oh, one last thing, most of them gals in the brothels ain't like yur sisters. So I would tell ya to stay the hell away from em' but I know ya won't. Have fun just don't come back to camp dead."

Cush, in a loud voice drawled, "I've spent so much time staring at the ass end of a bunch of cows I don't remember what a woman looks like. So, when we get to town, will you boys take me and show me the difference?"

Jim mockingly said, "All these boys getting a bath is gonna be something. I can only tell them apart on night herd by the smell their sorry ass throws off; usually cow shit, horse shit or their own shit. Sure hope I don't confuse them for some saloon gal on the way home."

Jim, never one to spend his hard earned money on booze, women or gambling used his time in Abilene to educate himself by speaking with some of the buyers. He learned they preferred steers over mixed herds of steers, cows and calves. Steers were usually bigger and stronger and could endure the long shipping times aboard the trains better than cows.

He decided that the smart thing to do before the next drive was sort the cattle, keeping the cows with calves at home and castrating the bull calves. This would allow three things to happen. The steer calves would reach maturity as a bigger stronger animal. The cows would wean the calves, breed again for a spring calf and the new heifers would be pregnant by the time they were yearlings. This methodology would expand his herd exponentially more rapidly than any other method.

Wheeler met with the buyers and the herd moved to McCoy's stockyards. A count made as the cattle passed the main gate showed over two thousand head. Lame and sick cattle deemed not fit for a long train ride, were culled by the buyers. McCoy would then sell the remnants of the herd for lower prices to other parties. Once that was accomplished, the drive was officially over and all that was left was the money changing hands.

Wheeler sent word to Jim and Cush to meet him at the Drovers Cottage Hotel to have a drink. The hotel, built by McCoy was the most palatial place Jim had ever seen. The floors covered in lush carpets made walking like stepping on air. Red wallpaper flecked with gold swirling decorations was stunning to the eye. Big comfortable cushioned chairs at each table greeted their aching backsides.

Jim said, "I gotta figure out how to mount this thing on the back of my horse."

They had no more than ordered their first drink than Wheeler said, "Jim here is your money for your cattle. I took out what I considered your fair share of the drover's wages, food and supplies."

Jim counted the money and blurted, "Why there is almost five thousand dollars here."

"Yes Sir! There is gonna be more next year. It seems like the market for beef in the East just keeps getting bigger every day."

"Now, I got a proposition for the two of you. McCoy has buyers for more cattle and he wants me to bring a larger herd up this next year. I propose we form three herds. I will take the lead and Jim, you and Cush will be trail boss on the other two herds. We can maintain contact with each other and in the event of trouble; we can help each other out. We will need to trail abreast of each other rather than following along behind. That way there will be fresh feed for all three herds. We will winter down in Texas and start gathering cattle for the summer drive. It is the first of October, and that gives us seven months to get ready. I promise you that the wages are lucrative."

Cush inquired, "Just how lucrative?"

"Well as a top hand I paid ya thirty five dollars a month for this drive. How does a hundred fifty plus a bonus depending on how much cattle are going for when we make the sale sound to ya? What do ya say?"

Cush demanded more information of Wheeler, "Just how big a bonus?"

"Using this last drive as an example I would say roughly five hundred dollars would be close."

Before leaving Abilene, Jim sold Joe Bob's pistol and his saddle rigging and collected the boy's pay from Wheeler for the drive. Wheeler threw in an extra hundred dollars and Jim passed the hat collecting a tidy sum for Joe Bob's mother.

It broke Jim's heart to have to break the news of Joe Bob's death to his mother. She was a woman not much older than he was, with four little children hanging on her skirt and a dead husband. Her face told the all too familiar story of the hardships facing many pioneer women, after Indians killed her husband. She was thin and haggard with few prospects for her future. As he rode away from the little shanty that housed her and her brood, he pledged that he would stop by after next year's drive.

Chapter 23

Making a Home

In February of 1872, Mary Ellen presented Tom with a baby boy they named Bill. The demands on the household grew exponentially. Milk Cow had another calf and Mary Ellen started selling cream to some of the surrounding families using the money to buy a large cast iron pot for laundry. She also churned butter and sold the excess to the neighbors.

They used her pot for scalding pigs from which they made sausage and rendered lard. She bossed the crew while rendering lard and made soap in her valuable pot too. Of course, Tom and Jim helped but it was not their favorite work. They wanted to work their cattle but as she pointed out in her demand, "We can't live on beef alone."

Mary Ellen had Orange and J. D. hitch one of the mules to a walking plow and a harrow. She picked out the piece of flat ground that had few rocks and directed the planting of the seed. Mary Ellen also organized the planting of a garden of green beans, watermelons and tomatoes.

Most of the time, she had a baby under one arm and another one clinging to her skirt. She and her husband worked at smoking and salting meat. Maintaining a constant smoky fire required wood be chopped and a fire tended for days at a time. She had the children search for fresh wild dandelion leaves for greens. They harvested beans in the fall and dried them on a tarp in the sun. She made a game of letting the youngsters take sticks hitting the vines to shell them.

Mary Ellen traded milk and cream to a nearby orchard for fresh apples in the fall. She used the big pot to the stew apples and put up apple butter. She planted corn and organized a picking, collaring all the men to help. A neighbor had a stone mill and Mary

Ellen traded butter for the opportunity to use it to grind their corn into cornmeal. They shucked and shelled the corn and made hominy with lye in her prized wash pot. Lu and Mary Ellen canned vegetables and fruit for what seemed like weeks on end.

She made dolls from rags and stick horses from corn stalks. She and Tom, and the rest of the family never missed the country hoedown where lots of fiddle playing and dancing took place. The men cooked several goats or a lamb in a pit and served it for dinner along with generous portions of corn on the cob and beans with salt pork cooked in Mary Ellen's pot. The women usually brought cakes or pies depending on the season. Moonshine, made from various recipes and consumed by the quart led to many hangovers. People traveled for miles and they usually danced until daybreak. They usually had breakfast before going home.

Mary Ellen also acquired a spinning wheel. When the cotton was ready to pick she gathered the children and commandeered as many of the men as she could find and they spent several days picking cotton. Mary Ellen befriended a woman in the area who had a loom. Bartering her milk and cream for use of the loom Mary Ellen made her own cloth. She always said the worst part was picking and carding the cotton as the bolls had sharp stickers. She wrapped her and the children's fingers to protect them from the prickly bolls but their hands felt like they had the flesh sliced and oozed blood for days.

A preacher moved to Forestburg and they had an old time church raising. All the men brought their saws and hammers and the women prepared lunch. The entire family attended services every Sunday after the building was finished unless it was harvest season. Even the preacher took time off from preaching during harvest and helped with the work. Some families came five or six miles to attend. The social life expanded over time to include a community theater at the church with poetry recitations and gospel singing usually after Sunday services with a picnic.

Lu lost another baby and she and Jim were devastated once again. Lu was so despondent that she stayed in bed for several days. Mary Ellen did her best to cheer her up saying, "Lu, you have to have faith. We lost a baby and I admit the hurt never really goes away but in time God has blessed us with more babies. You and Jim can try again. You are both young and healthy and God will bless you in due time."

They were completely at the mercy of the weather and the weather was ever a fickle flirt. Their hopes would be raised with a blessed rain only to be dashed by a late frost or a savage hail storm beating the fresh little plants to pieces. They planted again, and again, with a never ending, aching hope. Lightning storms sparked fires that burned homes and killed livestock. Whirling black funnel clouds would drop down from the sky and carve a path for miles taking everything in its wake.

At Mary Ellen's insistence, Tom dug a cellar behind the house big enough to shelter all of them from such a storm. During the day, if a storm was imminent, they rang a large bell to alert everyone. A major problem was they had no warning system at night. Mary Ellen insisted that everybody must sleep in the shelter during fierce storms. Sleeping was next to impossible in the storm shelter because of spiders and other creepy, skittering or crawling pests. Tom took a lantern down into the cellar before having everyone come in and chased most of the critters out. In all of this, the entire family remained eternally positive that the Lord would not abandon them and would provide for their sustenance.

The spring of 1873 saw J. D. return to East Texas to get married. When he rode into the old homestead and first spied Nan, he almost did not recognize her nor did she know him. She was now a young woman in full bloom. He was older and had filled out too. He had been a youngster of eighteen and she was only thirteen when he promised her marriage. She was but a child then but the same sparkling personality that attracted him before remained.

He loaded his new bride and a few possessions on a wagon and retraced the trail he and his brother had come five years earlier via Trinidad. Earhart had passed away the year before and a new owner now provided the ferry service to cross the Trinity River. The water level was low and they were able to make the crossing without a ferry or the drama of the first time.

Chapter 24

The Trail Drive of 1873

Jim sat on his horse on top of a rocky shelf at the crest of a long ridge with his leg crossed around the saddle horn. They were in Indian Territory. In another week, they would cross the Kansas line. He gazed intently at a herd of Buffalo grazing contentedly in the valley below. He tried to count the animals but soon gave up as the herd moved over the far side of a hill and revealed more buffalo than he had ever seen. A regal bull shaking his huge head from side to side lumbered leisurely along grazing from one patch of grass to another. His hide still glistened with the night's heavy dew reflecting the sun's morning rays.

Jim reached into his vest pocket and pulled out his smoking papers and tobacco. As he opened his tobacco pouch and began rolling himself a smoke, he heard riders coming. He turned to see his little brother J. D. and Orange loping up the side of the ridge.

When they stopped beside him, J. D. excitedly exclaimed, "What a sight! The entire valley is covered by buffalo."

"Yep, too many to count."

Orange joined in, "They, shor' nuff big! I'se thinks we ought to ride down there and take a closer look!"

Jim struck a match on his pants leg and lit his cigarette taking a long draw then exhaling said, "I don't think so Orange. We need to just let them graze on down the valley and hope they don't turn around since we have to take the herd on North from here. If we were to try driving the herd through the buffalo we might start a stampede and we could lose a lot of our herd and likely some of our crew too. If you look south behind us you can see Wheeler and Cush's two herds coming up behind us. Since we can't push through the buffalo we need to hold up here for a while and let them pass."

J. D. asked, "How long will that take?"

"Don't rightly know. Once we had to wait for a whole day but I have heard an old timer tell about waiting for as long as two days for the buffs to pass. I need to get word back to the two herds following us to not crowd up on our rear. Orange you go back to our herd and tell the boys to let the herd settle where they are for the night and have Cookie start supper. J. D., you ride back and tell Cush what we got here and then go on and get the word to Wheeler. I will scout ahead and try to see how long it is going to take the buffalo to clear our trail."

As both J. D. and Orange left to do his bidding, Jim remembered how they had evolved from snotty nosed kids to the men he was proud of. They had grown up a lot in the last year after returning from their sojourn with the Rangers. Enduring the hardships they faced on the frontier chasing Indians had tested them both but they had come through the experience as mature men.

According to both men, they fought two skirmishes with small groups of marauders. The first came after tracking the Indians for several days. On the second day of their pursuit, the Rangers discovered the Comanche had divided into two groups. Rather than split his forces, the Ranger captain decided to pursue, the bunch camped on the South Fork of the Brazos River in Shackelford County.

After scouting the camp, they found it was a small band of probably a dozen. The Rangers had about two dozen men most of whom were experienced fighters so they had the advantage. The Rangers decided to attack at dawn from the East so the sun would be at their backs. At first light, the Rangers attacked in a semicircle formation to try and control the flanks as the Indians sometimes tried to slip out of a fight by circling around behind their opponents.

As the sound of gunfire filled the air, J. D. and Orange found themselves on the receiving end of bullets whizzing through the mesquite brush. Suddenly Orange's horse went down.

An older Ranger rode swiftly up, held out his hand to Orange and said, "Swing up behind me!"

They raced toward more gunfire. It was all over in less than ten minutes. They killed four braves and just as importantly captured between forty and fifty head of horses.

The Ranger Captain told Orange, "Nigger boy, go pick yourself out a horse and if I was you, I'd try to find a fast one or that kinky hair of yours is going to end up on some Comanche's lodge pole."

J. D. overheard the comments from his Captain to Orange. Orange had not acted as if he sensed an insult but the Captain calling him Nigger Boy pissed J. D. off and he started to say something but decided that being in the middle of a fight was not the time to do it.

J. D. helped Orange cut out a strong, long legged buckskin gelding that looked to be four or five years old and then they went back to Orange's dead mount and pulled his saddle out from under the dead horse.

As they rode back to join the Ranger group, Orange spoke in a shaky voice, "J. D. did you'se get scared?"

"Not till it was over and then my whole body started shaking."

"Me too, I's still a shakin."

Jim smiled to himself remembering how he too had been scared to the point of vomiting prior to several battles in the war. He kept thinking he would get over it but he never did. Fascinated by human behavior, he knew there were as many different responses to fear as there were men. Some men cried hysterically. Some men got sick, vomiting uncontrollably. Some men simply could not speak and descended into a state of inaction and frozen in deep depression.

After the skirmish, the Captain told the Rangers that they would need to hobble the horses as well as tie them to a picket line saying, "I don't want to lose the horses we captured today. I expect all of you men to sleep tied to your own mount too."

Ten days later, J. D., Orange and the Rangers confronted a group of some fifty Kiowa Indians near the north fork of the Wichita River in Baylor County. The Rangers with twenty-five well-armed and mounted men stumbled on the group in broad daylight. The Indians were returning to Indian Territory from a raid in South Texas with several hundred horses. Twenty women and children traveled with them. The braves tried to fight a delaying action so their families could escape then they raced across a ridge to the west. Most of the women were on foot dragging their children with them and they scattered like quail hiding in the mesquite brush along the riverbed.

The Ranger Captain yelled instructions, "Let the women and children go. We can catch them later. Stay after the braves!"

A running pitched battle stretching over the next hour had a high cost for the Rangers. They lost three men killed and two wounded. Another was injured when his horse stepped in a prairie dog mound breaking one of its front legs. The Ranger fell, struck his head on a rock and was unconscious. The Indians lost ten dead. The Rangers were successful in capturing over two hundred head of horses. The Ranger Captain told J. D. and Orange to take the horses back to the river while the rest of the Rangers continued in pursuit of the fleeing Indians.

J. D. recalled a grassy plain that lay along both sides of the Wichita a half mile downstream, which would be a good place to take them.

He hollered, "Head'em up and push them to the wide place in the valley we came through earlier. There's lots of grass and water there and a good place for us to wait for the Rangers."

As they worked the horses slowly through the mesquite brush, a lone Comanche sprung up behind J. D. and tried to push him out of the saddle. A wrestling match started for his pistol. J.

D. was able to grab the brave by the arm and forced the brave off the horse with him as he fell to the ground. The impact of hitting the ground jarred the pistol from the Indians grip and the pistol lay between the two men. The Comanche saw the gun before J. D. did and flung his body at it scrambling to his knees. He quickly aimed and pulled the trigger. J. D. heard the hammer's dull click as it struck the back of the cartridge. The gun misfired. He watched in disbelief as the Indian cocked the gun again in slow motion. A gunshot rang out. J. D. did not feel the bullet. Then he saw Orange, pistol drawn, smoke curling lazily out of his gun barrel, ready to fire again. The Indian crumpled to the ground dead.

Both young men sat in the sandy soil of the river bottom sobbing. J. D. crawled over to where Orange sat, wrapped his arms around the young black man and said, "You saved my life! You saved my life! My God, Orange! You saved my life!"

Orange's face was ashen and covered in shock. He looked at the dead Indian, a youth close to his own age lying in the dirt, eyes vacantly staring, blood streaming out of his mouth.

"I'se ain't never shot nobody before. I'se gonna be sick." He rolled on all fours and retched for several minutes.

J. D. exclaimed, "Orange, I was dead if you hadn't killed him when you did. You saved my life."

From that moment, the bond between the two was cemented forever. What had been a friendship became a brotherhood. The memory was etched irrevocably in both of their minds.

☆ ☆ ☆ ☆ ☆

Jim finished his smoke crushing it out on his boot heel before turning to go back to the herd. The buffalo took their sweet time to graze west out of their path and did not clear the trail until noon the next day. The delay gave everyone time to enjoy a big breakfast and a few hours of lounging on their bedrolls.

Scouting along the Canadian river for a place to cross Jim came upon a small settlement of Negros living with a mixture of

Indians. One of the Negros owned a small store and as Jim rode by, the proprietor introducing himself as Rufus hailed him to dismount and have some watermelon. Jim noticed that the fella had on Union Army blue pants with a yellow stripe running down the leg. As Jim ate a slice of offered melon, he quizzed Rufus as to which battles he had fought during the war. After five minutes of rambling recollections, Jim suspected the ol' boy had not actually fought in battles. He was more likely a horse wrangler. Several horses in his corral carried brands from the Yankee army that Jim suspected had been stolen.

The Negro told Jim his wife died and he was now married to an Indian girl insisting Jim wait while he called her to meet him. Rufus brought out not only his wife but a passel of little Rufus's too. Rufus explained that his wife gardened and would be glad to pick some watermelons for the trail drive cowboys for only a nickel apiece.

Since it was late in the afternoon and the river was shallow without quicksand, Jim decided that this would be a good place to ford the river and overnight the herd. The boys took the opportunity to go for a swim in a nice pool in the river and had a watermelon feast after dinner. Rufus also sold them some corn, which Cookie roasted on a bed of coals for supper. Cookie also bought fresh eggs and sweet potatoes from Rufus providing some fresh fodder for the camp meals.

Orange did not come in for dinner that evening. Jim always did a head count of the boys and noticing that the lad was missing he sought out J. D. to find out what he knew. Smiling a knowing smile, J. D. reported that Orange had spied a young Negro woman in the settlement earlier when they brought the herd through. "He's over there trying to spark that gal."

Ever since J. D. married earlier in the year, Orange felt a little displaced. Nan took over his spot as best friend to J. D. and left Orange to fend for himself except when they were out on a drive. Jim also knew that Orange had matured into a fine looking young black man. His gangling gait was gone, and his shy approach to life replaced by self-assurance and a well-coordinated physique. It was close to midnight when Jim heard Orange unsaddle his horse as he tried to slip into bed unnoticed.

The next morning Orange did not volunteer anything about his activity of yesterday. Jim knew that to tease the boy would only embarrass him with the other cowpokes. He thought it best to let whatever happened come to light when Orange wanted.

☆ ☆ ☆ ☆ ☆

When they returned home, Tom and Mary Ellen excitedly broke the news of a new baby. A girl they named Mary Millie had been born November 12, 1873. The house was getting smaller and smaller. J. D. and Nannie had taken over the bunkhouse after their wedding as their abode, pushing Orange into the barn. Orange good naturedly offered the change and wisely knew that he could live in the barn easier than a newly married couple. During the spring, Tom purchased more lumber and they built a separate room on the side of the barn for Orange.

Spring in Texas can be a beautiful time of the year with bluebonnets and other wild flowers blooming and this year they were especially plentiful. It rained almost incessantly for the first month and a half of the year in 1874. The grass was good and the cattle were fat. The calves held back from the drive the year before matured and fattened into some of the best cattle they had ever seen. Tom and Jim accompanied by Orange and J. D. visited every rancher in a seventy-five square mile area to contract for cattle. Once bought, they branded the cattle and waited for the next drive to begin in July when Jim would lead one of the herds as the trail boss taking the cattle to Kansas.

Just as the time approached for the trail drive to begin Orange went to Tom and asked, "Massa Tom, I's got something important to talk to yous about."

Tom knew when he looked at the serious face of the young boy who was now a man standing before him it was something definitely important. "Let's go over here in the shade and rest a spell while we visit, Orange."

After sitting down on the side of a feed trough near the back of the barn Tom turned so he could look Orange in the eye, "So shoot, Orange, I'm all ears."

"Massa Tom, last year on the drive I met a nigger gal up on the Canadian River and I wants to go back with Jim again this year and ask her to marry me if she will. And If I can, I would like to bring her home with me and live with yous here."

Tom, startled by Orange's use of the word nigger, had never addressed Orange in such a manner. Surprised by how easy the word rolled off Orange's tongue, Tom looked at the serious expression on Orange's face and discerned that he had not intended the use of the word to be an insult. He immediately said, "Orange that is the best news I have had in a long while. I been watching you hangdog around all spring and wondered what was eating you. Now I know it was love. When you get back we will get the preacher over here and have a great big party."

"Well, Massa Tom, I don reckon her Pappi will let her come without getting married up thar. So if'n you don't mind we can tie the knot with her folks and celebrate with you'se folks down here later?"

"I think that would be great, Orange! Let's go tell Mary Ellen and the rest of the bunch. By the way, what's her name?"

"Latisha and she's mighty pretty!"

Chapter 25

The Last Cattle Drive in 1875

In December of 1875, Jim came home following his tenth trail drive to Dodge City. Lu was in the chicken pen gathering eggs. The noise of the clucking hens and her little girl playing obscured the sound of a horse coming into the yard until the horses nickered a greeting from the corral. She stepped out of the pen to see a thin, haggard and obviously sick man slumped over, holding on to the saddle pommel and barely able to stay mounted, his gaunt face heavily bearded. It was not until she heard her name called that she recognized her husband.

She wailed, "Dear God, Jim! What has happened?"

He slowly slid off the saddle to her waiting arms. Lu half carried him, half dragged him into the house to the bed. She pulled his filthy clothes from his body. A large bulging knot protruded from the right side of his spine just above his hip. Shocked, she said nothing. Fear filled her whole being. Lu heated water and lovingly bathed her husband like a child as he lay on the bed. When she finished bathing him she said, "I am going to shave those hairy whiskers. You don't look like yourself with all that fuzz."

He looked at her with teary pain filled eyes and said, "I have several bottles of laudanum in my saddle bags that the doctor in Dodge City gave me. I need it now!"

Lu quickly retrieved the medication.

"How much of it do you take?"

"Just hand me the bottle."

She did and he gulped a large amount, swallowing hard twice.

She propped Jim up in bed but because of the pain, he could only tolerate lying on his side. When she finished shaving him, she tried to feed him some chicken broth. After a couple of spoonful's, Jim shook his head, "No more." Her once strong husband fell asleep.

It was winter in North Texas and the weather turned ugly that night. Daybreak brought a cloudy, cold, windy day. Jim awakened panting and groaning in pain. The panic of the day before arose again within Lu.

Lu asked Jim, "What can I do to make you more comfortable?"

"Get me more laudanum then just sit here by me. I want to tell you how much I love you. I have worried about you the whole time I was gone. I have prayed that your pregnancy would produce a strong baby this time."

She smiled and said, "I think it must be a boy. He is kicking me harder each day and is probably going to be just like you. I am fine so let's talk about you. What did the Doctor in Dodge City tell you?"

Jim lay back on the bed bathed in perspiration while Lu placed a cold cloth on his face. Still panting in short shallow breaths, it took all his strength to answer her.

"The doc said I have a cancer."

"Oh my God!" She felt sick at her stomach. "Did he say there was any treatment?"

"No, he just gave me laudanum to help with the pain."

"When did you first know that something was wrong?"

"I started feeling a pain in my side and back just after we left to take the herd to Dodge City last July. I thought it was a pulled muscle or a strain in my back. Not that it matters much since the Doc said it was not something he could treat."

The painkiller began taking effect and he drifted into sleep.

☆ ☆ ☆ ☆ ☆

When the news reached Tom, he was branding calves on the West side of their ranch in Montague County. His little brother

J. D. rode a horse nearly to death to find him and share the bad news.

Tom rushed to Jim's home to find his brother unable to get out of bed. Stunned by Jim's appearance, he had to push back an impulse to collapse in uncontrollable grief. This could not be happening. It was a nightmare; only it was real. He felt a crushing helplessness. The former robust, heavily muscled man was almost unrecognizable. Tom searched his brother's face only to see dull eyes sunken into his skull. The dark dank room had a single small window making it difficult to see. Lu lit a lantern and held it up so Tom could see his brother's face.

Tom blurted out, "Damn big brother, what the hell is going on?"

Jim could not respond.

Lu spoke up, "He came home two days ago. I don't know how he was able to stay in the saddle. I had to help get him into bed."

Jim motioned with his hand for Tom to get close so he could talk, "You need to get my bedroll and open it up. There is a small coffee tin in the bottom that has our money in it, open it and take half the money."

Tom went outside to the barn found the bedroll and opened the coffee tin. There was almost five thousand dollars in it. At that moment, he would have gladly given it all away if he could see his brother a well man.

Lu's father and mother were waiting. They offered to stay and help Lu care for Jim while Tom went to get Mary Ellen and the children and bring more laudanum. Tom instead asked Wash to go get his family and let him stay with Jim.

Over the next forty-eight hours, the brothers, between Jim's lucid moments and the next swig of laudanum, talked about what to do with the ranch and cattle. Jim lay on the bed looking out the cloudy glass of the solitary window the bedroom possessed. "I see the sun is shining this morning and I shore would like to see the sun. I've been living my life mostly outside on cattle drives the last ten years and being inside during the day is tough to take. Do you think there is any way you could take me outside?"

"Yes sir, I sure can. Do you think you can sit up in a chair?"

"No, but if you can get the bunk from the back room I can lay down on it. Put a pillow behind my back so I can be on my side."

Tom moved the bunk and set it up in the front yard in the shade of an oak tree. Tom on one side and Lu on the other got under each arm and helped him to the bunk. The move exhausted Jim but after a few deep breaths and a shot of laudanum, the pain subsided.

Motioning to Tom to sit beside him, Jim said, "I want to give you some insights I have about the trail drive business. I have talked with people in the cattle business in most of the railheads in Kansas. I have taken note of things I see that portend big changes in how we need to do things to survive. First thing is, the large number of farmers that are flooding into Kansas and Oklahoma and they are beginning to pour into our country here in Texas too. The second is barbed wire. The farmers are fencing the whole damn state of Kansas. They will be fencing off land here too. We had a couple of confrontations with armed groups of farmers this last drive. Those folks are concerned about the Texas fever our cattle carry. It don't bother our cows because they have become immune to it but they are infecting the cattle coming from back east. It is making trail driving damn near impossible. The cattle trails are all moving further west. The Chisum and Goodnight-Loving trails out west are where everyone is headed. Third, the Texas Rangers and the Yankee Army have put the Comanche and Kiowa on reservations. Fourth, but not least is the restrictions we face from the Yanks not allowing us Confederates to homestead property. I have had a lot of time to think about this on the way home from this last drive. I think that our or I should say your future is brighter in going west and selling out here in Montague County. Take the money we have saved and buy up homesteads in New Mexico from sodbusters starving out on land God never intended

221

to be farmed. The ones you want to talk to are the ones who have yet to prove up on their land. They can patent the land sooner if they pay the government a dollar and a quarter an acre. I understand there are quite a number who are willing to throw in the towel due to lack of rain, if they can sell at two or three dollars an acre. We have each built up a nice nest egg over the last few years and even if you go it alone you got enough to put together a pretty good spread."

Tom listened patiently to what his brother was saying. Tom started to speak but Jim held up his hand. "I have got to have another swig of that laudanum. I don't think I can talk anymore right now. I need to rest for a while. Just let me take a nap here in this warm sunshine."

Lu prepared a lunch but Jim could not bring himself to eat it. While Jim slept a drug induced sleep Lu questioned Tom, "Do you think he will live?"

"Lu I just don't know. He is so weak now I think he has only a few days if that."

She started to cry, "He is still so young. He has never been sickly and I just...... don't know what to do."

She began to cry. She rose and walked into the house, saying, "I need to make supper. He always ate a big meal at supper."

Tom sat by his brother until it was late in the afternoon. He dozed and awakened to the sounds of his brother panting in pain. He took the bottle of laudanum and held it to his brother's lips. Jim eagerly swallowed the medication.

Tom looked at the setting sun and said, "Jim, let me take you back in the house. Night will be falling soon."

Jim nodded agreement saying nothing, just panting in pain. The evening fell into night. Jim did not eat supper nor did Tom. The night brought even more discomfort for Jim. Tom could feel every pulse of pain as it coursed through his brother. The next morning Jim was worse. He could only go for a few minutes between doses of the painkiller. Jim motioned Tom to sit close so Tom could hear his whispers.

Jim continued dispensing advice in a halting voice, "Just think about what I am telling you. More importantly I am dying. I am not long for this world. I want to leave Lu and our baby everything I have. It should be enough to keep her quite handily for several years. If she can hire a cowboy or two to work the ranch and brand the new calves then she might be good for the rest of her life."

Tom nodded. "I suspect her father will be more than ready to assist and so will I."

"Now I have another favor to ask. I want you to take me up to where we first saw the Red River the first time we came out to this country and bury me there. I have always thought that the knoll on top of that hill that looks down on the valley was the prettiest place in Texas I ever saw. Promise me that."

"I promise."

Jim closed his eyes and then spoke again, "Remember Cal Wylie from Fincastle, our cousin?"

"Yeah I remember him. Why?"

"I don't want to be forgotten like he was forgotten after he died."

Tom protested, "Jim, you are not going to be forgotten. Too many people love you."

"I knew after seeing the doc in Dodge City that I was going to die. I had the chance to think about what happened after Cal died, all the way home. He and I were the same age and we weren't just cousins we were close friends."

"I remember. You were just enough older than me to go get in a lot of mischief. I remember when the two of you got a paddling at school for smoking cigars at recess one day; then you got another paddling at home after Papa found out."

Jim smiled for a brief moment. "Yeah, I was lucky he only used a willow branch on my butt and not a board like our teacher Mrs. Lane used."

"You are right on that count."

"Give me another swig of painkiller. The pain is coming harder now."

Tom helped him, the effort exhausting for his brother.

"Anyway, after Cal died it was only a couple months before his wife got remarried. It always troubled me that she didn't wait longer. Just after she married, I saw her new husband riding Cal's favorite horse. He was trotting around town enjoying riding that fine animal. Then he rides home, eats dinner around Cal's table, sleeps in Cal's bed, makes love to Cal's wife and Cal's kids started calling him Papa. Hell, in no time at all, none of them folks remembered Cal ever existed, nor did most of the town. It was like Cal was never born."

Tom choking back tears uttered, "Jim, I will always remember you. You are unforgettable. So many people love you. You have many friends that will never forget you. You have earned the respect of every man you worked with on the trail drives. You will be leaving a legacy not of money, but the work ethic, integrity and skills you taught to so many young cowboys over the years. You will never be forgotten, not by them, not by me!"

Jim died two hours later. It was January 26, 1876. He was thirty-seven years old. Lu insisted that they bury him in Hardy Cemetery on the outskirts of Montague rather than on the Red River to make it easier for her to visit his grave.

Lu gave birth to Jim's son two weeks later. Lu already an attractive woman and with the land and cash Jim bequeathed her, she became irresistible. The sparking began shortly after Jim's death. Two months later Lu married Sam Fowler. Fowler sold Lu's land and they moved to Oklahoma. Tom never heard of them again.

Tom was devastated by his brother's death. All he could think of was Jim as the older brother had always been there for him. They grew up together. They fought a war together. They raised their families together. They were business partners. Now they were separated forever in this life.

Orange arrived with his new bride Latisha, from Indian Territory two days after they buried Jim. Their presence helped to lift the pall of gloom laying over the whole family. Latisha was a happy unsophisticated girl with a helpful attitude. Her father, a runaway slave escaped to what was now Indian Territory about ten years prior to the war starting.

The ex-slave possessed an entrepreneurial spirit and over time built a small camp that consisted of a store with living quarters in back where everyone slept. A barn and corrals along with chicken and hog pens were also out back. His main customers were the Union Buffalo soldiers stationed at a post not far from his place. He married a young Cherokee girl and they had brought a passel of half-breed children into the world.

Latisha inherited the same motivating personality, and immediately pitched in to help around the household doing the washing and cleaning the main house. The babies took to her immediately. She had a knack for making a croupy baby settle down and go to sleep. She did not seem to mind the tiny room Orange shared with her and Orange was happy to be back with his family. He was black and they were white but he knew this was his family and where he belonged.

On February 1, 1876, Mary Ellen gave birth in a difficult delivery to Julia, their fourth child. Latisha was able to help with the birthing as she chattered, "Massa Tom, I dun help deliver over a dozen young'uns in de last three years. Good thing I dun married Orange and come down here as the women folk all seem to be with child."

Not only did Latisha help deliver babies but she kept food on the table for the men and tended to the other children too. The biggest problem Tom noticed was Orange wanted to hang around the house all day so he could commiserate with his new bride.

It got so bad that Latisha told Tom, "Massa Tom, I been scolding my husband. I dun told him, Orange, honey, you best go back to doing your chores. Latisha has serious work to do and I don' want you chasing roun after me pinching me on the butt. Ya making me feel like my old pet dog. When she was in heat, the men dogs wouldn't let her be for a minute. Besides, Miss Mary Ellen and Miss Nannie are gonna be embarrassed wit ya rubbing yur hands on me all de time."

Tom resolved to have a conversation with Orange, knowing that over time the passions Orange felt would subside.

Chapter 26

The Trek West in 1878

In early January of 1878, Tom was sitting in the kitchen after breakfast with Mary Ellen when he broached the subject of moving to New Mexico Territory, "Quanah Parker's Comanches have finally accepted their new life under the Army at Fort Sill. Pioneers all over the West are welcoming the news and I feel the urge for something new. I need a new challenge. I have become bored with Montague County. Jim advised me to make the move before his death and that advice has rested in the depths of his mind for over two years. I have heard of the the Rocky Mountains and their lush forests and I want to see them. We need to make this move before we are too old to do it. I feel now is the right time."

Mary Ellen sat quietly after hearing his dream for a few minutes before saying sympathetically, "I suspect your brother's death plays a big part of how you are feeling. I know it still haunts me. Perhaps a move will help to heal us both."

Tom knew she too had felt the loss of his brother especially now with Lu gone. She rose, walked to the sole window in their sitting room, and stood there looking out at the barn and corrals that Tom worked so hard to build. She loved this man. She had borne him four children, three of them in this very house. She turned to him and said, "Sweetheart, I am ready if this is what your heart calls for. We can start over in New Mexico and I know it will be an adventure for us both."

☆ ☆ ☆ ☆ ☆

It had been a busy spring day and the women were all washing the dishes down in the separate kitchen. J. D. and Orange sat at a small table playing dominos. The room poorly lit by a single lantern hanging from the ceiling, emitted smoky soot that darkened the ceiling above it. Tom sat down at the side of the table and they looked at him expectantly. Not speaking immediately, Tom rolled a smoke, took a splinter off a piece of kindling, stuck it in the remaining coals of the evening fire in the fireplace until it flamed up and lit his cigarette.

He inhaled a long drag, held it for a moment, exhaling before speaking, "Boys, Mary Ellen and I have settled on moving out to New Mexico Territory. I think we need to make plans to leave by the middle of June. That is a little over four months away. We will have a lot to do before then to get ready."

Questions popped out of J.D.'s mouth, "What about the property here in Montague? What about the horses?"

Orange immediately, worriedly asked, "Is we all goin'?"

"Settle down! Settle down. Yes, Orange we are all going. A fella by the name of Donaldson, fresh out here from Missouri, is interested in buying us out and wants our cattle too."

J.D. asked, "We're taking all of the horses with us?"

"I only want to take the best animals. So we are gonna need to cull out the ones we need to sell. I think each of us can handle a string of twenty to twenty five head. The two of you will need to each take a wagon. The women will need to take their turns with the reins of the team so the three of us can manage the horses. Nannie can ride as good as anybody and she can help with the horses too."

J.D. questioned again, "What about the furniture? Are we leaving or taking?"

Tom jokingly smiled," I think you might be able to squeeze in those dominos. No, just teasing, we are taking our things."

☆ ☆ ☆ ☆ ☆

With the day of departure fast approaching, the buyer for the ranch brought his wife out to inspect the house and count the cattle. Tom and the boys helped the buyer's new wranglers push the cattle through the squeeze gates. The tally showed three hundred ten head of cows most of which carried a calf at their side, one hundred yearling steers and fifteen short horn bulls Tom purchased from a trader in Fort Worth two years before.

Tom and Mary Ellen went to the county court house and signed deeds to transfer the house, the quarter section of land they originally bought and for two other adjoining parcels. Tom acquired most of those parcels for little more than filing costs from people who starved out trying to dry land farm on rocky ground. They returned home thinking they were rich.

☆ ☆ ☆ ☆ ☆

It was early July and insufferably hot. They had been on the trail since the middle of June. The landscape and vegetation had changed from lush grasses and post oak forests to mesquite bushes in thickets that were difficult to navigate.

Nannie's baby, Little Tom, was only three months old. He was a source of concern for Nannie as he was a colicky baby. His crying at night became such a distraction that her husband had taken to sleeping away from the wagon to get some peace and quiet. Nannie and J.D. had three children, the youngest, Thomas Jefferson Pruit, was born April 7, 1878. He was just three months old when they left Montague County to go west to New Mexico Territory. The older two boys, Benjamin Franklin Pruit was four and his little brother John Alick was two years old.

Mary Ellen loved and admired her younger sister Nannie. She was however aggravated by her constant harping, about her health. Nannie watched as Mary Ellen strode quickly from the back of her wagon to climb up on the seat of the adjacent wagon and Mary Ellen heard her say, "Sis, I am just concerned that you take care of yourself."

"I am doing the best I can. The children need feeding, the clothes need washing the house and my husband needs me to be a wife."

Mary Ellen was pregnant again for the sixth time. Mary Ellen and Tom lost a little girl who died within just a few days of being born back in 1871 and it always made Mary Ellen sad to think of the innocent little Frances they buried back home on a cold miserable day with a strong wind blowing. Tom made a casket out of some oak lumber because he said it was the hardest thing he could find and it would supposedly protect the precious little infant from the elements the longest. She could not forget seeing her baby lying in the casket just before Tom nailed the lid shut, never to see her again. She held onto that memory because it helped her to know the value of the lives of her other children.

Nannie spoke whimsically, "Sis, your new little mischief will be coming soon now?"

"By my count not for another two or three months yet and don't call them mischief. They are blessings. "

Mary Ellen climbed up to the wagon seat and took the reins wrapped around the brake into her small hands, hands that were as calloused as any mans. She weighed less than a hundred pounds but was a strong woman both in body and will. She appreciated her sister's concern for her but sometimes it was irksome. "What do you think a woman is to do when her husband wants to sleep with her? Cross her legs and say no? Besides, I enjoy the feeling of oneness with Tom."

Still Nannie harped, "By the looks of you I wouldn't think it would be that long."

Mary Ellen ignored her sister and concentrated on the mule team pulling her wagon. She loved each one of the stubborn knot head mules as Tom referred to them. She made a practice of mixing up some molasses with barley and corn to feed to them each day, which was a trick Tom had taught her. She would take time to scratch each of them on the forehead after stopping every evening. Tom teased her that he thought she loved those mules more than she loved him.

When little Julia was wanting to nurse, Mary Ellen would hold the reins in one hand, unbutton her dress, drop the sleeve and neck down below her shoulder, gather the baby in the crook of her arm and let her nurse as the wagon rolled down the trail. Sometimes when they hit an unusually large rut the baby would bite down on her nipple causing excruciating pain. She never complained just accepting it as part of her normal routine.

Under normal everyday life, Mary Ellen knew a woman's work never ended and there were few moments where she could relax. Cooking to feed the camp and laundry on the odd days they stopped by a creek or river allowed little time for rest. While the men and children splashed away in the cool water she, Nannie and Latisha labored on, not stopping until they fell exhausted into their bed each night. Even then, they had to let the babies suckle, first one on one breast and then another on the other. Fortunately, a woman learned to sleep even with a little warm mouth pulling at her nipple.

☆ ☆ ☆ ☆ ☆

A detachment of Soldiers from Fort Griffin passed their small group heading north towards old Fort Richardson. Fort Richardson closed two years before but a small camp remained to provide provisions for troopers on the trail. Tom spoke to the Captain for a few minutes and the Captain mentioned another detachment going north from Fort Griffin should pass within two days. He said there had been no Indian activity for several months but stay on the lookout anyway. He said that most if not all Indian troubles were occurring in New Mexico where Apache Chief Victorio was raiding.

The next day a plume of smoke disquieted everyone, visualizing a wild hoard of Indians descending upon them, despite the information from the Army Captain. Tom gave the women loaded guns to carry in their apron pocket but the guns were so heavy they tore the pockets completely off their aprons. Mary Ellen and the other women quickly strapped gun belts on over their aprons. Tom did not know for sure if they could hit anything let alone an Indian racing along on a horse.

The smoke gradually died away leaving the question in Tom's mind. Was it an Indian attack or some innocent person's doing. Late in the afternoon, they rolled into a clearing where a former cabin was smoldering. There was a tent pitched a short distance away from the where there had obviously been a hot blazing fire just hours earlier. A wagon stuffed to the wall boards stood next to the tent. A man standing outside the tent hailed Tom and motioned him closer with a waving arm.

The man called, "Come on in everything is fine here."

Tom rode over to the man and said, "What happened here? Did you have an Indian attack?"

"No, stranger. We decided to move on west and we wanted to take our nails with us so we can build our next place. Just waiting for the embers to cool down then we can sort through everything and get our nails. Nails are too hard to buy where we are headed so we are taking them with us. Get down, have supper with us and visit awhile. I'm Rob Sheldon from Ohio."

Just after daybreak, Tom found Sheldon walking around the perimeter of his former cabin sifting through the ashes with a stick for nails. He joined the man and soon J. D. and Orange were stirring the black morass for nails too. Mid-morning Sheldon declared most of the nails recovered. It was time to move on.

The wagons, now numbering five, with the addition of Sheldon's, continued south and west. Sheldon told Tom of his plans to meet a wagon train at Fort Concho arriving from San Antonio

Fort Griffin sat on high ground above the Clear Fork of the Brazos River and was a busy crossroads. Before they arrived at the Fort, they pulled into the little village called The Flat. The settlement standing between the Fort and the riverfront had a number of businesses including the Beehive Saloon, the Occidental Hotel, a Masonic Lodge, the Glesk boot shop, the Conrad and Rath General Store and a newspaper, The Fort Griffin Echo. A motley collection of shady characters, gamblers, half-breeds, former slaves, Indians and saloon girls were present on the street and around the saloon.

Tom and the boys took their stock to a livery just outside of town and asked if they could put up for a couple of nights. The livery owner was a former Confederate Army sergeant named Phineas Browning. Browning whose biggest customer for feed was now the Union Army was a gracious host. He directed Tom to a level field close to the river behind his livery suitable where all the wagons made camp. Tom asked Browning if he knew if any maps existed of the trail west. Browning told them to go to the Fort and talk with Colonel Shafter. All immigrants were responsible for checking with the Army before setting out on a journey.

Stacks of Buffalo hides stored under shed roofs, out in the open in the street and alleys awaiting shipment, were scattered from one end of the town to the other. Various rough looking characters stood around the store fronts talking and smoking. A mix of white and Negro troops also in town concentrated at the saloon, their raucous laughter intermingled with the voices of soiled doves singing along to familiar tunes.

At the main gate, a sentry hailed him and asked their business. Tom said he needed to ask directions across the Llano Estacado. The sentry pointed out a white stone building constructed of Texas limestone near the commandant's quarters and directed him, "Sir you need to see Colonel Shafter the post cartographer."

The Fort consisted of approximately thirty nicely constructed buildings all built from Texas limestone and all looking so similar that they needed a sign telling the occupancy to identify what was what. The Fort reminded Tom how all military was the same and the loss of individual identity was so stupefying.

After tying his horse to a hitching rail, he strode through a door and was met by a peg legged Captain, the Colonel's adjutant. The Captain was a handsome blue-eyed man in his mid-thirties who was the epitome of a perfect Yankee officer even with the peg leg. The Captain smiled and asked, "What can I do for you sir?"

Tom, reciprocating the smile, reached to accept the officers extended hand asking, "War injury?"

"Yes, Indian wars to be exact. I caught a Comanche arrow. Damn Indian must have dipped his arrow in cow dung before shooting me, gave me a hellish case of blood poisoning. What brings you to our mapping office today?"

"Sir, my name is Tom Pruit. I would like to see if you have any maps available of the Llano Estacado?"

"Pleasure to meet you, Mr. Pruit, I am Captain Eggleston and we can definitely be of assistance to you. General Ranald Mackenzie, who defeated the Kiowas and the Comanches, directed Colonel Shafter to compile cartographic tools for the Army and now we make them available to the public. Tell me, what is your destination?"

"New Mexico Territory. I have heard rumors of homesteaders failing at farming who were eager to sell their claims to cattlemen in the Territory."

"Strange you should mention this. Just last week a man who served with me during the Great War, Captain Joseph Calloway Lea, stopped to see me. He told of buying a large tract along the Pecos River and suggested that if I had any inclination of joining the cattle business there were plenty of other claims to buy in the area. He swore the grasslands were enormous with grass belly high to a horse. Follow me into the map room and let me show you where he located."

Tom followed the Captain who walked with a slight limp, the telltale indication of his injury, the sound of the peg leg hitting the floor. There were several large tables in the room with various maps scattered about their surface. "Here we are," the Captain motioned as they stepped up to one of several map-strewn tables.

Pointing with a wooden dowel he said, "Captain Lea is locating here in the Pecos Valley. He indicated there are several tributary stream flows feeding into the Pecos where he would encourage settlement. Let me show you, the first is here along the Rio Hondo and another smaller one further south, the Rio Penasco."

As Tom studied the maps the Captain continued, "The trail up the Double Mountain Fork of the Brazos will take you to Yellow House Canyon then Buffalo Springs and eventually to New Mexico. It intersects the trail north from Fort Concho to Blanco canyon right here," pointing at the map. "The OS Ranch has its headquarters there."

Turning and walking to another map table the Captain said, "If you continue into New Mexico on the Mackenzie trail you will encounter the Bosque Grande Navajo Reservation on the Pecos River. From there you could follow the Pecos downstream until you hit the confluence of the Hondo River. The Famous Jingle Bob Ranch owned by John Chisum is just south of that point. I understand Chisum is an excellent source of information concerning property in the area."

"You seem to be very confident concerning the accuracy of the maps Captain, but I am taking my family through this wilderness and I have not been there before nor do I wish to put them in any more danger than necessary. Is it possible to obtain a copy of your map?"

"Yes, but I would also suggest that you consider joining a wagon train. There are usually competent wagon masters bringing other westward venturing immigrants through our area."

"Do you know if any wagon trains are scheduled to depart on this route in the near future?"

"You will need to speak with Lieutenant Jackson; he is responsible for tracking all departing settlers and the route they follow. He's next door. Let me introduce you. I will have a copy of the map brought over to us."

Tom left the fort with a map and news of a wagon train arriving from San Antonio in the next few weeks they could join.

Several weeks later Colonel Luke Jordan, a proud Tennessean, led a group of over fifty wagons into Fort Griffin from Fort Worth. Jordan had earned a reputation as a man who knew his way through the perilous combination of desolation and Indian threats. Tom was impressed with the man after meeting with him to discuss joining the wagon train. Jordan enlisted in the Confederate Army as a private and was a decorated southern hero who commanded a brigade for the Confederacy at the end of the war. After his service with General Ranald Mackenzie, he began leading trains west. Tom estimated his age to be fifty. His clear blue eyes bespoke a man who was used to command and tolerated little disagreement and reminded Tom of his commander in the war.

Tom, Sheldon, J. D. and Orange met Jordan at the Beehive Saloon. Jordan told them, "I have four conditions for joining the train, first, payment of one hundred fifty dollars for each wagon, second, all wagons need to pass inspection, three, you acquire the necessary supplies and finally you agree that my authority is absolute or the guilty party will be banned from the train."

Tom had anticipated a higher price and he was pleasantly surprised at what he considered a fair charge. Jordan usually traveled the Southern Immigrant Trail from San Antonio to Fort Concho. There the Goodnight Loving Cattle Trail took a south and westerly course to the Pecos River. Crossing the Pecos at Horsehead Crossing the trail turned west to El Paso then to Tucson. From Tucson, the road led across southern Arizona to San Diego. After listening to Jordan for over half an hour Tom asked, "Sir, why have you decided to change your route and go across what has been a largely unexplored land."

"Son, Texas is the big empty, a land full of desperados, little water and inhospitable weather. However, I learned a long time ago the shortest distance between two points was a straight line. If you look at the map, you will see that this route cuts off at least a third of the distance. The secret to using this trail is knowing where the water is located. I know! I made this trip with Mackenzie twice and have led four other trains through," he assured Tom.

Even with the Comanche and the Kiowa at Fort Sill there are still plenty of reasons to make the trip with a proven wagon master. Renegades and Comancheros still roam the vastness out of the reach of the Army and there are sometimes no landmarks to guide you. If you try going it alone or in a small group and do not have an innate sense of direction, stay home or go with someone who does."

Jordan paused to let everyone digest his comments then began again, "Most of the wagons are going on to California. So we will take you as far as the Bosque Grande and then you can head south down the Pecos. The Mescalero Apaches are on their reservation in New Mexico and even when they were raiding, they seldom came east of the Pecos, as they were afraid of the Comanche. As bad as the Apaches are they were no match for the Comanche."

Tom queried the Colonel, "We have almost a hundred head of horses with us. Is that a problem for you?"

"Actually it is an asset because where we are going there aren't many replacement animals. We may be your best customers. Horse thieves and Comancheros will have high interest too so it is best that you keep a sharp eye on your stock. Rather than trailing them on drag, you should consider staying abreast of the first wagons on the trail. We will be traveling a slow enough pace your horses can graze during the day, so keeping them on a picket line inside the perimeter of our wagons at night would be a good idea too."

Tom nodded, "I think we can do that Colonel. I will have your money first thing in the morning. When do you plan on leaving?"

"Day after tomorrow."

Tom felt a surge of excitement and relief knowing that he and his family would be in the company of such experienced Westerners.

Chapter 27

Llano Estacado

The wagons stretched out one behind the other for well over a mile. Tom had not seen a sight like it since the war. Painful memories were evoked which he pushed aside to concentrate on the many tasks required. Orange, J.D. and Tom took part of the time each day to drive the wagons since just two of them needed to herd the horses. This gave the women folk time to tend to the needs of the babies and get some rest from wrangling the teams. Sometimes everyone was walking alongside the wagon to get some exercise. The roughness of the road and the stiff ride were brutal on anyone riding in the wagon. They found that the pace was very comfortable for the mule teams since the oxen pulling most of the other wagons were so slow.

Two days out of Fort Griffin, they forded the Clear Fork of the Brazos River without incident and continued west. In another two days, they passed the Magnus Swenson ranch headquarters located on the banks of Paint Creek where Jordan had the train camp. Swenson was the first Swedish immigrant to Texas in 1846. He built an immense ranch over the next twenty years. Quite an active farming community existed in the area because Swenson encouraged other Swedes into coming to Texas by paying their passage in exchange for their labor. The Swenson's sons, Eric and Swen, welcomed everyone with an abundance of hospitality. They hosted a barbecue and the women prepared potluck dishes to accompany the fresh beef.

The day after they left the Swenson Ranch, Mary Ellen who was seven months pregnant, started experiencing nausea, cramping and a bloody discharge that started in late afternoon. Latisha hovered over Mary Ellen all that day telling Mary Ellen, "The baby is a coming."

Mary Ellen insisted that it was too soon. Latisha told Tom, "Massa Tom your wife needs to rest. This rough ride is going to cause the baby to come early. We need to drop out of the train and let yur wife be still or we may lose the baby."

Orange and J. D. chimed in, "You can catch up later if you don't have to keep pace with the oxen. We can manage for a few days."

Tom approached Jordan to get his opinion, "Where we are going there are no doctors. Your best bet is to take her back to the Swenson's place and then send for the Fort Griffin doctor. There is water and a telegraph office at the OS Ranch headquarters. We should be there in about five or six days. Send a wire there to let us know how she is doing. You have two choices after your wife is better, stay in Fort Griffin and I will be back in six months or try to catch up with us. We will stay at the OS for a few days and wait for you if you send a wire that you are coming. The trail will be fairly easy for you to follow unless we get a gully washer of a rain."

Tom broke the news to Mary Ellen and Latisha who volunteered, "Well then, that is where we is gotta go. I is going wit you to nurse Miss Mary Ellen while you handle the team and we needs to go right now!"

Upon their return to the Swenson Ranch, the Swensons graciously welcomed their guests with Mrs. Swenson saying, "You come in this house this minute young lady, bouncing around in that wagon is hard on anyone let alone a pregnant woman."

Once they were in the house Mrs. Swenson took Mary Ellen into a private bedroom, "Let me have a look at you. Goodness my dear girl you are about to have a baby! Latisha, go with Swen and he will help you get some clean towels and set water on the stove to boil."

In the middle of the night on the fourth of October, 1878, Charles Thomas Pruit, "Charlie" came into this world. It was a breech birth and Mary Ellen lost a significant amount of blood.

241

Mrs. Swenson comforted her by saying, "My Darling, we will have you up in no time after giving you some of my husband's favorite dish of liver and onions, that's the sort of meal that will strengthen your blood fast as anything."

Tom dispatched a Swenson's cowboy to Fort Griffin to send a telegram to Jordan in Post, Texas informing him they would be leaving Swenson's after a stay of 5 days.

After leaving Swenson's, Tom made camp each evening and after supper, saddled his stallion to scout the trail ahead looking for any obstacles. During one of his forays ahead of the wagon, Tom saw fresh tracks of an unshod pony that seemed to be lame crossing the main trail. He followed the tracks for a short distance but lost the sign after he came to a rocky shelf of land. He reasoned that there were other people pushing west ahead of them or it was a lone animal that had been left behind by a cattle drive and was not concerned. That was a common practice because the cowboys could not nursemaid a horse that was ailing and he soon forgot about the tracks.

Before sun up the next morning, Tom became aware of an eerie silence. The sound of horses grazing, snorting and hooves shuffling across the hard pan was lacking. The instant he threw the canvas back to get out of the wagon his heart stopped. The horses and the mules were gone. He jumped to the ground and found the hobbles cut and lying in the dirt.

It was still too dark to see any sign or where they might have gone. It was not until he lit a lantern and surveyed the area that he saw a trail of hoof prints that led south accompanied by a set of human tracks which appeared to be moccasins. Because there was no heel imprint, they left a rounded look. Had it been boots the print would have been much sharper and deeper.

With his brain spinning, he yelled for Mary Ellen and Latisha to get out of bed. He was trying to come to grips with their predicament. Whoever took the horses was mounted now and he was afoot making it difficult if not impossible to catch up with them. His mind was racing. He assessed his alternatives. They had a limited supply of water, perhaps stretching it; they might make it last six or seven days. He even considered riding the milk cow but knew she could not bear his weight and besides Mary Ellen would need to have the milk for the children. He knew that to go back east for help he would not have time to walk the distance and come back before his family would be dead.

Tom reasoned that their only chance was for him to follow and overtake the thief. He collected his Sharps carbine and a bandolier of cartridges. His Colt pistol he gave to Mary Ellen with a quick lesson of how to aim, shoot and reload the gun. Tom had taught her to shoot the pistol several years ago in Forestburg but in her current hysterical state her hands shook so badly he hoped she would not shoot herself or Latisha. She understood the predicament they were in was life threatening and finally managed to calm down enough to make a reasonable effort.

Tom retrieved a sawed off shotgun from under the wagon seat. He spoke to the two women, "Listen up, both of you. Latisha, do you know how to load and shoot a shotgun?"

"Yessa, I shor do. My Pappy done taught me to shoot it. I knows to hold on tight and shoot only one barrel at a time and eject the shells and load more shells. Ain't nobody gonna mess wit us while ya gone Massa Tom."

"Well this one is loaded with double oo buckshot. It will cut a man in half at ten feet. Now I want the two of you to listen to me. If I'm not back in three days I want Latisha to start walking back to the Swenson ranch. We are two maybe three days walk from the Swenson ranch and they will help you. We have enough water for five or six days and that gives us a margin of safety. Just follow the wagon tracks. Mary Ellen you need to stay here. You and the children will be better off here than exposed to the elements."

She wanted to protest but knew he was right. Walking and carrying a small baby after such a difficult delivery would be disastrous.

243

He filled a canteen with water and put some jerky in his saddlebags along with extra cartridges, his spyglass and a short catch rope that he could use as a hackamore. Tom left as soon as early morning twilight allowed him to see the trail. As soon as the sun rose over the horizon, the day burst into full daylight. Tom trotted at a pace, which would cover a lot of ground if he could maintain it for several hours.

The hoof prints were easy to follow. Three miles down the trail, he noticed a lot of ground had been disturbed and when the tracks continued he no longer saw any footprints. The thief was either riding one of the horses or perhaps one of the mules. Star had a shoe on each hoof that had a wing like look to it. Legs had a shoe that had a bar across the back to help her with a soft heel on her right rear hoof.

Tom suspected that the thief had tried to mount Star but the stallion apparently would not let him. Morning stretched to midday. The wide brown plains flowed like an ocean to the horizon. As the sun climbed, the horizon became a moving mirage of heat waves rising to the sky. He was not sure he was gaining ground and it was imperative that he push himself to continue. His motivation came from the thought of his wife and children struggling for life without water.

Tom spent a sleepless night. He made a depression in a sandy place in which to lie and cut bear grass stems for cover from the night chill. As soon as twilight showed the trail he continued his pursuit, hopeful that the perpetrator was confident in not being followed and would soon stop to rest.

It was mid-morning when Tom found the remains of a small campfire. Holding his hand over the still warm ashes, he knew he needed to pick up the pace. His feet already bloody from broken blisters were hurting. To preserve water he sucked on jerky to generate energy and just as importantly wet his mouth with saliva. His determination increased when he found a place where the thief had defecated and was still fresh. He pushed on harder than ever.

As night fell, he smelled the smoke of a campfire. He slowed his pace to approach without alarming the thief who did not yet know he was now the prey. Slowly Tom crept low to the ground toward the direction of the smoke smell. A rise afforded him a view that encompassed two small arroyos that converged into one larger one. He removed his hat and hugged the ground. Using his spyglass, he could see the light of a small fire and a man sitting cross-legged before it. Three horses were grazing nearby but the small lame pony was not visible.

Tom's attention diverted further down the hill by some crows circling in the early twilight exposed the small pony laying stretched out on the ground. Tom could make out bloodstains on its haunch. He knew the pony was in bad shape but did not realize it was close to death. While he puzzled on the dead horse, the thief rose and walked over to the remaining three horses to check their hobbles. The thief was a small man dressed in a black vest over a bright calico shirt. He wore a loincloth over what looked to be soldier's pants with a rifle slung over his shoulder. He had to be a Comanche, possibly an Apache, or perhaps just a renegade.

Tom decided to move slowly east during the night to put the rising sun behind his back to maximize the opportunity for surprise and a good shot. Tom was going to kill him. He could not afford not to kill him. There would be no negotiation, no warning when the time came. The stakes were too high and he did not have the luxury of making a mistake. He had killed before during the war but the men he had killed had been faceless and impersonal. The reason he would kill now was for the most valuable thing a man could ever have, the love of his family, his life and the lives of his wife and children depended on it.

It was a long night for Tom. His only thoughts were of his dear Mary Ellen and their precious children dying of thirst or worse. He wanted to rush down and take the Indian by surprise and choke the life from his body but he knew the consequences if he could not totally surprise him. He watched the fire flicker in the night until it slowly went out. He could not sleep. The thought of awakening and having missed the opportunity to make the kill burned his mind awake. He knew that he needed to wait until daybreak and darkness disappeared.

☆ ☆ ☆ ☆ ☆

Back at the wagon, Mary Ellen waited fearfully and was grateful for Latisha's presence. Night came. She tried to sleep with the children wrapped in her arms to no avail. The only sound she heard was the milk cow's bell as she grazed near the rear of the wagon. Suddenly, the mournful howl of a wolf reminded her of the peril they faced. She made herself focus on her and Tom's courtship and of the excitement of being with him on their wedding night. She remembered his touch, told herself that he was alive, and that he would return to them.

During the second day, Mary Ellen asked Bill and Belle to take turns standing on the wagon seat, the highest point available, and scan the horizon as their lookout. The children took their assignment seriously watching for their father or any other man or beast that might approach and give a warning. The chores of being a mother never ended and she busied herself trying to take her mind off Tom's whereabouts.

This morning she took one of her most useful kitchen tools, a fork nearly as long as her arm. She walked around their camp spearing dry buffalo patties lying on the ground. Pulling them off the fork, she stacked them on her arm until she had a supply that stretched from her wrist to her chin. A tarp slung underneath the wagon provided storage. Buffalo patties provided the fuel that she used to cook meals burning hot and with a little flame. Unfortunately, they did not build a bed of coals.

Latisha prepared meals and helped with the newborn baby. Mary Ellen read the Bible aloud, prayed and darned clothes. She had not prayed so fervently since Tom had come home safely from the war. She did her praying silently so as not to alarm Belle and the other children. She and Latisha took turns to be the lookout to let little Bill and his sister have time to play. Bill played with a stick using it as a make believe gun. He ran back and forth using a Yucca stalk pretending to ride a horse. At night, they lit a single lantern and hung it from a pole tied to the side of the wagon to shine as a beacon in the event Tom was nearby.

☆ ☆ ☆ ☆ ☆

During the night, Tom crept to within approximately a hundred yards of the Indian's camp at the head of the arroyo. The incessant yipping of coyotes rolled across the prairie. Attracted by the smell of blood from the dead horse the coyotes were sitting impatiently on the crest of the hill above the Indian.

In the twilight, the Indian rose to his feet and stirred up the coals to his fire. After putting more cow chips and small brush branches on the fire, the Indian stood with his arms outstretched and gazed in the direction of the rising sun. A woeful sound echoed down the arroyo to Tom. The Indian was chanting what Tom assumed to be a morning prayer. The Indian did not know that death lay before him concealed by the bright rays of light streaming across the sky.

His Sharp fifty's heavy barrel was supported by a rock to help with the elevation. He pulled the ladder gun sight up into position, made an adjustment for the estimated distance then put the bead at the end of the barrel in the middle of the man's chest. Tom drew a deep breath and let it out and then drew another and held it. His Sharps belched a cloud of smoke. The bullet hit the Indian low in the belly near his groin. The impact knocked the man down and the slap of the impact echoed back to Tom.

The Indian was screaming and writhing in pain on the ground. Tom reloaded and ran as fast as his legs could carry him toward the camp. The Indian tried to get to his feet but his pelvis was shattered. He could only crawl awkwardly across the ground. He was dead by the time Tom stood over him. The large fifty-caliber bullet killed by creating a wound that was so large death was mercifully only a few seconds away.

Tom immediately ran to the saddle horses and the mules. They were excitedly rearing up and wanting to bolt. The horses calmed down upon recognizing him. Their hobbles were secure. He saw the slashed throat of the dead pony oozing a pool of blood. The Indian had carved off a piece of the flank and cooked it. It made sense; the horse slowed them down and was more valuable as food.

Tom walked over to the dead man's blanket near the fire. He took the toe of his boot to kick it aside to see if anything of value was there. There was nothing. An old musket lay near the fire whose best days were behind it. He let it lie where he found it. He went back to the Indian and rolled him over. A knife with a bone handle inlaid with turquoise tucked in the Indians waist sash caught his eye. He picked it up and stuck it in his boot.

Concerned that the sound of the rifle shot might bring unwanted company, Tom scanned the surrounding horizon and saw the coyotes pacing back and forth waiting for a meal of horseflesh. He quickly gathered some stones to cover the dead Indian but there would be no time to dig a grave. He used his catch rope to make a hackamore for Star and fashioned a lead line from the Indian's ropes for the others. Releasing the hobbles of the horses and the four mules, he swung up on Star by holding onto his mane. He turned north toward his loved ones. He would be home before evening.

☆ ☆ ☆ ☆ ☆

Bill quarreled with Mary Ellen when she told him to take the watch on the wagon seat this afternoon saying, "No! I want Belle to take the watch. It's her turn." He continued playing with his make believe gun and riding his imaginary horse.

Mary Ellen trying to nurse her newborn baby, lost her patience snapped, "Bill, do as you are told before I take a switch to

248

your bottom. I need Belle to watch Millie and Julia while Latisha and I make supper."

Climbing reluctantly up to become the lookout Bill knew his mother was upset and knew she had the capacity to spank and spank hard. He did not question her further. The sun was settling low into the western sky now and he had to squint to see anything in that direction so he would only look that way for a short time and would pivot his stance to see in all the other directions.

When Bill looked back to the south and west, he thought he noticed movement on the horizon. Slowly the shape of a man and horses formed on the horizon.

Bill pointing to the setting sun shouted, "Momma! Momma! Momma! Daddy!"

Mary Ellen dropped the pot she was preparing to cook dinner in, quickly scrambled up and stood on the seat of the wagon beside Bill. She squinted hard into the sun and immediately burst into tears of relief. Mary Ellen grabbed Bill and wrapped her arms tightly around him and said, "Your Daddy is coming Bill, Your Daddy is coming!"

Chapter 28

New Mexico Territory

It took five days for Tom and Mary Ellen to reach the OS Ranch. A lookout saw them coming and notified Jordan who rode out to meet them. "I am shor happy ya showed up today cause we were going to break camp in the morning.

"Sorry to be behind schedule but we had a little Indian problem. Set us back a couple of days." Tom continued, "We lost our mules and horses but everything is okay now."

That night everyone gathered around the campfire to hear about the excitement. Jordan said, "Tom you were mighty lucky that all you got was blistered feet."

The next day the wagon train ran head long into a cattle drive of several thousand head of cattle and had to stop until they cleared the trail. The trail boss rode up to where J. D. was herding the horses. The man waved and said, "That is the best bunch of horses I seen in a long time. Where ya takin 'em?"

"New Mexico Territory."

"Name yur price but I would shor like to own the stud horse over there."

"Ya gotta talk to my brother. This is him coming now."

Tom rode up and was met with a smile and handshake form the stranger. "Howdy, John Slaughter is my name, just admiring yur stud horse."

Tom touched his hat brim, "Tom Pruit. I appreciate your interest but the stallion is the foundation of my dreams and without his blood my mares would be foaling much weaker horses. Come out to New Mexico in a couple of years and I will sell ya one of his colts."

"Where do ya think ya are gonna settle?"

"Headed to the Penasco River Valley. Did you say your name was Slaughter?"

"That's right John Slaughter."

Tom pulled out his tobacco and paper and offered some to Slaughter. The stranger accepted and began to roll a cigarette. Tom said musing, "Slaughter, Slaughter, mighty familiar name. We are from Montague County. Did ya ever get up there?"

"Yep, and damn near got scalped by the Comanches near Victoria Peak." Slaughter finished rolling his smoke and handed the makings back to Tom.

"I think you may have known my brother Jim, Jim Pruit. He was a trail boss on several drives up to Kansas."

Slaughter's eyes showed recognition, "Well I'll be damned. He is a good man. Is he with ya?"

"No, friend he died two years ago of cancer."

"Sorry to hear that. He and his hands helped us out after a big storm started a stampede. We spent a week sorting cattle. I got to know him some but never saw him again after that."

Looking out at the horses Tom said, "Jim and our little brother J. D. here put this bunch of steel dust horses together."

"They are a right fine looking bunch. Next time I get over to Roswell I will look ya up. Best I get back to my cows. My pleasure to meet ya."

The wagon train reached the Bosque Redondo in New Mexico on the west side of the Pecos River. Tom and his family said their goodbyes to Rob Sheldon and his family as well as Colonel Jordan who were going on to California. Jordan gave Tom directions to find both Chisum's South Spring Ranch and Captain Lea's ranch near the settlement of Roswell.

When they arrived at Chisum's ranch headquarters, Tom told everyone to rest until he visited with Chisum. The hacienda stood in a grove of Cottonwood trees along the course of a spring. Tom could not help but admire the structure with large verandas and vowed he would build one like it. Irrigated fields lush to the eye extended away from the house in every direction and spoke of the dedication of the owner.

While tying his horse to a hitching rail, a Mexican house-keeper greeted him. She ushered him into a sitting room and went to fetch Mister Chisum. When Chisum entered the room the man's energy impressed Tom. He was slightly shorter in stature than Tom but he was a man of unmistakable physical strength. A hand-some, sunburned, weather beaten face pockmarked by smallpox portrayed a man who suffered little doubt of the world. A large mustache covered his upper lip like a roof. His steel gray eyes seemed to penetrate to Tom's core. Tom estimated the man's age to be early fifties. An obviously self-confident man, Chisum ex-tended his hand in greeting and said, "Pleased to make your ac-quaintance Mr. Pruit. What can I do for you?"

"Thank you for seeing me, sir. We just pulled in from Tex-as. I was told that you are an honest, fair dealing man and I was hoping to get some advice on where I could find some suitable property to start a cattle ranch."

"You are not a sod buster I take it?"

"No sir, cattle is my main ambition."

"Where in Texas are you from?"

"Montague County, near the Red River."

"Small world son, I hail from Paris about a hundred miles east. So tell me what kind of land are you looking for?"

"Well sir, if I could find land with a water source like you have here it would be heaven indeed. I planned to put in some gardens and perhaps some pasture grasses but my main idea was to raise beef cattle. Any farming would just be supplemental to the cattle."

"You said your family was with you?"

"Yes sir, we have three wagons and a herd of steel dust horses with us. I need to find pasture tonight so we will be moving on as soon as we finish talking."

"No need to move on. You might as well stay here. Steel Dust horses ya say? I am always looking for prime horseflesh. I'd like to take a look."

"Yes Sir, it is always good to look."

Looking outside, Chisum said, "You have children with you?"

"Yes sir, we have seven little ones between me and my brother and our wives."

"I love children and would take it as a personal accommodation for you and your family to stay and have supper with us. I have some good Tennessee whiskey we need to drink as well. My niece Sally will enjoy having some women folk to visit with too."

After a supper of steak and beans, Chisum freely gave advice to Tom, concerning where he thought it would be most advantageous to buy property.

"Son, I have to ask a very personal question but I must ask it to give you the right advice. Do you have some money to wave under the nose of folks who need to sell and move on?"

"Mr. Chisum we sold our place in Texas for a fair sum and while we don't consider ourselves rich, lots of folk might."

"Let me cogitate for a while and after dinner perhaps I can give you some names of folks to approach."

Before, during and after the meal Chisum kept up a running dialogue about soil types, grass varieties, weather patterns and water. Tom tried to suck up all the knowledge presented to him by this man who fought the Indians, the Comancheros and the desperados that proliferated in the area as he worked to develop his cattle business.

Chisum finally came back to Tom's inquiry about land to settle, "Most folks think they want to push west up the Rio Hondo. It is a great little valley that flows a nice stream down from the confluence of the Rio Bonito and the Rio Ruidoso. One thing to be mindful of, it is mighty close to Lincoln County and the problems going on there between the McSween and Tunstall people on one side and the Dolan Murphy people on the other. Been many killings and it ain't over yet. The Army stepped in and tried to calm things down but there is still a lot of animosity. William Bonney and his cohorts continue to rustle cattle including some of mine."

After they had eaten dinner, they moved to comfortable chairs on the veranda. Chisum offered Tom a cigar, struck a match on his pants and lit both cigars. Exhaling he continued, "I think the better choice would be the Rio Peñasco. It is similar country to the Rio Hondo, it heads up in the same mountain range as the Hondo and it is generally a year round stream. There are quite a few homesteaders farming down there but the only place that is viable is the bottomlands along the river. Trouble is there is not enough irrigable land along the river bottom to make a living farming. Now, if you primarily raise cattle then you would have some nice irrigated fields to supplement your dry land pastures. Let me give you some names of folks that you should see."

Tom interrupted Chisum asking, "Pardon me sir but what does Peñasco mean?"

Chisum smiled, "It is Spanish for boulder or rocks. I suspect it garnered the name from the rocky, boulder strewn mountain country it passes through."

The next morning Chisum pointed out two nice brood mares saying, "I've got a stallion with Arab blood and I think he would be a good sire for these good looking mares if you will sell them to me. How much would I owe you?"

Pointing to the pasture Tom asked, "Mr. Chisum is that your stud horse?"

Chisum responded with pride in his voice, "Yes, a beautiful piece of horse flesh, don't you agree?"

"Mr. Chisum, I want the first foal, either horse colt or filly from each of the mares as payment."

Chisum smiled and held out his hand saying, "Son, ya got yourself a deal."

The Pruits said their goodbyes and gave thanks for the hospitality provided by Chisum. Their next stop was at the adobe general store in Roswell. The interior, dimly lit by two kerosene lamps, was ill equipped to display merchandise on dark winter days. One lamp hung in the front of the building and the other in the rear. The local post office was located in a front corner of the building. The one and only hotel in town was named the City of Bright Lights and its attic served as sleeping quarters for all guests no matter their social status. The hotel's name was apparently a hopeful vision rather than a description of its current state.

Tom introduced himself and asked to meet the proprietor. A tall man, well over six feet came to the counter from an office in the rear and said, "Mr. Pruit, I am Captain Lea."

Tom, slightly startled, said, "Captain, I have been referred to you by Captain Eggleston of Fort Griffin and recommended by John Chisum to be a source of good information."

"Chisum has been a friend since I arrived in the Territory but he inflates my ego at times. So you are a friend of Eggy? Did you serve with him during the war?"

"No sir, I was on the other side and just met him a few weeks back and he gave me your name and said I could use him as a reference."

"What can I do for you Mr. Pruit?"

"I have several things Captain, the first is I want to open an account with your store by depositing two hundred dollars with you for us to draw upon. I would like you to honor orders from my wife Mary Ellen, my brother J. D. and an employee, a former slave called Orange."

"We can certainly do that Mr. Pruit. What else?"

"Captain, I am aware that most merchants know which of their customer's credit has worn thin and needs to sell their land. I am most particularly interested in folks in the Rio Penãsco Valley. The land needs to be suitable for running cattle but river bottom would be welcome. I would be very interested in parcels that would be contiguous that I could assemble into a property capable of supporting me and my family."

"I have a condition which I would expect you to honor."

"What is that Captain?"

"I know of several people that are struggling and they have asked me to help if someone came to the Territory who wanted to buy property. Most of these poor unfortunate people live in dugouts along the river like burrowing badgers. Most tried to farm and failed but if you are of a mind to run cattle, you can possibly change the dynamics of their property. If you are able to consummate a transaction, I would like you to conduct the closing here in my store so I will be assured of collecting any open accounts. I will not be taking a commission of any kind, I just want my accounts paid. This may sound severe to you but most of these folks are going to lose their homesteads if they can't pay the government for them. When they default, I lose too. The cattlemen have been hit hard as well. Prices are down to eleven dollars a head from eighteen dollars ten years ago. One other piece of advice, when you find a homesteader ready to sell out get proof of his filing and have him accompany you to the Post Office in person to pay the commutation for the property. Only after that, pay him the bounty of whatever you agree to in your purchase. Most are selling for three dollars or less per acre."

Tipping his hat Tom said, "Thank you for the advice Captain. I am sure we will see each other again."

☆ ☆ ☆ ☆ ☆

Before they left town they stopped at the Post Office and obtained maps showing he locations of homesteads filed along the Rio Peñasco. Tom and the family continued down the Pecos River until they were at the confluence of the Pecos and the Peñasco. They turned west proceeding upstream on the Peñasco seeing several dugouts protruding from the side of the mountain. Tom stopped to talk with some of the people who were trying to farm in the rocky soils.

Asked if they would sell their property, most responded enthusiastically in the affirmative, as Ramsey Smith said, "Why hell yes, I'll sell and so will most of the folks trying to scratch a living

256

out of this worthless piece of dirt. Mister, if you got the money you can pretty well own the whole damn place."

Not wanting to appear eager, Tom deferred and the family set up camp further up the river. He needed to explore the land prior to making a decision on which outfits he would attempt to buy. The land lay in broken arroyos and was mostly arid and barren except for the river bottom. Tom realized he needed to control a lot of the river frontage, which ran west to east and decided he would push west upstream while he sent J. D. south of the Rio Peñasco and Orange north. Their instructions were to find settlers and talk in general about their circumstances.

It took several days for Tom to feel comfortable knowing where they should locate. Most of the best river property already filed upon left little available property. After engaging in conversations with several persons, Tom was able to visualize in his mind the parcels best suited to his needs. Evenings he studied the map from the land patent office listening to input from J.D. and Orange.

Like most business deals, those most anxious to sell held the poorest property. Tom knew he would need to convince some of the owners holding the better property by offering a higher price. At the end of a week, he felt confident in the plan he mentally prepared. J.D. and Nannie planned to homestead two one hundred sixty acre plots adjacent to Tom and Mary Ellen's by building a house spanning the property line so they could prove up on the land all at the same time. Orange and Latisha would do the same.

Tom acquired every parcel he wanted but had to pay the high price of five dollars an acre for two of them. He justified the price because both parcels straddled the Rio Peñasco and water was critical to his success. In the end, he was able to buy contiguous quarter sections totaling over twelve hundred acres.

Tom and the boys enlarged an existing dugout into the side of a hill for shelter from the winter blast of winds. They cut logs and replaced the existing roof. Since a sod roof always leaked, they laid down several pieces of canvas and then placed the sod on top.

Mary Ellen was not happy sleeping and cooking in a dugout but she knew it was only until they could get a house built. The men added a log cabin structure they used in later years as a bunkhouse. The next spring Tom hired Filiberto, a young Mexican, an expert in making and laying adobe. A new adobe house expertly built, laid, strong and tight was much easier to heat and offered more fire protection.

The Pruit women continued to have children. Between Charlie coming in October of 1878 and Buck in October of 1880, Mary Ellen birthed a stillborn boy they named Allan. Mattie was born in October of 1883 and Lillie was born in March of 1885. "Bud" was born in March of 1888. His real given name was Samuel with no middle name. He had been given the nickname "Bud" as he always wanted to buddy around with his older brothers. When he got to school, he was the only kid in the entire school of sixteen students that didn't have a middle name. One day after studying about Columbus' discovery of America "Bud" announced he was henceforth Samuel Columbus Pruit. Nothing much changed as everyone still called him "Bud".

Nannie and J.D. preferred naming their boys after Presidents of the United States, Benjamin Franklin Pruit in 1874, Thomas Jefferson Pruit in 1878 and George Washington Pruit in 1880. John Alick Pruit slipped in between two of his brothers in 1876. How he missed being named for a famous president no one ever figured out. Their last two children were girls, Nan Elizabeth in 1884 and Sally Ann in 1885. Tom was amused at his brother and sister-in-law's use of Presidential names. He ribbed J. D. that the kids would grow up with an uppity attitude with such famous names.

One afternoon Tom stood on a hillock he and Mary Ellen selected for their home overlooking the Rio Peñasco. The majesty of the valley to the East and the pine and spruce covered mountains to the West where the Rio Peñasco, fed by melting snow, flowed clear and cool in the valley below was absolutely beautiful. Tom knew this was where he could be happy.

When Tom and the family arrived in New Mexico, West Texas and Eastern New Mexico were open range. The closest barbed wire fence was five hundred miles away. Tom and his fellow ranchers liked open range mostly because that was all they had ever known. It had the advantage of allowing cattle to roam freely, migrating to wherever the forage was best. The disadvantage was at roundup time all the neighbors had to participate in a roundup covering an area of immense acreage. Tom estimated the area to be one hundred fifty miles long by seventy-five miles wide.

Roundup was a time of excitement for the cowboys who normally led a dreary lonely life. While everyone was cooperative, there was an element of competition between the individuals showing off their skills of roping and riding.

Every roundup started by gathering and sorting the cattle according to owner. The cowmen divided the range into sectors usually moving south to north and west to east. The Rio Peñasco Ranch sent all men available, as did every other rancher.

Men on horseback cut calves out of the main bunch, threw a loop around the critter's neck and pulled him to the branding fire. A team of men waited, a flanker flipped the calf on his side immediately kneeling hard on the calf's shoulder. As soon as the calf hit the ground, a second man grabbed the top rear leg pulling the hoof to his chest, placing his boot against the lower leg and pushing away.

A third man earmarked with a sharp knife cutting the owner's preferred design. A fourth castrated the bull calves by cutting the bottom of the scrotum off like the toe off a sock. He then pulled the individual testicles down stretching the cords taut and cutting them off. This action caused many a non-cowboy to faint. The testicles were thrown in a bucket of water, and later fried for lunch were always a favored menu on the range.

A fifth cowboy took a hot iron and held it to the animals hide applying the brand. The smoky smell of scorched hair and burning flesh wafted through the air. A sixth dabbed a mixture of carbolic acid, kerosene and pine tar on the freshly cut scrotum and checked ears, eyes or other orifices for evidence of worm infestations doctoring any visible wound the calf might have.

Babies bawled for their mother. Mommas bawled for their babies, lunging at the cowboys as if they were evil attackers. Running threateningly, towards any man standing between her and her baby, she tried her best to save her baby from calamity. Once the calf was branded and released, he would stagger away to find his momma. Momma would lick the calf trying to comfort it until he started to nurse again.

The work was intense, the weather hot. Dust filled the air. It was a sight, smell and sound, of back-breaking, bone-weary work only a stockman could love and they branded over twenty thousand head that spring.

In 1896, the roundup was close to winding up the year's work and the last branding was on the bank of Ranger Lake. Ranger was normally a dry lake most of the year, but this particular year, the area received an abundance of moisture during the rainy season. The rain-swollen lake stretched almost ten miles long and a mile or so across.

In mid-afternoon, about five days before the roundup was to wind up, a lone cowboy rode out of the Eastern horizon stopping on the far side of the lake. This fella sat there for a few minutes then climbed up and stood in his saddle looking first one direction and then another. Climbing down again he rode south first and returned to a point directly across the lake from the branding. He sat there for a few minutes and then rode north. Soon he was back again. Dismounting, he began to shuck his clothes until he wore nary a stitch except his hat, then mounted up and struck out across the lake with his clothes wrapped around his neck.

The work slowed until every eye was fixated on the cowpoke. He ventured out into the water and a murmur rippled through the group starting as surprised comments, and ending in a crescendo of raucous laughter. The poor fella rode that damn horse across the lake never even getting the horses' fetlocks wet. Once across, he dismounted, took his clothes from around his neck, coolly bowed, mooning the entire group. Every man present was rolling on the ground in mirthful laughter, tears running down their faces.

When the man had pulled his pants and shirt on, Tom walked over and said, "Mister, you just provided a much needed break for all of us. I take it you don't swim."

"No sir, I never learned, too many gators in the water."

Where ya' from?"

"Beaumont."

"What brought you out here?"

"Lookin' for work."

"What's your name?"

"Shorty, Shorty Dolan."

"Well son, as soon as your boots are on come introduce yourself proper and have lunch with us."

Chapter 29

Memories

It was Sunday morning July 22, 1906. The sky was stained pink by a swelling sun that lay just beyond the eastern horizon. The day would be boiling hot with a cloudless sky, if it were like yesterday. It needed to get hot to precipitate the monsoonal flow of moisture. There had been no rain for weeks and the thirsty earth was crisp.

Out of habit, Tom awakened before dawn every morning. He sat in a wooden chair holding a cup of steaming hot coffee. The chair's curved back swept round to support his arms. The wood strained and creaked as he leaned back against the adobe wall. It was the kind of chair found in any good saloon; saloon keepers knew that a comfortable man was a profitable one.

He was older now and in the winter of his life. Stiff joints and aching muscles stayed with him even after a long night's rest. He was a tall spare man with a shock of white hair. A face lined and tanned framed still keen eyes conveying a sense of competence and trustworthiness. The white of his forehead began about an inch above the top of his nose. His hat kept the blistering sun off that part, whereas the rest of his face was brown and darkened with age spots here and there.

Newspaper journalists were coming today to interview him as a pioneer on the Llano. Mary Ellen insisted that he wear his best dark trousers. The pant legs were tucked into a pair of almost new boots. The boots had a lower heel than he liked while in the saddle but the higher heels made walking uncomfortable. His best long sleeved white shirt adorned with pearl buttons, and a turquoise bolo tie completed his outfit. The journalists expected to be regaled with stories of his adventures; adventures which in his mind were not extraordinary. He was not sure exactly what coddled, soft, city folks wanted to hear. He had slept little during the night trying to collect his thoughts of what they would find interesting.

A Winchester lever action carbine rested against the wall of the house within easy reach. It was there every morning and every evening when he sat on the porch. It was in his saddle scabbard anytime he was horseback, which was most of the time, as he abhorred walking any distance at all. When asked by strangers why he felt the need to be armed, he said that he just wanted to be ready besides an occasional Apache could be slipping around trying to steal his prize horses. He overlooked the fact that the Mescaleros had not put out a raiding party in over twenty years. In 1906, they were more interested in stealing whiskey than horses.

Coyotes provided Tom with target practice most mornings and evenings. Just last week he saw two of them working as a team running one of his calves. Coyotes were smart, one would run a young calf in a circle and the other would sit resting until his cohort tired. Then they would trade off and the race would be on again. Unfortunately, the coyotes would run the little bugger until his tongue was hanging out. That was when the predators moved in for the kill.

Tom had sighted the Winchester in on the sitting coyote because he did not figure he could hit the running one, as he could a few years back. Just as he pulled the trigger, the running coyote came to a sudden stop directly behind the sitting coyote. He killed them both with one shot. He would brag about that shot for a long time.

The chill of the air slowly retreated as the sunlight silhouetted a wagon wheel atop a head gate announcing the "Rio Peñasco Ranch" in Southeast New Mexico. A sign hung from the center inscribed with an old Mexican proverb or "dicho" saying, Entren en Paz, Viver en Paz which in English means Enter in peace, Live in peace.

He used this quiet time to reflect on his life. He had but few regrets and still nurtured dreams for the future. The regrets he maintained were focused on his inability to express his love to his family to the depth he felt it. Unintentionally, his taciturn manner kept people at a distance and discussions with his loved ones suffered, yet family was everything to him. The love of a woman and the children they shared made his life complete.

He and his wife's sons and daughters were married now, beginning their families. He enjoyed watching his grandchildren play under the big cottonwood tree near the front of the house. The toddler's laughing and playful squealing filling the air brought him great pleasure. He especially loved it when they would crawl up in his lap with entranced eyes and sit spellbound as they listened to yarns he spun for them.

The family was finally beginning to prosper and hopes were high for the future. Much had been accomplished in his life but much remained to do. His prayer this morning thanked the Lord for the many blessings bestowed upon him and asked the Lord to grant him a few more years to finish what he started.

He waited patiently for the rays of light to reach across the sky until it blinded him and he had to squint and look away. As darkness lifted, the first light cast shadows along the arroyos that scarred the earth like fingers. Dun and violet bluffs appeared against the blue horizon tricking his eye. This always filled him with exhilaration in anticipation of what the day would bring. The sweet scent of sage, pinon and juniper filled his nostrils while a white wing mourning dove coo, coo, cooed a message of serenity in the cool morning air.

The vast treeless plain the Spanish explorers called Los Llanos Estacado lay to the East. Twenty years ago, he and his family had paid the price to traverse that lonely, desolate land. The melodic name rolled easily off the tongue but in reality, it was at best a hard callous country and at worst a death trap for unsuspecting pioneers. Once ruled by the Comanche and Kiowa Indians, the Great Staked Plains revealed the bleached bones of both man and beast; victims of a brutal environment of hostile weather, white outlaws and red savages.

Thirty-eight years ago, he married a dark eyed, raven haired beauty of seventeen. He was ten years older. To this day, she still made his heart palpitate. Mary Ellen was a fertile woman who bore him eleven children. Two babies died shortly after birth but nine survived to adulthood.

His son Charlie married Ada Stamps in Seminole, Texas, in April 1906. They were living with Tom and his wife, Mary Ellen, until the new house they were building on the other side of the mountain was habitable. Charlie was a good cowman and Tom was glad to have his help on the place as well as Charlie's younger brother, Buck. Buck married Ada's sister, Eunice Stamps, a year earlier in Monument, New Mexico. Brothers marrying sisters made a most cohesive group but when an argument came up which was infrequent, the women seemed to have the superior position over the hapless fellas.

The incessant bawling of a bull penetrated the serenity of the early morning. It evoked a memory from years gone by of his favorite bull, Lethal Weapon. Lethal, a prime Hereford bull, had always performed his job flawlessly. He had been a powerful creature, muscular, heavy and beautiful, for a bull. Lethal with amorous intent pursued a group of ten, virginal, yearling heifer calves, as they gathered at the barn. Tom kept them in a pasture close to the barn and as far away from the bull pasture as possible. His plan had been to hold them back and let them cycle through their first estrus without breeding until they could reach full maturity. They congregated at the barn every morning to water and eat a mixture of corn, barley, molasses and hay designed to get them off to a good start.

The bawling had grown louder and louder. Lethal had something sweet on his mind and it was not molasses. The wind must have been just right to carry the scent of a cow in heat to his sensitive nostrils as he moved with deliberation across the pasture toward his prize. Lethal jumped the fence dividing the pastures and headed down the lane to the heifers. He stopped briefly, head down, smelling fresh urine puddled on the dry dirt. The bawling became incessant.

Everyone else was still asleep and if the yearlings were to be saved from the bull's instinctive desires, it was up to Tom. There was no time to saddle a horse. He had bolted down the hill running at full gait, which was awkward for a bowlegged man used to sitting a horse. The bull was in the lane headed for the barn and the young heifers. Tom climbed the fence and ran waving his hat, screaming like a banshee. At first, Lethal was startled to see a mere mortal challenge his primal pursuit of propagation.

Normally a gentle giant, Lethal often let Tom give his head a knuckle rub when standing out in a pasture. Now he put his head down pawing the ground, first one front foot and then the other throwing dust in the air that drifted into Tom's eyes. Tom shouted and ran at the bull, finally getting the animal to give way until he could close a gate leading into the lane.

Lethal again caught the heat scent, curled his upper lip, rolled his eyes back in his head and issued the guttural sound of a mighty god. Undeterred, the bull simply moved down the fence and flatfooted, jumped it. The force of gravity was impotent against the instinct of procreation. It was a beautiful thing to watch this huge animal display such effortless, graceful, athleti- cism. Tom prayed that the bull's testicles cleared the barbed wire as they swung out in the air behind him or he would have to shoot his prize bull for only doing what came naturally to him.

Lethal hit the ground turning toward Tom, bawling ever louder. The virile animal lowered his head, pawing the ground menacingly, as though Tom was a deadly enemy. Tom knew he was defeated. Lethal strode in the midst of the heifers, as if a lo- thario, confident in his prowess, smelling first one and then the other until he found the object of his affection. His lips curled up while drooling frothy streams of saliva, his eyes rolled back in his big skull. Mother Nature's law of multiply and replenish the earth was fulfilled. The memory brought a smile to Tom.

His thoughts drifted to ten years earlier when he sold a hundred head of steel dust horses in exchange for a note to a slick fella from Tascosa, Texas. Tom always prided himself in being a judge of character but this fella fooled him. Normally a handshake would have sealed the deal but at his wife's insistence, he spoke with his Priest, asking him to draft a written note document to support the sale. The due date came and went. By then, of course, the horses were in Navajo country in northwest New Mexico. The only value in having the note was as a reminder not to sell horses to strangers on credit.

Charlie, age nineteen, and Buck, seventeen at the time volunteered to traverse four hundred miles of New Mexico Territory to see if they could salvage any remnants of the horses, get the money back or turn the dirty SOB over to the local law.

Naturally, the guilty party was long gone by the time the boys rode into Junction City on the San Juan River in Northern New Mexico. The horses, with the exception of four or five head found at a livery stable, had all been sold to unsuspecting buyers.

Several times before in Tom's life he found it necessary to deal with horse thieves. The first time was when Tom killed a renegade Indian. The second time, a stranger rode into their homestead looking for something to eat in exchange for work. Mary Ellen, always the first to help the down and out, told the man that she would feed him but insisted he take a bath down at the river. He hung around doing odd jobs, chopping firewood or weeding the garden for a few days. One morning they awakened to find the man gone, along with Tom's favorite gelding.

Tom and J.D. followed the culprit for two days. The dirty bastard roused from a sound sleep by Tom nudging him in the ribs with the barrel of his Winchester, cried and begged for his life. After securely tying the man's hands, J.D. threw a rope over a stout limb of a cottonwood tree slipping the noose around the man's head and neck. Tom took a dally around his saddle horn and slowly tightened the rope. The poor devil pissed his pants and pled for his life as Tom put just enough pressure on the rope to make the man's eyes bulge.

A memory of another man kicking wildly at the end of a rope, thirty years before, so revolted Tom that he let the rope have slack. Hanging a man just was not in his blood but he intended to make a believer out of this miscreant. He asked for a declaration that the man would leave the country under threat of death if he came back. After nodding his head affirmatively, they cut him loose. A few months later, they got word of the same scoundrel strung up in El Paso for stealing the Mayor's horse. Hearing the news, Tom thought justice prevailed.

Sometimes horse thieves and rustlers won battles in the struggle of taming the West. Such was the case of the enforcer the cattleman's group hired in late 1893 as the rustler problems grew beyond a single rancher's ability to deal with it. Tom and his neighbors called a meeting to try to come up with a solution. After much consideration, they interviewed several prospective hired gunmen. They settled on a fifty something former ranch manager. He came with a reputation of being an uncompromising hard man who did not hesitate to use harsh methods in addressing supposed bad men. The Association made a deal with the railroad that allowed the man to flag down any train, jump his horse into a boxcar and ride up and down the rails giving him the element of surprise to the rustlers who would not know when or where he might show up.

The Cattleman's Association convinced the Territorial Governor to deputize the man. Word spread around the area that rustlers needed to clear out or face the hanging tree. Activity stopped for a while. Until one morning when Tom and Juan Sepulveda were riding in the south pasture. Upon cresting a small hill, they could see a short distance away a seed sack tied to the cross bar of the pasture gate. A stiff breeze was blowing but the sack did not sway back and forth. It just hung there. Clouds of swarming flies surrounded the sack and it smelled damn bad. A rope tied round the gathered cloth and thrown over the arch pole held it. Tom held the reins to Juan's horse as he climbed up to stand in the saddle, since it was too high to cut down while sitting normally.

Upon severing the last strands of the rope, the sack, flies and all, plummeted to the ground striking with a sickening thud. The stench was so bad Juan was gagging by the time Tom had the sack open and was puking when the enforcer's head rolled out, eyes staring blankly. Juan, an old caballero from Mexico said, "Oh, muy malo. Thees hombre es no bueno por mi ojos." (Oh this is very bad. This man is not good for my eyes.)

A rooster crowed, interrupting Tom's thoughts and, snapping him back into the present. He gazed down at the valley below. His horses and cattle grazed contentedly on the green fields whose straight and neat furrows he himself had plowed. It was moments such as this that he knew true happiness. Every hardship endured was worth the difficult journey across the Llano Estacado.

An acequia (irrigation ditch) meandered lazily along the valley floor carrying life sustaining water to his fields. Sunlight reflected off the water created a shimmering mirage as it spread across the pasture. Tom watched the image dance lazily across the landscape.

Building the ditch had been a communal effort of hard manual labor. Each landowner contributed time and money in proportion to their holdings. Every year they elected someone, usually a volunteer, to be the Ditch Boss. This individual would monitor the usage and schedule work details in the spring to clean the ditch and make everything ready for the irrigation season, which ran from mid-March until mid-October.

Tom himself had been Ditch Boss several times and it required work and diligence. There was one particular landowner, an old Mexican man, Cesar Norero, who had never taken a turn being ditch boss even when the opportunity arose. Cesar was an irascible old fart who seemed to enjoy stirring things up between not only the ditch users but also everyone in the valley. He tended to drink too much on a regular basis and when drunk he wanted to pick a fight, usually with a gun. The old man kept several jugs of whiskey stashed along the bank of the irrigation ditch so they were easily accessible. Every time Tom found one, he pulled the stopper, poured out the liquor and refilled it with water.

Tom would go to divert the water to the next user and it would already be running to Cesar's fields. Other times, the gate not closed completely created significant seepage running down the ditch leading to Cesar's property. Tom figured that Cesar thought he could pilfer more than his share of water and nobody would be the wiser.

There were three things that could get a man killed in New Mexico Territory, stealing a horse, stealing water and stealing a woman, not necessarily in that order. The other two users, Pasqual Jimenez and Mike Duval met with Tom and decided that they had tolerated enough of Cesar's shenanigans. Tom had to convince them that they needed to warn him first before they hung him. They began patrolling together to check the ditch early in the morning. The day before the water was to be released by Jimenez to Cesar, Tom, Jimenez and Duval were all hidden in the thick shoulder high willows at the junction gate where most of the diversions were occurring. Along comes Cesar, ambling up the ditch from his property. He opens the gate about half way thus diverting significant water down to his fields a day early. It would have been hard for Jimenez to miss the water unless he was checking the junction gate regularly.

Cesar was standing by the ditch watching the water flow when all three of his ditch partners came out from behind the willow branches. Tom said, "A donde va Cesar?" (Where are you going?) The old man almost had a heart attack.

Tom spoke before the man could formulate a response, "Cesar you are up and at'm early this morning. Is this your day to be getting water? I thought today was Pasqual's water and yours would start tomorrow."

The three men stood abreast, hands on pistol butts facing the water thief. Cesar heard the hammer on a six-gun being cocked, he stuttered and stammered but could not get any words out. In shock, with guilt all over his ashen face he began to weep and told them he was just mistaken about the day. Strangely enough, the water theft ended there that day.

At the next annual meeting of the ditch users Tom queried Cesar why he never volunteered to be Ditch Boss. Using some psychology on the old reprobate Tom thought if they gave the man some responsibility he just might turn over a new leaf. Cesar reported, "Well, I no want being called Deetch Boss."

"Why not?"

"Bosses all sonsabeeches. I no like bosses."

Tom surprised, looked at Cesar and queried, "Well what do you think we should call the ditch boss then?"

"Mayordomo."

"Well Cesar, what does Mayordomo mean?"

"Well señor, it means boss."

Mayordomo or boss? Mayordomo or boss? Tom was perplexed. He could only shake his head in disbelief.

"Ok Cesar, you are the next Mayordomo."

A toothless smile broke out on the old man's weathered face. "Gracias señor, muy gracias."

Several half-broke horses nickering at the corral brought Tom back to the present. The horses were greeting Juan, his friend and old Mexican remudero (one who tends a herd of horses). Juan placed a ration of corn and oats in each stall's feeder then took a pitchfork and filled the feeders with hay and then opened the corral gate for the waiting horses. Each horse knew the pecking order and deferred to those with seniority as they made their way into the barn. One gelding always ate his ration faster than the other horses, and would then proceed to force his way into an open stall and try to steal the unlucky horse's meal, so Juan would close each stall gate to stop any thievery between horses.

Juan, who was pushing seventy, was a wiry little fella. He and his wife, Rosario, twenty years younger and fifty pounds heavier than Juan, lived at the bottom of the hill next to the river. Rosario cooked, did laundry and cleaned Tom and Mary Ellen's house. Juan cared for the horses and helped with the cattle. If there was anyone Tom trusted to handle his horses, it was Juan.

A while back Juan had expressed his concerns about dying. Juan wanted to be buried within earshot of the Penasco River. When he showed Tom the plot he wanted, Tom said, "Juan, you might wash away in one of the flash floods if we plant you there."

"Señor, jest geet my bones and deeg another hole, por favor."

"Don't you want me to move you further up the hill if that happens?"

"No señor, same place por favor. My ears no hear too good so I need to be close to the rio to hear the water."

Simple pleasures made Juan immensely happy. He rose with the sun, ate a hearty breakfast and worked throughout the entire day, never quitting until the sun was casting long shadows across the low foothills. He never seemed to break a sweat but worked steadily accomplishing as much as most any two men half his age could do. A dead shot, he loved hunting mule deer roaming the area. He shared his venison jerky freely and brought all sorts of wild game to the house for Tom.

One afternoon Tom and Juan were taking a spool of new barbed wire and cedar posts down to the south pasture to do some fence work. As the wagon rattled down the rutted dirt trail, they began discussing a recent senseless unsolved murder of an old Mexican man in the valley. All the ranch families were shocked about the terrible event and Tom and Juan were speculating on whom the guilty party was when Juan said, "I was shot once."

"I didn't know that, Juan. How did that happen?"

"Well señor, I go to thee bar in San Ysidro and I flirting with a señorita working there when her boyfriend who is my good amigo come in. When he see the señorita keessing me, he go outside to my caballo and geet my gun from my saddle bags, come back inside and shoot me with my own gun."

"Damn, Juan! Where did he shoot you?"

"Well señor, his hand shaking so beeg when he pull the trigger, the gun she pointing at my leg. It went straight through, no hitting the bone. I fall down and our amigos tackle him before he pull the trigger again."

"Did the constable arrest him?"

"Nooo, señor. The constable, he standing right beside me when I shot and he say he not going to arrest nobody cause we all amigos and I no should beeen flirting with the señorita."

"I bet your friendship with that hombre ended right then."

"Oh no señor, We still amigos. I like him better than the senorita."

"Did you learn a lesson about women that day Juan?"

"Oh si señor, I learn to never keep your gun where another man can find it."

Tom chuckled loudly and shook his head. Such was life in the Penãsco valley.

A door opened and slammed shut breaking the tranquility of the morning. His Granddaughter poked her head around the corner of the house and said, "Don't forget, today is the day those reporters from the Dallas newspaper are coming to interview you about the olden days. They ought to be here about noon. We will have lunch after they arrive. You need to wash up and shave to look your best. Don't make a mess in the bathroom and put on your new suit that is laid out."

Her mentioning the bathroom brought forth a memory of building Mary Ellen's house almost thirty years ago. They selected this knob of a hillside nestled at the base of steep, rugged, ten thousand foot high mountain peaks. It was where the juniper and pinon began, the grassland of the Llano Estacado ended, and the view to the east carried to the horizon.

Adobe construction was not his forte but his hired hand, Filiberto, was an expert. He was a small thin man with dark skin and a big toothy smile. Making adobe bricks and Saltillo tile from mother earth was an art. He used both adobe and Saltillo tile to create a beautiful structure that would stand for decades. In the end though, the adobes and tiles would one-day return to dust just the same as the men who made them. That was what Tom liked about it. The earth was forever.

Tom sketched out a plan in the dirt for Filiberto explaining he wanted a long house built in three sections. On each end would be four rooms with a center breezeway of equal size but open to the elements on front and back. They would use the open-air room for dancing and partying. After the first winter, Mary Ellen insisted the room be fully enclosed telling Tom, "It is time for civilization to come to our home and time to keep the weather out."

Bringing running water into the house was simple enough. An acequia up-stream from the home site, flowing out of the Rio Penasco, brought a continuous stream of water down and diverted into and through the open porch that was later enclosed.

A master artisan, Filiberto made adobes from a formula passed down for generations from his father's father to his father to him. He found just the right deposit of clay close to the Penasco River, which cut through the little valley below. He threw in some dried straw, a significant amount of horseshit mixing it all with water and clay, until it was just the right consistency. They shoveled the thick slurry into forms and let the sun dry it into perfect bricks four inches thick, eight inches wide and sixteen inches long. The adobes laid using mud mortar created walls ten feet high.

Tom, Filiberto and two other men climbed the side of a mountain on the western side of the ranch covered by stands of tall ponderosa pines. They cut mature trees Juan called vigas for the roof, limbed them and dragged them to the home site with a team of horses. What bark was not knocked off along the way they removed with drawknives. The vigas, after curing in the hot southwest sun, for a year still dripped sap during the hot summers.

The wide veranda's floor and the interior rooms of the hacienda covered with Saltillo tile cast a rose-colored glow throughout the entire house. The formula for Saltillo tile was a treasured secret and Filiberto shared it with no one. Tom asked Filiberto why he was so closemouthed, "You no need me no more if I tell you."

"Not need you? Hells bells man I ain't no mud dauber."

Filiberto made the tile on the South side of Lewis Peak where the mountain possessed abundant red clay soil. There he built a horno to fire the tile to a smooth glazed finish. After a significant amount of tile was ready, he carefully hauled the fragile pieces on an ox cart to the building site.

Filiberto, down on hands and knees, was tirelessly laying tile one afternoon, when Tom discovered dog footprints in several tiles. Pointing at the dog prints Tom said, "Filiberto, these tiles are ruined."

"No! No! No! Es muy fortuna, señor Pruit! Muy fortuna! Theese perro steps bring us mucho good luck."

The dog print tiles, more likely coyote print tiles since Filiberto did not own a dog, stayed.

Many people in the valley thought the veranda to be an ostentatious accoutrement but in reality, it was a practical and useful addition. Its roof provided shelter from a scorching sun and because it was on all sides, it provided shelter from powerful winds sweeping down from the surrounding mountains. One big advantage New Mexico weather possessed over East Texas was low humidity. Even on the hottest day, a man could get in the shade and cool off.

Rough sawn lumber hauled from Blazer's Mill, located on the bank of the Tularosa River, provided the roof decking and door and window jambs. Filiberto hand split shingles from sections of pine logs and nailed them in place over the roof decking. The shingles tended to warp over time and if rain persisted for a couple of days, the roof eventually leaked. About ten years ago, corrugated tin roofing material brought in by train to Roswell and installed on the roof made it watertight and wind resistant.

Filiberto plastered the interior walls with lime mixed with sand and horsehairs. Tom marveled at how tough the little Mexican was because he did it with his bare hands, refusing to use a trowel. Filiberto said, "I have to feeel it so I no can do it with the trowel." The finished product was indeed smooth and pleasing to the touch and the eye.

The most recent change was indoor plumbing. Tom could not imagine why anyone would want to shit in their house where they slept and cooked. His wife insisted. What does a man do when his wife is adamant about such things? To keep peace he relented. Plumbers from Roswell installed the complicated pipes that he did not understand. That next winter was extremely harsh. That was when he began to appreciate shitting inside rather than freezing his butt off sitting in a drafty outhouse that stood fifty feet from the back door.

The next modern improvement his wife wanted was electricity. As soon as she heard the new electric company in Roswell was planning expansion to the valley in 1904, she wanted it. One positive would be the cooling boxes to keep food fresh. A cold glass of milk before bed was a luxury he would enjoy.

Tom thought kerosene lamps worked just fine although he admitted that it was hard to read after dark with one of the smoky old lamps. Reading after dark was low priority for Tom. He enjoyed sitting in front of a roaring fire of good juniper logs listening to the popping and sizzling as they burned, plus the pitch generated a wonderful smell.

The morning sun was high enough in the sky to expose a dilapidated rotted wood cemetery fence. It was leaning but still standing on the side of a hill a half-mile distant from where he sat. It spoke many truths after enduring the harsh sun, wind and freezing cold of the Llano Estacado for over twenty years. Cows pushed against it trying to eat a few wisps of grass hidden between the iron posts. There were several grave markers. One leaned precipitously as it seemed ready to give up and simply fade into the dry earth. He intended to fix that every time he looked at it but always something more important needed doing. After all, the dead would still be there when he got around to doing it. He would lay there too someday alongside the stillborn baby he and Mary Ellen lost over thirty years ago. They buried his wife's unmarried sister there after she died of consumption in 1902. She had lived with them since 1885. The disease simply wore her down until she could no longer breathe.

Tom carried scars of hate from his days in the war. Time had lessened the pain but the memories lingered still forty years later. He still felt the anger and the frustration of a lack of closure. His mind flashed back to the Franklin battlefield. The sunrise this morning reminded him of that day in Tennessee. He could taste the dirt coating his lips. It was a gritty mixture of gunpowder and earth. He touched his mouth to wipe it away but it was not there only the smell of the Llano Estacado remained.

Tom kept another group of chairs on the West side veranda too. It was the perfect place to say goodbye to the day. Majestic sunsets frequently streaked the sky various shades of red, orange, yellow and sometimes purple above the mountain. Starting in July, magnificent thunderstorms filled the summer sky with flashing lightning dancing across the horizon. He loved the smell of moisture permeating the air, which foretold the rain they needed so badly. The pitter-patter of the raindrops hitting the tin roof of the house sometimes lulled him to sleep sitting in his chair.

A path meandering among large cottonwood trees, led from the veranda on the west side down to the bunkhouse. Filiberto slept there when he was not in Mexico visiting his family. Most summer evenings he sat on the porch of the bunkhouse gently strumming his guitar and softly singing melodic Spanish tunes.

Tom encouraged Filiberto to bring his family across the border but Filiberto said his wife was reluctant to leave her large family. He was a free spirit who persisted in an annoying habit. He would simply wake up in the morning, say to himself, it was time to go home and then without a word to anyone, leave. He would show up again in a few weeks as if he had never been gone.

A few months back Tom and Mary Ellen made an announcement that a new grandbaby was soon to be born.

Filiberto upon hearing the news said, "My wife, she going to have a nino too."

Mary Ellen said, "Why Filiberto, we didn't know that! I bet you are excited too."

"Noooo. It's no my nino."

"How could that be?"

"When I go home last she have big belly. I ask, when nino be coming. She say in tres mes mas. (Three more months.) Es muy poco tiempo." (It is too little time.)

Startled and then embarrassed, Mary Ellen could not find words in answer to his statement. Stranger things had happened.

Possessing knowledge of local medicinal herbs was another of Filiberto's talents. A few years back one of the horses was injured when a tree fell, scraping the hide off its rear leg. Tom thought they would have to put the animal down since keeping a lame horse was not in the cards. Upon seeing the injury, Filiberto volunteered he thought he could heal the wound.

Tom asked, "How ya gonna do that?"

"*Well señor*, I use Hierba de Indio." (Herb of the Indian)

"Yerba de Indio?"

"Si señor. I use the root of the plant. I cut the root muy poquito until it is like dust and I will make a tea in muy caliente aqua to wash the laceracion. Then I will take the remaining root and make emplasto de medicamento por su caballo's leg. Then I will wrap it in clean rags. I will do todos los dias por ocho dias. (every day for eight days) Su caballo esta en buen estado." (Your horse will be in good health,)

"Where do you get this Yerba?"

"No se Señor, no se." Filiberto's avoidance of answering Tom was irritating but Tom knew that it was important to the little Mexican to maintain exclusive control of the folk ways of his ancestors safe from heretics. Sure enough at the end of the eight days, the wound was well on the way to healing.

Suddenly the tranquil morning was interrupted again by the voice of his Granddaughter calling him, "Grampa, breakfast is on the table. Come and eat while it is hot. Are you ready?"

This was a different Sunday. Normally he would hitch a horse to the buggy and take Mary Ellen down to the Catholic Mission for mass. He felt that their priorities were confused this Sunday. Skipping mass to entertain some city folks irritated Tom.

Tom and Mary Ellen were Baptists when they first came west but since no Baptists were in the area they started attending the little Catholic mission down the valley. Tom's memory of the Baptist preachers preaching until the cows came home was painful. Half the congregation was usually asleep before it was all over; proof, in his opinion, that hellfire and damnation did not put the fear of God in folks.

The little mission La Iglesia de San Ysidro shared a priest who served several communities. The priest, Father Alejandro, a Mexican who came to the valley in 1875 from a seminary in Mexico City gave a good, short, sweet and to the point homily. Tom liked that and he always felt his soul restored after partaking of the blood and body of Jesus Christ.

Tom believed in confessing his sins to his God, but not to another man even if he was a priest. This precipitated many philosophical discussions with Father Alejandro. Tom reckoned his sins were not big serious sins but rather little sins like his exasperation with folks. He and Father Alejandro had a running dialogue about that, with the priest saying every man is filled with sin and every man needs absolution through confession. As far as Tom was concerned, absolution was between him and his maker and no one else.

Father Alejandro retorted, "Senor Tom, when you are in the confessional you are talking to God and not to anyone else."

Tom smiled and said, "Padre, you are a mighty wily coyote."

Their nearest neighbor, a matronly older woman owned a ranch with a round knob of a mountain. It was a significant landmark to the Mexican caballeros. They called it Chiches de Weta, (The Blonde's Tit) because it looked exactly like a woman's breast. When Mary Ellen first heard of her neighbor's namesake mountain, she gasped and rushed into the house telling Tom she did not want to hear those words said in English or Spanish. In a private moment, she admitted later to her husband that she always thought of the name every time she saw the mountain or her blond friend.

A great example of a sin for Tom at this stage of life was his detested snoopy widow neighbor who complained about everything when he thought she had no complaints. Her husband had been a good provider and left her with a sizable estate but that was not enough, by golly. She constantly complained about the lack of decent dress boutiques in Roswell. For pity sakes, how many black dresses did any one woman need? He dreaded the Sundays the widow woman came to lunch after mass and found any excuse to go to the most distant pasture to look for lost calves.

Even though the Bible told him to love his neighbor, he thought the Lord would understand even if his wife did not. After all, he offered no vindictiveness toward the woman, just his absence. He confided his dislike for the widow to Father Alejandro. When the Priest told him he was being judgmental, Tom was surprised. Father Alejandro then informed him that to judge another person was a sin and he needed to ask God for forgiveness and come to confession. Tom listened and resolved to try to give the widow some leeway but was unmoved to attend confession.

Father Alejandro made a big production of baptizing all of the youngsters every spring on Easter in the river and any other heathen he could find. The river serenely flowed through the valley creating pools easily approachable by wagon. Several years before, the Priest showed Tom where he wanted to perform the baptisms and asked Tom to smooth a road down close to the water. Men of the church cleared brush and undergrowth to allow a sizable group of people to observe the goings on. A large bonfire would be laid to take the chill of the water off the celebrants and afterwards, a fiesta was held where all the women of the congregation served their favorite food in a grand potluck or Matanza in Spanish.

A day earlier, Filiberto, Juan and men from the church excavated a deep pit, filled it with dry oak wood, lit a fire and let it burn down to coals. They then placed a sheet of corrugated metal roofing over the coals. Two cabritos (goats), two borregos (sheep) and a side of beef basted with a mix of vinegar, honey, salt, pepper, garlic and onions wrapped in burlap bags were placed on the meat and then another piece of metal was placed on top of the meat. Then the entire affair was covered in dirt. After the Easter Service and baptisms, they would dig the meat up. Tender and roasted to perfection, it was the absolute best meat on earth. A grand banquet of every type of potatoes and bean dishes followed by cakes and pies left no one hungry.

Interrupting his thoughts, Tom's Granddaughter again called, "Your breakfast is getting cold Grampa. Its time to come and eat. Gramma says if you don't she will slop the pigs with your breakfast."

His usual meal consisted of two eggs cooked over medium until the yoke was almost firm, not runny and sowbelly with sourdough biscuits and gravy, followed by more black coffee. When he was finished eating he went back to his chair on the east veranda affording a clear view of the dirt road leading across the plains to his property. Shortly before noon, he saw a tiny speck leading a rooster tail of dust. It had to be one of those newfangled automobiles. He sighed, dreading talking to some person who could not possibly understand his point of view about life in the West.

Stretching to a seemingly god-forsaken horizon, the flat arid landscape of the Llano suffered from a long drought. Dust devils carried tiny specks of earth up into the sky forming funnels that rose several hundred feet in the air. He envisioned them to be a staircase to the past life of the many people who struggled against everything Mother Nature threw at them.

Sure enough, the smoke belching, backfiring automobile lurched to a stop at the front of the house in a cloud of dust a few minutes after noon. It scared the horses, upset the milk cow, the mules started braying and Tom thought the chickens would probably stop laying for a couple days. It was a hell of a cacophony of noise. As far as Tom was concerned, the interview was already a disaster.

Two men, obviously city slickers with their two fancy women emerged from a dirty, dusty car that would have been shiny black, had it been clean. During conversation at lunch, Tom learned it was a brand new 1906 Ford Model "K", with seats for four and a canvas top stretched over a flimsy frame. Tom considered the automobile or for that matter any automobile to be an abomination and vowed to himself never to own one. Tom's curiosity was mildly aroused as the women took wraps from over their faces. They complained loudly as they dismounted about the roughness of the road and the dusty conditions leading to this godforsaken destination. From the bridge of their nose to their forehead was matted in dust the color of fresh cow patty. That brought a smile to his weathered face as he muttered under his breath, "If only they could see themselves right now."

Mary Ellen, all a dither with such highfalutin company, assumed a cosmopolitan air and escorted them into the house saying, "Come ladies, I know you need to freshen up before lunch."

After lunch and meaningless small talk, Rosario, their cook and housekeeper followed by her naked toddler, brought the newspaper people hot tea. Seeing the naked child elicited gasps from the petticoated ladies of, "Oh!!! My dear child, you must put some clothes on."

Tom rather enjoyed seeing the matrons in shock and wondered what they would do at a branding when the castrations took place and mountain oysters were served for lunch. Only sissy men drank tea in Tom's opinion. He smiled, refusing the offered tea asking for coffee instead.

The head newspaperman stood and retrieved a writing pad from his case and said "So Mr. Pruit, why don't you give us the highlights of your life you feel are the most important. Start with your war time experience."

Tom thought it impossible to tell the story so that this pompous ass could understand it, let alone appreciate the hardships and lives lost in the dream of owning a piece of God's country.

Chapter 30

Sunday evening, July 22, 1906

Mary Ellen and Tom watched the newspaper folks' new-fangled automobile bounce from one rut to the next, jostling the occupants until it was out of sight. All that remained of the visit by the journalists was the dust hanging in the air. Turning to her husband, Mary Ellen gave him a hug and said, "It meant a lot to me to hear you tell our story today. I realized all over again how much you love me and how much I love you. Our lives are so inter-twined with this country and the people who live here and I am so very proud of you and what you have done for me and the children over the years."

Tom put his arm around her waist and stooped to give her a kiss, "I am proud of you too. You have been the strength of our family through every crisis. You have nurtured not only me but also raised nine babies to adulthood. If anyone deserves apprecia-tion and thanks, you do."

They turned and slowly walked to the house. Then the moment was over as she said, "Best I go help Rosario clear the ta-ble and put things away."

"If you are going to be busy, I saw Charlie, Buck and Juan rounding up the yearling heifers down in the south pasture. Still a couple of hours of daylight left so I think I will ride down and check on those rascals."

"You never know when to quit do you, Tom Pruit. I under-stand how much you enjoy that so go ahead and go check on those rascals that don't need checking on." Flashing a coquettish smile, she quickened her step and in a swishing of her skirts opened the door to the house, and left him smiling at her.

When Tom rode into the pasture, he found Charlie and Juan trying to cut a rank bull out of the group of heifers. Buck was just riding in from the south pasture where this bull was supposed to be. Several of the heifers were in season and the bull did not want to give up his presumed right to breed them. He stood pawing the ground and snorting slobber that rolled down his jaw.

Charlie raced alongside the huge animal whipping the bull in the face with a lariat. Finally, the bull turned and ran down the fence away from the gate. Tom jabbed his spurs into his mount and raced alongside the bull pulling even with him. Abruptly the bull doubled back. Tom's prized cutting horse instinctively followed the bull. Tom leaned into his stirrup as the horse whirled changing direction. A loud snapping noise occurred. The stirrup leather broke. Tom immediately fell down and under his horse. The horse's hooves struck him in the head.

Charlie, Buck, and Juan rushed to Tom lying deathly still in the dust. Blood was running down his forehead and into his eyes, down to his mouth and then down his neck into his shirt collar. Buck who was first to get to his father said, "He's still alive. Juan get the wagon!"

Juan rushed to the house screaming for Mary Ellen. They gently loaded Tom into the wagon and took him to the house with his head swathed in Mary Ellen's lap and her skirt. After they carried Tom into his bedroom and laid him on the bed Charlie turned to Juan, "Juan take a horse to San Ysidro and see if you can find Doc Ellis and get him over here fast!"

Two hours later Juan returned, driving the doctor's buggy at breakneck speed, the Doctor hanging on for dear life. The Doctor was ushered into the house to Tom's bedside by the anxious family to find Tom unconscious on the bed. Mary Ellen had already removed his clothes and cleaned the blood from his face and head. The doctor looked at the wound and turned, slowly shaking his head saying, "Mary Ellen, I am sorry but there is nothing I can do. He has a fractured skull."

For six days, Charlie and Buck never left Mary Ellen or Tom's side. They slept on the floor and in chairs as close to their Father and Mother as they could. Early, on the sixth day, Tom's breath became uneven gasps and grew more labored; then they stopped. A mournful silence fell over the world of everyone present. It was Saturday, July 28, 1906. Samuel Thomas Pruit was buried at the ranch on the Llano Estacado.

The End

Epilogue

Charlie and Buck continued to work the ranch for their mother for nine years. A disastrous blue norther in the winter of 1906/1907 brought snow, wind and ice that punished both man and beast. Cattle turned their tail into the wind as the storm pushed them south and many froze to death. Charlie and Buck weathered the storm, tightened their belts and survived nature's brutality but many neighbors gave up, sold out and moved. The next disaster a few years later was a manmade financial panic. The price of cattle crashed causing the ranch to fail. Charlie became the Marshall of Lovington, New Mexico, for the princely sum of forty dollars a month. They moved Mary Ellen into a modest home in Lovington where Charlie could keep an eye on her. She died in January of 1936. Daddy Charlie and Mama Ada produced nine children, seven survived to adulthood. Charlie died in 1943. He was sixty-four. Ada died in 1954 at age sixty-nine. They lay at rest in Lovington, New Mexico.

Buck punched cows for various ranch outfits until he moved to Odessa, Texas. Buck and Eunice had five children. Eunice passed away in 1920. Buck died at age 86 in 1966. J.D. and Nan farmed in eastern New Mexico for many years. He, like his father, was a farmer and a darn good one. They acquired a three-room frame house with barns, corrals and an Eclipse windmill near Causey to be near their daughter Sally. J.D. loved horses and his pride and joy were a pair of perfectly proportioned pure white horses of obviously thoroughbred heritage named Ben and Buck. While they were both special, Ben was a speedster winning many races at fairs and horse shows and was never beaten.

J.D. and Nan's children, George, Nannie and Sally were all married in Monument, New Mexico in 1904 and 1905. Sally's new husband, Emzy Roberts, was a young man with grandiose ideas. They promptly moved to Causey in Roosevelt County where he owned a ranch. Causey is located about five miles west of the new Mexico-Texas line about ninety miles northeast of Monument. J.D. and Nan decided to follow them. Emzy had an ambition to build a complete town and name it after himself. He did, building a grocery store, a dry goods store, a post office, a barbershop and a large gristmill to serve the area's farmers. One of the buildings caught fire and a strong west wind spread it rapidly. Within a matter of minutes, the Town of Emzy disappeared in smoke. Later Sally's brother, George Pruit, built a general store-post office but Emzy Roberts did not rebuild his dream town on the prairie. Emzy and Sally were divorced in 1916 or 1917.

J.D. and Nan lived completely at the mercy of the weather on the Llano Estacado, which was an unpredictable and fickle mistress. Frustrating as it was, J.D. loved the life despite the uncertain rain, the freezing cold in the late spring and the scarifying wind-driven sand. One evening while preparing for bed he and Nan decided to share an apple. She brought his half and then went back to the kitchen. When she returned he was lying crosswise on the bed, asleep forever. It was February 20, 1933. Nan passed away four years later. They are resting at Causey cemetery.

Orange and Latisha moved to Oklahoma to be near her family after Tom's death and were never heard from again.

Our family endures. Each new generation has contributed successful business people, schoolteachers, physicians, geologists, college professors, journalists, attorneys, and patriots who serve in our military as pilots and soldiers.

We still have grit.

Illustration 1

My Grandfather, Charles Thomas Pruit

"Daddy Charlie"
Born October 4, 1878, Died March 16, 1943
City Marshall, Lovington, NM
Circa 1942

Illustration #2

My Great Grandfather,

Samuel Thomas Pruit

Born 1842, Died July 28, 1906